Crosscurrents / Modern Critiques / Third Series

Edited by Jerome Klinkowitz

Critical Angles
European Views of Contemporary American Literature

Edited by
Marc Chénetier

Southern Illinois University Press
CARBONDALE AND EDWARDSVILLE

Edited by Barbara E. Cohen
Designed by Bob Nance, Design for Publishing, Inc.
Jacket design by Quentin Fiore
Production supervised by Kathleen Giencke

89 88 87 86   4 3 2 1

Library of Congress Cataloging in Publication Data
Main entry under title:

Critical angles.

  (Crosscurrents/modern critiques. Third series)
  Includes index.
  1. American literature—20th century—History and
criticism—Addresses, essays, lectures.   2. Criticism—
Europe—Addresses, essays, lectures.   I. Chénetier, Marc,
1946–   . II. Series.
PS225.C75   1986   810'.9'0054   85–2075
ISBN 0-8093-1216-6

In memoriam
René Tadlov
(1892–1977)

Contents

Crosscurrents/ Modern Critiques/ Third Series

Jerome Klinkowitz

I N THE EARLY 1960s, when the Crosscurrents/Modern Critiques series was developed by Harry T. Moore, the contemporary period was still a controversial one for scholarship. Even today the elusive sense of the present dares critics to rise above mere impressionism and to approach their subject with the same rigors of discipline expected in more traditional areas of study. As the first two series of Crosscurrents books demonstrated, critiquing contemporary culture often means that the writer must be historian, philosopher, sociologist, and bibliographer as well as literary critic, for in many cases these essential preliminary tasks are yet undone.

To the challenges that faced the initial Crosscurrents project have been added those unique to the past two decades: the disruption of conventional techniques by the great surge in innovative writing in the American 1960s just when social and political conditions were being radically transformed, the new worldwide interest in the Magic Realism of South American novelists, the startling experiments of textual and aural poetry from Europe, the emergence of Third World authors, the rising cause of feminism in life and literature, and, most dramatically, the introduction of Continental theory into the previously staid world of Anglo-American literary scholarship. These transformations demand that many traditional treatments be rethought, and part of the new responsibility for Crosscurrents will be to provide such studies.

Contributions to Crosscurrents/Modern Critiques/Third Series will be distinguished by their fresh approaches to . established topics and by their opening up of new territories for discourse. When a single author is studied, we hope to present the first book on his or her work, or to explore a previously untreated aspect based on new research. Writers who have been critiqued well elsewhere will be studied in comparison with lesser-known figures, sometimes from other cultures, in an effort to broaden our base of understanding. Critical and theoretical works by leading novelists, poets, and dramatists will have a home in Crosscurrents/Modern Critiques/Third Series, as will sampler-introductions to the best in the new Americanist criticism written abroad.

The excitement of contemporary studies is that all of its critical practitioners and most of their subjects are alive and working at the same time. One work influences another, bringing to the field a spirit of competition and cooperation that reaches an intensity rarely found in other disciplines. Above all, this third series of Crosscurrents/Modern Critiques will be collegial—a mutual interest in the present moment that can be shared by writer, subject, and reader alike.

Introduction

Marc Chénetier

I WISH BRITISH NOVELIST AND CRITIC of American literature Malcolm Bradbury had been able to participate, as he so often has in the past, in yet another collective European endeavor; the title of his latest novel, *Rates of Exchange,* might have served nicely for this introduction. If one considers the cultural "rates of exchange" between the United States and Europe, in effect, disappointment is the order of the day. Thanks to the odd chance investment of this or that publisher, to the benedictine dedication of a handful of researchers and translators, or to the enthusiastic endorsement of some suicidal literary magazine, here as well as there, such and such a novelist, poet, or playwright, eventually gets introduced to the reading public of the other continent; but one can hardly hope to get any sense of the general scene. For one Calvino, one Eco, one Robbe-Grillet, one Michel Tournier, one Handke, one Grass, or one Angela Carter published in the United States, how many worthy European writers never make it to these shores? What fraction of the American public has ever heard of Julien Gracq, J. M. G. Le Clezio, Leonardo Sciascia, or Ian McEwan? Conversely, if writers as strikingly diverse as Styron,

Singer, Bellow, Hawkes, Brautigan, or Bukowski have managed to emerge haphazardly in France, Germany, Italy, or England, one cannot help mourn the dozens of excellent American writers whose names are totally unknown in Europe. Well, not totally. And not exclusively in Europe. Chances are that important living authors unknown to Europeans are also little known to Americans.

This book not only endeavors to demonstrate the awareness on the part of European critics of a large variety of American literary productions; it also wants to encourage the development of other types of exchange. The curious, mutually patronizing, mutually suspicious, mutually admirative, and slightly arrogant love-hate relationship between European and American criticism is no new thing, but recently, over the last twenty years, the age-long misunderstanding has at times taken on strangely disquieting proportions. To most mainstream critics of American literature in the United States, adjectives are easily translated: French means slightly batty, British staid and dusty, and German ponderously philosophical, and so forth . . . To most European critics, on the other hand, the American scene is strewn with philologically inclined editorial jobs and blatantly impressionistic or idealistic critical productions. Only in very distinct circles is there any specific cooperation and discussion. Such contacts more often than not fruitfully emphasize and highlight fundamental differences in critical approach and philosophical assessment. Poe's image in Europe and in the United States will serve as a hackneyed example, but so could divergent approaches to Melville, Thoreau, the Gilded Age, or Henry James. When it comes to contemporary literature, the eternally puzzling time-lag that has separated American from European judgments and criticism tends to surface more dramatically. Melville, Faulkner, and Dos Passos had a name in Europe before their own country paid attention to them. Today many of the authors European academics interested in contemporary American literature may talk about when they visit or teach in the United States will be largely unknown to their students and often despised or looked askance at by their colleagues. Donald Barthelme and Thomas Pynchon might occasionally grace coffee tables along with copies of the *New Yorker,* but few English departments in this country offer courses on contemporary American literature, and writing one's Ph.D. dissertation on William Gass or Robert Coover is hardly the best way of landing a job. The scenes are so drastically different that one feels the need for a variety of real exchanges and introductions.

This essay, in other words, aims to be, in good metafictional logics—an introduction to introductions.

But the general introduction that this collection of essays constitutes would not have been possible without years of intense preparation of the ground.[1] A good friend, whose name appears in the following pages, is fond of saying that he loves international meetings, conferences, and publications because they so effectively strengthen prejudice. His tongue-in-cheek remark does not prevent him from being extremely active in American-European cultural exchanges, and all the participants in this volume have, at some point or another, been enthusiastic instruments of ever more open communication.

The 1970s, in spite of a number of depressing features, was a magic decade. Looking back simultaneously on literary production and critical output, on the work on contemporary literature being done at the time in European and American universities it is indeed possible to witness the gradual conception of the present book.

I was then teaching at Paris III–Sorbonne Nouvelle and taking part in a seminar created and directed by Professor André Le Vot. A number of his own doctoral students, writing on contemporary authors, were there, but the place was open to all other interested parties. Open and alive. There was hardly a bimonthly meeting without the news of some recent publication: Hawkes had published this and Coover had written that, the latest stories by Barthelme were out, Purdy had struck again, Pynchon had presented us with another fat book, Brautigan had changed, Kosinski evolved, and Nabokov was still around. Not only that, but every meeting had also somehow to be prefaced by summaries and exchanges of impressions on the new Genette, the new Barthes, the new Deleuze, the new Iser, the new Todorov, or the new Lyotard. Early students of Lacan and Derrida introduced their work to that group. Those of us who had carried their political and historical consciousness from the 1960s into the new decade talked of Macherey and Althusser, of a Baudrillard who had not yet gone out for "seduction," and the perspectives opened by "Les Annales." Linguistic theories were being refined and tested, narratology was riding high, and Levi-Strauss, Foucault, and the Russian Formalists were nourishing literary critical thought anew. Authors came by: Hawkes, Styron, Baumbach, Coover, Federman, Kosinski, Mirsky, Charyn, Sontag, Reed, Sukenick, and Spielberg at first; Gass, Major, Irving, Barth, and Elkin later. Came and came back and read and talked and answered and debated and, I think, enjoyed themselves as much as we enjoyed them. An uncommon sense of liberation and pleasure presided over our explorations. A lively literature made for lively involvement. Simultaneously, in Italy, in Germany, in Britain, and in eastern Europe, similar groups took shape and worked.

By the mid-1970s, enough contacts had been established formally and informally between the various centers of activity, on contemporary American fiction in particular, for them to engage in fruitful cooperation. Relations existed very early on between the Paris III Research Center and the Center for Twentieth Century Studies of Milwaukee. Thanks to a grant from the European Economic Community, the administrative efforts of Gerhard Hoffmann, and the work of his team of assistants and graduate students, new contacts were established and institutionalized between the universities of Paris III, Würzburg (West Germany), and East Anglia (Great Britian), and then with the University of Venice (Italy). For four years programs in contemporary American literature were developed in common at these universities, and meetings were held every year at each of them. Trilaterals were held, then quadrilaterals, then multilaterals as colleagues from Belgium, Holland, and other western European countries joined in. Two conferences were organized in Poland at the initiative of Polish colleagues and regrouped other specialists from eastern (Hungary, Checkoslovakia, and East Germany) and western countries.

By the time the 1970s were over a rather pleasing network of friendships and cooperation had been established, boosted by the growing importance and frequency of contacts afforded by a rejuvenated and expanded European Association for American Studies. By the time the 1970s were over a number of specialized journals, such as *Delta, Trema,* and *Granta,* had seen the light of day and a host of others, such as *Ranam, Amerikastudien,* and *Revue Française d'Etudes Américaines,* had dedicated special issues to contemporary American fiction. By the end of the decade there were courses on contemporary American literature in most departments of English in European universities. By the end of the decade several books on contemporary American fiction had been published by Europeans (Tony Tanner and Manfred Pütz among others). By that time, Paris III having no longer a senior specialist in the field, the research center lost its original institutional bonds and reappeared in 1981 as the "Groupe René Tadlov" under the aegis of the Maison des Sciences de l'Homme in Paris. Moreover, numerous contacts had been established with some of the best American specialists in the field and with a number of international theoreticians. Meetings held in Munich, Venice, Paris, Wisconsin, Nice, Montpellier, Norwich, and Würzburg allowed the European teams the pleasure of their collaboration and the benefit of their insights. Ihab Hassan, Thomas Le Clair, Jerome Klinkowitz, Patrick O'Donnell, Jack Hicks, Geoffrey Hartman, Dominick La Capra, Ralph Cohen, Wolfgang Iser, M. Calinescu, and R. Warning—all, and many others, participated in several colloquia discussing contemporary fiction, critical theory, or both.

With the opening of the 1980s, everything points to the incontrovertible fact that contemporary American literature now has a firm hold in European academic circles and curricula and that European research, far from having subsided after a very active decade, has found a more visibly productive cruising speed. The increase in the number of special issues dedicated to contemporary American literature published by *Delta* and other French journals—linked with the second life and developing activities of the "Groupe René Tadlov" in Paris, with its thirty active members, monthly workshops, and yearly *inter campos* seminar—is one example. The increasing number of German books and dissertations in the field is another. A third is the birth of the Contemporary Writers Series, edited in England by Malcolm Bradbury and Christopher Bigsby and published by Methuen. Another set of examples could include the several publications of Italian researchers from Venice, Bologna, and Rome principally, and the important work (particularly on Saul Bellow) accomplished in Belgium by our late friend Edmond Schraepen and by scholars concerned with fiction (Johan Thielemans and Pierre Michel) or with the theatre (Gilbert Debusscher).

Following the trails blazed by specialists of classical American literature, modernism, and most notably Southern writers over the last fifty years, a sizeable number of writings and analyses by European students of the contemporary literary scene now regularly find their way into American publications in the form of articles or chapters in collective books, as a quick survey of the last six or seven volumes of *American Lit-*

erary Scholarship (Duke University Press) easily demonstrates. But, from what impressions and remarks I have been able to gather in discussions over the years, the particularities of European angles of approach do not often make much of an impact on and are neither always fully convincing to nor very much appreciated by American students of contemporary literature. Theoretical inclinations and pragmatic drives have a hard time mixing in this country, as many Yale-inspired works of epigonic criticism keep demonstrating. For some extraordinary reason, the picture of American criticism available today to the European observer keeps illustrating the following paradox: whoever is interested and trained in Continental critical theories turns most of his or her activities to the literatures of the past and hardly ever touches contemporary authors. Let Harold Bloom endorse a contemporary author and it is more likely to be a formally conservative one, one whose writing practice thrives on the general sentiment that language is securely anchored and its transitive uses beyond reasonable doubt, someone, say, like Saul Bellow or Gore Vidal,[2] rather than a more innovative voice. Conversely, the ever more numerous pieces written in this country on contemporary American literature are overwhelmingly couched in rather traditional critical terms. For the few most stimulating exceptions, such as O'Donnell, Le Clair, Molesworth, McCaffery, Graff, or Stevick, we must trudge through endless series of humanistically inclined commentaries that hardly allow us to seize the novelty of the many authors who have emerged over the last thirty years. Some of the very best American critics of the contemporary scene are actually writers themselves; William Gass stands out but he is not alone.

A visibly contrasting—and I hope enriching—set of views is what this book, for all its modest proportions and concomitant lack of total representativeness, may be able to afford. Its original plan made for roughly even representation of the various European countries involved, but the pressures of time unfortunately did not allow all of the colleagues approached to contribute their particular critical views.

Angles

"All is angle: the capacity of the observer to receive. And incidence: encounter, repetition, moment," Adriaan van Hovendaal notes in Guy Davenport's story "The Dawn in Erewhon."[3] And if I have grafted the adjective "critical" onto this fundamental notion, the reader of these lines is asked to believe that it is not for the mere pleasure of a disputable wordplay (although I have certainly never been above that). The accolade in fact springs from the most respectable of definitions: "*Critical angle:* 5.1.: (Optics) the least angle of incidence at which a ray is totally reflected."[4] And in effect the regrouping particularity of the analyses that follow may well lie with the specific degree of aperture afforded by distance. *Révérence parlée,* critical acuteness of perception can and must often oxymoronically accommodate a modicum of geometrical obtuseness. Stretched across the Atlantic, the angle of perception grows straighter as one is displaced from the immediacy of things to contemplate them at a distance; what seems most important when apprehended from up close becomes somewhat peripheral, while previously unnoticed asperities loom large on a horizon illuminated by lower beams of grazing light. The immediate temptation to read national texts as documentary evidence or social commentary is necessarily dampened; instead, their *textual* features feed the reflection of critics for whom their informative or expository quality is filtered and reassessed in the light of foreign concerns. If "misprision" (to use Harold Bloom's notorious concept) indeed has its worth, the swerving or clinamen of the texts included in this collection from the "native" apprehension of American literary texts can no doubt come as enrichment. Not that cultural dimensions are ever absent from European analyses of contemporary American literature. But the ratio of their importance to that ascribed to formal features and writing strategies is radically altered when compared with American commentaries. The temptation to go comparative increases as the awareness of the intertext afforded by other literatures is stronger and relativizes parochial enthusiasms; so does that of drawing on and drawing parallels with other aesthetic and theoretical fields. Clearly, if the angle of perception becomes "critical" in these essays, it is because the "least angle of incidence"—the texts analyzed can hardly be said to be of immediate relevance to largely different cultural contexts—allows for a greater "totality" of reflection; to cultural and literary historical concerns are added the foregrounded preoccupations of form and epistemological impact, as well as vivid reactions to cultural questions and particularities often occulted by proximity. To each point of view belong its particular scotomazations and perceptive advantages.

It may well be, of course, that the "ray" reflected here illuminates a certain grain or quality of European thought and intellectual habits (tics?) just as much as, or more than, the variety of American literary productions examined. "Tell me how you talk about texts and I'll tell you who you are" seems to be a valid aphorism for this situation. The exercises involved may explain more about European literary and critical sensibilities than they do about the authors and questions examined. But our collective vain assumption is also that they point out a variety of features in American texts too often left aside by American practitioners of literary criticism pressured by a different set of demands and expectations. "Where one speaks from" is of necessity made more conspicuous with cultural distance, all the more so as the Continental tradition has long been partial to the explicit foregrounding of ideological choices and standpoints, whereas American criticism tends to

flow along with the deeply embedded—and possibly inau-
gural—American idea that ideology is bust, history bunk, and
critical moves natural and unproblematical. Clearly the "era
of suspicion" has shaped European approaches to a much
wider extent than it has influenced critical gestures in the
United States.

It is not my desire or intention to exhibit here, with a different perspective in mind, the hilariously self-destructive
mental configuration I once heard vocally illustrated by a
militantly feminist upper-class lady at a cocktail party: "Men
always generalize." I hope I can avoid the temptation, in other
words, to lump neatly into distinct and homogeneous bunches
critical traditions of equally rich internal variety or to conclude
on the necessary predictability of critical reactions on both
sides of an ocean that, all told, aesthetically unites more than
it separates. Stimulating transatlantic collaborations and innumerable personal contacts long ago dispelled the suggestion
of an eternally insuperable gap. But the trends exist and a
number of features illustrate them in the following essays.

The price to pay for the breaking down of stereotypes and
a fairer balancing of the going "rates of exchange" in the
intellectual sphere must be candid exposure and honest re-
ceptivity. I believe all the authors in this volume would agree
with me—their response to this initiative must constitute the
sign of a degree of acquiescence!—on a number of positions
on which this volume is predicated.

No clinometer is readily available to register the angular
differences illustrated by the critical essays in this volume. But
it will be clear, I think, that they all reflect a very personal
and very deep commitment to literary texts. Not only are these
texts viewed as a source of pleasure and intellectual challenge
and enjoyment, but they are also viewed in a manner betraying
the conviction that texts matter, in close and intimate ways,
that the problems they pose, *qua* texts, go infinitely beyond
their contents and more or less explicit subject, and that their

study is much more than a professional activity from which status or dividends of various kinds may be obtained, indeed that they represent something against which most of our everyday ideological, existential, and behavioral choices have to be sounded.

Behind this rather passionate European involvement there seems to me to be an institutional backdrop differing widely from the American scene. For all the toll an imported "publish or perish" situation may have taken of late on the European stage, I believe it still holds true that the institutional pressures to which we Europeans are submitted remain of a very different sort. Our academic politics have not yet taken on quite the quantitative dimension so often bewailed—although also encouraged—by American selection committees, and I am particularly receptive to the sense of free-roaming fun and pleasure that emanates from the papers presented here. Here also lurks the implicit conviction that the study of literary texts is not one intellectual exercise among others and that crucial stakes are in play depending on the approach or approaches one chooses to take. Over and against an MLA type of ossification that derives from institutional pressure and engenders a politics of the well-made essay devised to satisfy formal criteria in the production of periodically mass-buried stillborns, over and against the creation of critical pieces as something one just has to do not to be thrown back into the cold Tenebrae that lie off every bend along the tenure tracks, and largely in defiance of the commodified and market-oriented academic and intellectual situation that gradually takes over most of the Western institutions of higher learning, it seems to me these essays indicate in varying degrees an often playful and Pelagian, albeit earnest and uncompromising, sense of the intellectual and aesthetic pleasures and lessons to be derived from a critical expression freed of codified molds.

No less clearly, most of these essays gleefully cut through a number of entrenched positions that, to a certain extent, paralyze expression in the field at hand in the United States. One will find no agonizing—nor agonistic—concern, in these pages, over the strange debate generated in this country around the issue of the "postmodern." The issue in question is largely beclouded by the fact that modernism and modernity are expediently, but confusingly and misleadingly, collapsed for the sake of a neutered adjective—"modern"—that never really confesses to its chosen semantics, "aesthetic-literary," as in "Joyce, Pound, Faulkner, Futurism, Surrealism, and all that," or "philosophical," as in "following the mideighteenth century mark chosen by Hegel." This internally hybrid adjective relinquishes instead all embarrassing particulars for the sake of a lifebuoylike prefix that keeps the present floating uncommittedly on the indeterminate and the provisional. The obstinate practice of anathema on which reputations are made and unmade on each side of the bizarre and manipulatively crooked fence dividing the pro-innovative, postmodern, and "anti-Aristotelian" factions from what can then only be "gardnerites" and "diehard conservatives," in the dubious language of cultural radicalism, will not be found here. Nor will a clearcut choice be discovered to underlie essays dealing with authors who cannot easily be pigeonholed according to often terroristic canons. Welcome to the demilitarized zone.

I do not wish to insist here on the various critical methods used, on the particular clinometrics pertaining to individual endeavors. Only a wearisome catalog could ensue and the reader is, I trust, both aware enough of the tags at hand and in a position to judge what influences have come to bear on the various discourses that follow. But it seems legitimate to point out that while repudiating standard "New Critical" and "explication de textes" approaches, most of the "practical" essays included in the second part indicate a willingness and an eagerness to tackle the texts at hand on the level of particulars, while the more "general" essays of the first part concentrate on the specifics of strategic moves. Most of us indeed believe that microanalysis reveals at least as much about over-all strategic literary choices as placated and, as it were, im-ported macrogrids might in the ritual attempt to check out how this or that particular theory can be made to fit. The text cannot be fodder for critical theories, which must at all times retain their ancillary quality. For all the variety of theoretical tools employed in these pages—not because each critic has forever decided to stake one particular claim of the critical territory and apply it to all he or she touches but because the tool chosen seemed to be the best available under the circum-stances defined by the text under scrutiny—one may be struck by the general reluctance to flaunt flashy "isms" and to handle labels as heavy artillery. It may be fitting to puzzle here, par-enthetically, over the more or less faddish and more often than not blundering vogue of "structuralism," "poststructur-alism," and "deconstruction" in the United States (a thick hail of such words provides the curtain for many a regional con-ference, but the curtain seldom rises), whereas the most im-portant practitioners of the disciplines roughly confused with or subsumed under these terms never dreamed themselves of endowing them with such sledgehammer power. It may also be fitting here to wonder about the ferociously pragmatic energy that has come to characterize the American use of such labelled fields for immediate and forceful application to all visible texts under the sun, a fact that puzzles Europeans to no end as, for most of them, all such theoretical explorations are meant to feed literary reflection rather than to dictate recipes for the shaping of its practical output. Some influences are obvious in these pages, from that of linguistic models in Maurice Couturier's sprited and idiosyncratic essay or Pierre Gault's search for the common tropes underlying artistic cre-ation in different media, to that of Derrida in Johan Thiele-mans' and Claude Richard's papers, via that of Levi-Strauss, Lacan, or Gadamer in others. Yet, for all their importance, these methodologies do not use the texts at hand for their own defense and illustration, choosing rather to expand the range of potential readings and enrich preexisting ones. Theoretical preoccupations loom large in these texts but they seldom preempt upstage positions rightly held by the literary texts under consideration.

For all this defiance, theoretical notions and a certain accompanying technical lexicon are not absent from the following pages. Only the most hackneyed partisans of an elusive and eternally naturalized common sense could object to the use of a jargon used for brevity and convenience under the assumption that all activities need a vocabulary of their own. Jargon more often than not describes the way the other guy speaks. If the indiscriminate users of "human nature," "dense plotting," "brief and powerful sentences," "beautiful imagery," and "highly convincing piece" see no problem with the words they use, they will nevertheless tend to object to a set of critical tools that go against the grain of their own intellectual choices. But since no surgeon and no mechanic likes to describe his working instruments in detail hundreds of times a day, every time he needs the nurse or the apprentice to hand over a "catheter," a "sphygmomanometer," a "camshaft," or a "head gasket," we can have recourse to fairly common critical terms without much of a bad conscience. Similarly, if metaphor and anecdote will serve, if science and painting can be of use, if epistemology and philosophy are found illuminating, if psychoanalytical concepts come in handy, and if hypothetically simplified categories will do the trick, none of these essays cringes before them. The beauty of it, as I see things, is that these essays have no shame.

A further common bond is probably furnished by the conviction, not always shared by Americans themselves, that contemporary American literature is now as rich as it has ever been, that fiction, in particular, has capitalized on and transcended European experiments of the period 1945–1965, and that after a rather lame post–World War 2 period, formal innovation and imaginative renovation are making for a most lively scene. The overabundance of American poetry—there are now more than 3,000 published poets in the United States—is too dependent on a prevailing confessional mode to make the period anywhere akin to the explosion of poetic production that characterized, say, the 1920s; but the fiction to come out since 1960 will no doubt hold its own when compared with that same period. Writing the history of the present is no mean gamble,[5] but the list of authors examined in the following pages most certainly includes the names of many writers who are here to stay.

This book of essays is offered to the American public as a cordial token of the genuine interest taken by European scholars in one of the richest literatures of our day. It will be found, we hope, to be highly idiosyncratic—to be made out of "views" or "takes" that, for being rather different from American approaches, can fertilize a field in need of more numerous and ever deeper explorations. American friends and colleagues who have worked with us over the years will recognize the spirit in which they are offered and will hopefully grace us with uncompromising reactions, will help us break down a few more barriers of suspicious parochialism, and will make sure we are made aware of their sentiment, favorable or adverse, on the question. As an academic friend of mine used to end his lectures, "now is the time for questions, queries, comments, [and] general insults."

Meanwhile, I hope the reader will draw as much pleasure from these pages as was involved in thinking about them and writing them, and with thanks to all concerned, I shall run back somewhere into the pages of this book, among friends, where, more than here, I really belong.

Part 1
Wide Angles

1

The Real Thing

Notes on an American Strategy

Alide Cagidemetrio

> *They went off with an evident increase of comfort, founded on their demonstrable advantage of being the real thing.*
>
> —Henry James, *"The Real Thing"*

I N GILBERT SORRENTINO'S *Mulligan Stew*, a host of "characters" wait "in a remote enclave 'down the river' " to be reemployed in novels-to-be. They also claim a decent salary as just remuneration for the name they have made for themselves in a lifetime/fiction time. The literary market is where they belong; living palimpsests, these characters' role is to lend themselves to as many rewritings as are demanded and, given the status of contemporary fiction, many of them are frustrated and gape for "a decent job in some reasonable book."[1] Like the models in Henry James's story they seem to know that the real thing for them is to be their roles, to achieve perfection within a system—a literary system. They know how this system works and are on a par with the author: *"we* are as real as he is," states one character in reference to the character who plays the author in Sorrentino's above-mentioned novel. They pretend to be as real as Scheherazade, Don Quixote, or Frankenstein, sharing Jorge Luis Borges's epocal belief that it is the characters who are real, not their flesh-and-bone authors and readers, and that they achieve reality as functions of the written world, the ever-open library of Babel. In other words, their being real is connected with their functions, their names, and their roles in an infinite number of stories, and their *effet de réel* is obtained through the exhibition of their fictional statute. Signs of a system of illusion, characters in contemporary experimental fiction show how far the compromise between life and fiction has gone: the author as character and the character as character obstinately act out in performance a world vision that is as compact as that of the Balzac-era: reality is an illusion, we are fictions, and disbelieve in words.

"Nothing changes, yet everything must change. . . . It is a long story,"[2] comments Clarence Major's narrator in *Reflex and Bone Structure*. What does not change is the obsession with the nature of reality and of what would seem its opposite, illusion. The poetics of fragmentation, reflexivity, and repetition—from Robert Coover to Ronald Sukenick, Clarence Major, Gilbert Sorrentino, and Jonathan Baumbach—posit themselves as the "real thing." Metanarrative motives, such as the author's struggle to capture reality, are main narrative issues, and the mimetic or "realistic" superiority is openly denounced as impending darkness: "this realism is their darkness so powerful that it lasts for the rest of . . ."[3] To scare away realism is to enhance the sense of reality, to make fiction reality itself. The ideal fiction would then be, in Sorrentino's words, that which "mirrors the process of the real, but, being selective, makes a form that allows us to see these processes with clarity."[4] Fiction as process is a major category in the poetics of the avant-garde. Gertrude Stein would have agreed with Sorrentino and company, the value of the real is in the process. And to say it within the novel itself—which is to exploit its metanarrative possibilities—is not new either. One could go back to Henry James's *Sacred Fount,* or, to remain in the purely American tradition, even to *The Scarlet Letter.*[5] What is new is the degree of involvement with showing or reflecting the arbitrariness of any discourse, from that of literature itself to that of films or television. The "real thing" is arbitrary, and fiction has first of all to expose the arbitrariness of its own rules, decomposing the elements that constitute its main quality, illusion. The thing critics lament as a loss, the disappearance of the dividing line between literature and theory, becomes the necessary structuring principle. Arbitrariness, as Emile Benveniste has shown, lies in the relation between the sign and its object. Fiction builds itself as the topos of the relation of the sign to its system, literary and paraliterary, but also acts out the epistemological problem of the creation of meaning in the sign object process. Fiction then claims to represent a salutary antidote to fixity, to tradition, and to the nonfiction mythos of the contemporary American scene, an antidote that the ideal reader will take in order to dispel "negative hallucinations"; or "when you don't see something that's really there" this novel can help you, so a disruptionist slogan could run.[6] Frankenstein's children and Sukenick's readers are taught to consider the novel and its mechanisms as the only reality, that is, as a self-contained discourse. At the same time they are invited to take an active role in the interpretation of such a reality, thus connecting signs to objects through the reading experience. So Major, commenting on his novels and those of Sukenick, Steve Katz, Charles Wright, Walter Abish, and others, stresses the importance of the experience of the reader when confronted with what he calls the "nonrepresentational novel."[7]

Pragmatic theories of literature have made us consider the text as an event, a happening, and "happening is the hallmark of reality."[8] Sukenick confirms, "What's happening here is the novel." Textual strategies, such as the position of the narrator and the use of the narrative present, tend to assert another pragmatic principle: "the condition of *con*ception and *per*ception which enable the observer to construct the object intended by the signs."[9] A narration in the present aims to destroy story and assert discourse, to stress the relation between the *persona,* very often overt, responsible for the narrative voice and its implied or virtual reader. Simultaneity is the value elicited by this practice.[10]

It makes the identification of the processes of reading and writing possible: "Cora is putting on a dress. It's blue with white flowers. Her lips are pressed together. Canada is leaning with his back against the mirror and Dale is leaving. I *think* he's leaving. He's headed for the door."[11] In this opening fragment of *Reflex and Bone Structure* the effect of simultaneous conception and perception is obtained by transforming the witness function of the narrator into an active interpretative function. "I *think*" indicates the interplay between witnessing and working out the relation of the object described to the subject detaining the narrative voice. It is more than a device for signalling the position of the narrator; it is also an invitation to the reader to share in building up hypotheses of meaning within the narrated world or, rather, within the narration in process. The narrated world tends to derive its reality from the process of narration, which is a tautology for the workings of fiction in general. That is to say, experimental, nonrepresentational, or disruptionist fiction seems to identify itself with the very notion of literature as represented by narration. From the arbitrariness of illusion and the value of its experience for the production of meaning come the structural principles of their texts. They are the "real thing" insofar as they aim primarily at reflecting the fascinating and mysterious world of fiction, where the teller, the word, and the listener cooperate in transforming illusion into reality.

A Detective Story

The novel, *Lionel Trilling* maintained, "is born in response to snobbery". Snobbery, the product of illusions generated by the social context, is characterized by "emotions", such as "uneasiness, self-consciousness, self-defensiveness, and the sense that one is not quite real but can, in some way, acquire reality."[12] If the great tradition of the realistic novel to which Trilling is referring was an answer to snobbery, that same snobbery and its associated emotions have come to constitute the very texture of contemporary experimental fiction. The self-reflective novel aims at detecting its own nature and its own making, at exposing that which is concealed in its illusion, at revealing an uneasiness and, at the same time, at functioning as self-defense. The uneasiness occurs when confronted with that which is still the tradition of narration, the grandeur of literature as represented by the masters of the past, whose books still figure on the best-seller list—from Balzac to Conrad, from Dickens to Tolstoy. The self-defense consists in showing that the new novel is literature itself. Like all parvenus, self-conscious narrators and characters inquire into their own role in the actual story-world. Or rather their inquiry constitutes the true story, that is, the impossibility of consequential (illusory) narration of a story. Only "fragments" of narration are allowed to make their appearance to show the interplay between the representational code and the means by which the code is constructed. The neat consequential story of tradition is turned into a puzzle, as is appropriate from the point of view of those who investigate forms and relations of a system of discourse in order to represent it.

Within the literary system the detective or mystery story seems to provide an apt referential code for self-reflective fictions. Both *Mulligan Stew* and *Reflex and Bone Structure* stage a murder as the central incident in a fiction whose object is to investigate itself. In both cases some doubt remains as to whether any murder has been committed at all. To merely name the word *murder* is enough to start an investigative process no longer aimed solely at finding a culprit, since there may be no corpse, but to explore the possibility of the construction and deconstruction of meaning. The word *murder* originates a plot: a detective novel begins with a murder and its narrative development inevitably leads to the discovery of the truth. But the grammar of this development, as Todorov has shown, is dependent on "the antagonism between truth and verisimilitude."[13] In the end what is true is not verisimilar, and what is verisimilar proves not to be true. A high degree of verisimilitude would prove a maximum degree of illusion. The detective novel, then, is a convincing instance of the way narration works. It is appropriate that in *Mulligan Stew,* Martin Halpin, the disobedient alter-ego of the author, refuses to consider his supposed victim dead (ironically "characters must look alive"), while at the same time he is made to carry out his investigation as if the victim were dead. In *Reflex and Bone Structure* the "dead" Cora and the "living" one are alternately substituted for one another in a jigsaw movement ("She moves closer. Away."). The novel itself begins in a reversal. The very first fragments present us with Cora "well and alive" in an action in the present tense, then a sudden switch to the past tense initiates the narration of the discovery of her corpse. The origin of the novel, its beginning, is in the "life" of the victim, not in her death. There is no progression or regression in time, but there is the copresence of a possible storyline and an imaginary discourse on what Cora means as an object of representation. Murder then is not a point in time, an origin, but a reference with no statute in fact or incident. In the detective novel, moreover, verisimilitude is achieved through the slow evidencing process of a concealed mechanism of cause and effect, which is confirmed by true or apparent motives justifying the relation between fact, murderer, and victim. "I have no motive. Not really a motive," announces Martin Halpin.[14] And if motives make murder verisimilar, then in lacking them murder itself is nonexistent. The pact between text and reader as to what is "real" is exposed to ridicule by means of a narration that exploits the distance between the referential literary scheme of the genre and what it conceals, which is that truth in literature (as in life) is something agreed upon by general consensus. What Gérard Genette calls the Valincour theorem has its paradoxical application here: no motives are necessary where general consensus is denied, and what is true is purely subjective.[15]

It is the detective's eye that usually sees what others do not see; it is a "private eye" peering through the veil of appearances, setting up new and unexpected relations. Dashiell Hammett is the father of Ned Beaumont, Sorrentino's would-be victim in *Mulligan Stew,* and it was Hammett who shaped the archetypal private eye, a man "capable of any action, endowed with godlike immunity and independence."[16] The "private eye" is a suitable metaphor for the role of the narrator as represented ironically in *Mulligan Stew* and more functionally in *Reflex and Bone Structure.* It is the subjective eye that provides its own logic to the text; it is the organizer of time and space:

The most amazing discovery is that it is always nighttime *inside* the house; that is, when one ventures outside, it is day. It is only in here that Lamont has managed to arrest time. . . .
It is a rather odd house, to say the least. There is the living room and the den, but we have not been able to find any other rooms. It *seems* as if there were other rooms—I don't quite know how to put this—they are simply *not there!*[17]

Within Antony Lamont's novel, Martin Halpin experiences the limitations of time and space he has set and tries to overcome them in his own private investigation. The house of fiction is explored by him in order to establish the relation between the *chronotope* of the genre and what would be a "real" house, or a different type of house in a different novel. Major abandons the novel-within-the novel investigation to show how continuity works when the fixity of time and space is overcome: "I'm back in bed. The late show comes on. It's 1923. *The Bright Shawl*. Dorothy Gish, Mary Astor. I'm taking Mary Astor home in a yellow taxi. Dorothy Gish is jealous."[18]

Spatial contiguity between the narrated world and the referential one (as in the movies) matches temporal homogeneity. The *chronotope* turns out to be that of the subject's mind, the mind of the detective who tells the truth—his own truth—beyond verisimilitude and, at the same time, exacts a new pact between the reader and himself as to the very nature of reality. The surrealists had already asserted the possibility of such a "supernatural" function of the subject as detective. His mind can blur the difference between the real and the imaginary, between subjective and objective. The contiguity between the "imagined" world and the "real" one is qualified here by referentiality, to the novel and to the movie. That which is narrated, without what Todorov called the "hesitation" of the fantastic, [19] comprehends the transition between the codes of the verisimilar and the marvelous, [20] in a continuity enhanced by tenses being paratactically connected. Syntactic regularity contrasts with and thus sets in relief what would seem to be a semantic aberration in the narrated world, [21] that is, its being both probable and improbable. Truth is not dependent on probability or, rather, what is probable is a construction that depends both on representational codes and on the combining function of the "private eye." The detective's function is to make us see unexpected coincidences; as Major's narrator says, it is a "mood of mystery" that shapes the novel. From micro- to macro-structures, reference and combination seem to be the structural principles of much experimental fiction, as if the real investigation of the mystery of what the truth is should take place in the interplay of the code of the "real", of verisimilitude, and the code of the marvelous, that is of the imaginary. The post-Freudian novel makes no mystery of the central importance of dreams as a suitable parallel for fiction. And it finds its objective correlative in films. Films become the referential pattern for a larger response and, as popular art, are the best interpreters of the collective imagination. Jonathan Baumbach extensively "remakes" movies in his novel *Reruns*. His investigation into the meaning of a life purports to be a sort of autobiography that would have started in earlier times with "I was born. . . ." His narrator reruns fragments of his past life as if they were old movies or excerpts of them. The text is organized in a double reversed movement: the narrator as character is either in the "movie" or out of it, as if watching it happen or even making it. Narration develops in the continuous overlapping of the "movie" and the "novel" code, combining them without solution of continuity. It is not a mere translation of one code into another, but the coexistence of two levels of discourse that gives origin to a third. "A neutral territory," Hawthorne would have called it—a territory where the improbable and the probable could meet; or it is a means of coping with reality. It is, in Baumbach's words, to "tell the guys . . . that in America anything is possible."[22]

Call Me Ishmael

A name given to a person or an object identifies it and makes reference to it possible. Names of characters are a constant grudge in recent fiction, from Thomas Pynchon's mysterious *V* (1963) to Sukenick's *Out* (1973), where the hero changes names at each chapter, to the explicit parody of the naming process staged in *Mulligan Stew*. Martin Halpin introduces himself and, at first, his identification seems casual and matter-of-fact: "The police should be here soon. It is I who called them. Halpin's the name." The reader is directly and in a friendly manner addressed soon after: "Call me Halpin—

Martin Halpin. Some of my friends call me Marty. Some few
call me 'Chuck'."[23] Martin Halpin's real introduction follows
the first appearance of his name as a clichéd answer to a
hypothetical question during the mentioned "official" telephone conversation: "What's the name?" "Halpin's the name."
The question/answer pattern is implicit in the very naming of
a character; an identification is needed as a reference within
the narration, and the character as *opérateur de lisibilité* requires
the certainty of an appellation.[24] Yet "Halpin's name" could
also be somebody else's name, just as "call me Halpin" is not
exactly "I am Halpin." The name of the character can be any
name, since it is the name as function and not the name as
signifier that matters. Any name has to be "semantically" filled
by the relation between character and text: "Let's say that I'm
Martin Halpin. Who cares? For the purposes of my story that
name will do as well as any. If you'd prefer to call me by
another name, that's all right, but remember what it is you
chose to call me so when you hear the name "Martin" or
"Halpin" or even "Marty" or " Chuck," and so on, you'll know
it's I."[25]

Characters and their names belong to a fictitious code—as
Sorrentino shows by calling Lamont's characters Ned Beaumont and Daisy Buchanan—and they help to sustain the referential illusion. No matter if the narrator advises us to accept
the lie, no matter if names change: in their apparent innocence or undisguised malice they transform a function into a
persona and are responsible for the relation between fiction
and reality. This is especially so when they are names taken
from reality itself, as is often the case in the historical novel,
where the mere name of a historical man or woman is one of
the main strategies of verisimilitude. Robert Coover's *Public
Burning* (1976) proves how extensively this use of the referential "historical" illusion can be used within a nonrealistic
code. Uncle Sam's show piles up the most "representative"
names of the time (and not only), together with names from

the collective imagination (Uncle Sam is one of them himself). A double referentiality is staged, to history and representational codes, thus playing upon the ambiguity between reality and fiction.[26] At the same time that he exposes it, Coover manages to show the compromise, the compromise of the name as well as the compromise of fiction insofar as the text is always bound to be somehow *lisible,* that is, interpreted according to the terms of the real. The obsession with the naming process is then another form of the obsession with reality—a reality whose references inside the text prove to be, differing in this from the surrealists, socio-historical. They are names from literature as well as names from the American scene. The writer himself wants to be identified in his own fiction with his own name, as Sukenick does or as other contemporary writers' names and (that of their works) peep into the narration. There are also the names of movie stars, film directors, and politicians. Self-reference or socio-historical reference tends to show how much America matters as an extratextual reality. Writers quoting each other's names ideally establish a self-advertising corporation whose referents are themselves in the marketplace (overwhelmed by "realistic" well-made fiction); names of people and objects alike tend to represent symbolically what is immediately perceivable as reality. The well-known name, be it a character's or an object's, "hyperrealistically" exploits the direct collusion between signifiers and their referents in social terms, so that a car is not a car, it is a Ford, an actor is not an actor but John Wayne, and, of course, a soft drink is a Coca-Cola. The signifiers are not common names but proper names; the *effet de réel* is delegated to a prior identification given by extratextual systems. Once again the contradiction between being and naming is implicit, a contradiction that is on the contrary evident in contemporary advertised, mass-communicated reality (how many times have you ordered a Coca-Cola and been served something else?).

The referential necessity of the text becomes the stylization of itself. Reduced to their essentials, names stand out, thereby causing their referential function to become paradigmatic of the double working of the text. It is now clear that "Call me Ishmael" or call me such and such is an explicit acceptance of the rules of the naming game, an acceptance of the co-existence of the certainty of what reality is—"My name is Ishmael and I am your reference for the real "— and of its opposite—" Ismael is only a fictitious name, of somebody else's making, it's not me." Names are made to reflect the compromise between reality and illusion that characterizes any literary text. In contemporary experimental fiction instances both of reality and of illusion are obsessively exhibited and reflected upon, as if the ambivalence of literature itself were the obsession and not the characteristic of the text. A "compulsion to repeat" is what seems to be the "method of reality" as text, thus suggesting that the experiment in writing is a sado-masochistic love act with the literary word, as well as with the contemporary American scene or with the unshakeable present of the "great American novel"—the ideal "real thing."

2

Modernism/Postmodernism

Continuities of a "Split" Repertoire of Narrative Themes and Strategies

(A Provisional Restatement of a Traditional View of Twentieth Century Literary Avant-gardism)

Hartwig Isernhagen

IN THE DECONSTRUCTIVE and postmodern attitudes that have, during the last ten years or so, become prominent in discussions of literature and criticism that aspire to any degree of contemporaneity, three distinct, though certainly related, intellectual and literary traditions appear to converge. On the most general level, such negative approaches to the text can be based on a nominalist philosophy of language that stresses the schematic and arbitrary character of any utterance. They may also be grounded in the axiom that a national literature can be distinguished by its negative intention and function from traditionally more affirmative ones; such was, for example, D. H. Lawrence's view in *Studies in Classic American Literature.* And finally, such readings can proceed on the assumption that there is something in a particular text's use of language that makes the deconstructive approach the only correct or adequate interpretation. This is obviously the case where a text foregrounds its own negation of preestablished patterns of meaning, as happens, above all, in postmodern texts.

The last statement, though, is close to tautological. In it, what one might call the hermeneutical adaptation of deconstructivist tendencies exhibits that circularity that is both the logical problem and the enabling strategy of hermeneutical approaches in general; and it raises the problem of the proper historical horizon for the interpretative act. The critic, in order to judge the adequacy of his deconstructive reading, needs to recognize and classify the text's use of language, that is, he needs to know its *Systemreferenz*[1] or the kind of repertoire from which it draws its strategies and, indeed, its general intentions.

This is the question I shall briefly attempt to deal with in this essay. In doing so I am isolating it from the other two questions, with which it is obviously not unconnected: Lawrence's view of American literature postulates that it is characterized by a nominalist attitude towards modern European cultural patterns and the rhetorics that embody them. And nominalist skepticism is a trait and the basis of those texts and those types of criticism to which I shall refer.

The problem of the uncertainty of a given text's repertoire is compounded, in the case of postmodern texts, by a general—though certainly not generally acknowledged—uncertainty as to whether a specifically postmodern repertoire does at all exist. The answer depends largely on the critic's view of modernism. If he accepts the perspective established by the New Criticism and related movements, he will ascribe to modernism an overriding concern with the creation of new and alternate meanings, such as Stephen Spender's outline of the aims of modernist writing in *The Struggle of the Modern:*

1. *Realization* through new art of the modern experience;
2. The invention through art of a *pattern of hope,* influencing society;
3. The idea of an art which will fuse past with present into the modern symbolism of *a shared life;*
4. The *Alternate Life of Art;*
5. *Distortion;*
6. The *Revolutionary concept of Tradition.*[2]

Postmodernism will then easily be conceived of as a movement that does in some ways continue the basic trends of modernism, but that above all reacts negatively against all those *affirmations* alluded to or implied by Spender.

It is not surprising that in some ways this is the majority view, since it claims, for our own historical moment, a radical newness, and since it gives the critical enterprise an aura of adventurous avant-gardism. In spite of these pragmatic assets, which it undoubtedly has, I wish to argue here for the merits of the opposite view, according to which modernism itself, rather than being predominantly the affirmative making of the New, was a movement whose historical impact can only be understood if one recognizes that it was at least as much a negative destruction of conventions. The argument, which is implicit in many of the critical self-reflections of modernism itself, was put forward again, after what one might call the New Critical barrier, by Frank Kermode.

In an essay from the very early 1970s, which perhaps makes his point most clearly because it is informed with a reflex of the radicalism of the 1960s, Kermode asserts that "the middle-aged are the victims of their own historical mistake"—perhaps because they "were taken in by what may be called the Hulme tradition, the authoritarian attitudes struck by some of the most influential writers":

From this we derived a model of modernism which included a large and impressive requirement of order. It was not an order that one could easily perceive . . . But literary order was demanded and related to more familiar forms of order, social and theological.

What we had forgotten, of course, was a modernism much more radical than [that one]. We had forgotten a modernism which ridiculed 'order', rejected the models which included it, and helped to invent the world we are going, for some time hence, to have to live in.

What we forgot was, to put it briefly, Dada.

In the course of the ensuing argument, Kermode refers to "desacralizing the arts," to giving "a violent kick at the entire notion of Art," to a "switch of attention from the environment to the instrument," to the fact that "the novel must make its way without the aid of the old, shared belief that its arbitrarinesses somehow represent a knowable world," and to the enumeration of several rejections: "rejection of restraints, rejection of the culture, rejection of the past."[3]

Modernism, in this view, has a repertoire of affirmative and negative strategies and intentions—a split repertoire. Postmodernism, the negations of which are of a kind contained by Kermode's argument, is then characterized by a different use of that same repertoire: provisionally put, by a more consistent and insistent use of its negative components. But this is a matter of degree, not of kind. Modernist and postmodernist texts and readings should be viewed as belonging to one and the same continuum of discourse.

It must be clear that this type of discussion is less interested in the strategies used by or the elements contained in a text, or in any combination of such components as such, than in the text, in its entirety, as a strategy for order. The question is whether and how and in how far the text sets itself up as a source of meaning; for modernist texts, I would like to suggest, the answer should be that the well-known concern of modernist writings with privileged moments of meaning and with the power of privileged forms of language to create or recreate a (communicative and communicable) sense of reality is balanced by a despair of all cultural forms, and particularly of language. If we have learned—largely, I think, under the influence of the New Criticism—to regard the relationship between despair and creation as a sequential one, with creation coming out of an overcoming the despair, this is quite simply an attempt to view such creation as a solution of problems and as a *product*, rather than as an ongoing *process* of trying to deal with the problem. There may be in this attitude something of the many reflexes of romantic thinking that one does find in modernist thought; but it is also possible to find more of Freud and (particularly) of later and simpler forms of psychoanalysis in it than of Romanticism.

The following view of modernism may, then, recommend itself as a basis for further reflections.[4]

If one of the besetting problems of modernism is the fragmentation and partialization of modern life, then the modernist work of art presumes to heal that deficiency (absence) through the creative act. It sets itself up, in the face of destruction, as a form of construction; but thereby it does not overcome the lack or solve the problem. Rather, the wholeness of the creative act remains abstract; it exists in uneasy interaction with notions of destructiveness that place it in jeopardy and prevent it from ever achieving a status of complete concreteness. In the tension, the theme of the guilt of language (and all cultural patterns) is present as an implicit criticism, not just of the general loss that characterizes the cultural situation, but also of the very attempt to deal with it in any concrete way. If the modernist text—as a historical phenomenon or a period "genre"—says yes at all (and I will admit that it does just that), it primarily and in the last analysis says yes to its own inability to say yes in any simple or concrete manner. This is what we mean when we talk of the abstractness of the implied values of modernist texts—an abstractness that we have learned to place historically and to recognize as a clear-cut cultural pattern.

Given this outlook, the profusion of different traditions, all of which seem to have become available to the modernist writer (in the spirit of a visitor to an imaginary museum), acquires the significance of a central fact. It is not an irritating anomaly in a tradition that really aspires to a more rigidly unified repertoire of textual strategies and a unified ideal of textual meaning; for even less than for other historical periods can we define the ideal text of modernism. What this uncomfortable fact points to is that modernism is a way, or a number of ways, of dealing with traditions and conventions, rather than being itself a single tradition or convention.

The formal disruptions of which we are all aware in modernist texts, then, are not entirely unified by the creative impetus. The absences of meaning to which the text is an answer of sorts are not entirely filled, through an act of transcendence, on the level of symbolic forms of thought or language. Art, specifically, does not provide a unified form that copes with cultural disruptions rendered mimetically on the level of content; nor is it an ultimate and over-arching strategy or rhetoric of unification for formal disruptions that mimetically render the lacks and problems of the socio-cultural situation; and the formal change from one work to the other, and—in a wider historical perspective—from premodernism to modernism (that is, the creation of the very notion of the modernist text), can itself not be read simply as an adequate and final solution of the problems of social change. Rather, on all levels—that of the objective historical existence of the work, that of its contents, and that of its form—there appears to exist the same opposition of negatives and positives, of negation and affirmation.

To show—very briefly and provisionally—that this is so on the level of themes (or overriding thematic concerns) and on that of narrative strategies, to show how this is so, and to show that this disposition is shared by modernist and post-modernist texts will be the concern of the remainder of this discussion.

The characteristic spiritual malaise of the twentieth century—that unprecedented loss of cultural cohesion that Spender sees as the source of innovation in the first half of our age[5]—can be talked about in terms of a loss of identity. In order, however, to arrive at a notion of the themes and textual strategies elicited by and developed in answer to it, it may be more fruitful to break that concept down into its components. It is less the self as such that is being endangered, according to the central texts of modernism/postmodernism, than the self in certain respects and relations, of which—I would like to suggest—four are of fundamental importance.

1. Vital contact with the other, and hence the meaning of that other, is lost. The frame of reference of personal inter-action—above all in sexuality—and of the spontaneous experience of a living nature breaks down; the well-known "death-in-life" results. The entire complex generates the theme of sexuality, of a psychology of sex, of the 'mind' of the body.

Sexuality, then, may take the form of a depersonalized or anonymous force outside the individual that determines his or her actions and reactions. As such, it may destroy the "upper" or properly "human" self and lead into a downward movement like the transcendence downward in the Black Mass at the end of Djuna Barnes' *Nightwood* (1937), or it may simply destroy a part of the self, like "Karintha" in Jean Toomer's *Cane* (1923). A similar destructiveness of depersonalized sexual forces is characteristic of the rituals of obscenity in Thomas Pynchon's *Gravity's Rainbow* (1973) and also of some of the gratuitous sexual rituals in Richard Brautigan's formulaic fictions. The attempt to transform this destructiveness and the destroyed sexuality of the individual itself into a more creative one through a willed involvement and a conscious acceptance of the risks it entails is a central theme in the fiction of D. H.

Lawrence as well as in John Barth's "Dunyazadiad" (1972) or William Gass's *Willie Masters' Lonesome Wife* (1968). The enterprise tends to be associated with notions of play, and obscenity is again and again used both in a spirit of playful infringement of decencies and as an attempt to break through barriers and to achieve a positive primitivism. The notion of a return to the level of animal existence through sexual encounters with animals, whether in true copulation or in mere sexual play, then does not appear as farfetched [See *Nightwood* or Stanley Elkin's "The Making of Ashenden," *Searches and Seizures* (1973)].

2. The meaning of action in an overarching metaphysical, religious, or spiritual context is lost. Social or group action as such can no longer be regarded as a source of meaning, nor does there exist a socially accepted form of individual action that can replace it. To generalize, patterns of action have become arbitrary in that they have lost all transcendent sanction. This generates the theme of myth and ritual.

The radical isolation and virtual or actual nihilism of so many "lost generation" characters and the aimlessness of many of their actions and movements result from the absence of such sanctions; the hectic increase in activity and mobility manifests that debilitating lack rather than overcoming it. Fitzgerald's *Great Gatsby* (1925) is as much a case in point as Hemingway's *Sun Also Rises* (1926) or Pynchon's *Crying of Lot 49* (1967). In the symbolic gestures of Gatsby's looking out across the bay and towards the green light *and* of the "boats [beating on] against the current, borne back ceaselessly into the past," at the end of *Gatsby,* there is the same attempt to capture the essential quality of the American dream as an expression of the human desire for meaning as there is in the rituals of bullfighting and trout fishing in Hemingway's works from the 1920s and 1930s and in the artificial mythical patterns constructed and acted out by Oedipa Maas.

It might be objected, at this point, that myth and ritual are ultimately affirmed in the works of Fitzgerald and Hemingway and that they appear as paranoid constructions in those of Pynchon or as arbitrarily repeatable empty formulas in those of Barth. But this is exactly the point under discussion: had one not better go back to those modernist texts and discover not only the destruction of Gatsby by his adherence to an obsolete myth and the provisional nature, the artificiality, and the brittleness of the order that only momentarily sustains Jake Barnes or Nick Adams, but also the thematic implications of these traits? And does one not need to see also the life-giving aspects of paranoid delusions in Pynchon's works and the playful creativity that goes into the reenactments of myths in Barth's works, from *The Sot-Weed Factor* (1960) to *Letters* (1979)?

3. The theme of history arises out of a loss of the very idea of historical action as meaningful action. This entails, it seems to me, a loss of time and space as frames of reference.

Both immobilization and randomness result from that predicament, until history is recreated as fiction—or as a series of fictions that, in their very proliferation, indicate that a common, shared, intersubjective, or even objective history for all has been irretrievably lost. All attempts at reconstruction, whether in Faulkner's Yoknapatawpha cycle, Dos Passos' "contemporary chronicles," Hemingway's *In Our Time*, Gass's fragments, Barth's attempts to write a history that will contain all his creations, Coover's satires, or Pynchon's apocalyptic fantasies of World War II and its aftermath, therefore, contain indices of their own provisional nature, in the form of the montage/collage construction of their juxtaposed subtexts, in the fantastic nature of their form and content, or in the deformation of many of the subjectivities "contained" in them on some level or other.

4. Finally, the meaning of language and other cultural instruments has become dubious. The mind (obviously) continues to work, but both its tools and the results it achieves through their use lack validity.

This view, of course, endangers the very process of artistic creation, and there arises, within the fiction, the theme of language and fiction-making. Whether the basic tendency is to withdraw into silence or to erupt into compulsive loquaciousness, whether the presentation of the theme takes place through self-reflectiveness or metafictionality, whether the formula of everyday language or of high and low art are exploited and simultaneously held up and exposed in all their historical emptiness—there is in the repetitive patterns-and-variations of Gertrude Stein and Samuel Beckett the same ambivalence of a destructive and, in a residual manner, still constructive play that the reader also encounters in Brautigan's hybrid combinations of fictional patterns, in Barth's forceful combination of styles and (human as well as non-human) languages in *Letters,* or in the interlaced fictions of Barthelme's "Views of My Father Weeping" (1971).

It is possible to view the four problem areas, which (as I have indicated) generate four thematic complexes that are perhaps in some ways characteristic of the experimental literature of our times, in strict analogy as areas in which the following frames of reference have been lost: vital communication between self and other; transcendent schemes of order and their reflexion in social patterns of action; historical action in time and space; and language and story. These are frames of reference in that they provide a context for the living-out of individual selfhood and in that they provide patterns of referring to something outside the self or directions in which that self can reach out.

If these frames break down, the act of referring becomes impossible and the self is isolated in alienation/anomie/autism, which is what the general (or super) theme of identity in modernism and postmodernism concretely means. And this is the way in which it is made up out of the more specific themes, or the way in which, conversely, it generates them.

At this point it becomes possible to connect theme and form—which, after all, is the basic tenet, postulate, or even axiom of modernism and postmodernism, or, perhaps, of all forms of experiment in writing. For these problems of reference, of context-building, recur in the text also as problems of contextualization and of language. I hope this is not an empty juggling of metaphors, but rather a valid way of going beyond the general postulate that the language of the text should not or must not deny the problems raised on the thematic level, but that it must also in some way remain enmeshed in that guilt of language that is a central aspect of the cultural crisis thematized. It is true—and one should insist on the validity of this perspective—that the text cannot simply arrogate the right to ignore, through its language use, the linguistic skepticism, the uncertainty about the historicity of actions, the metaphysical despair, and the loss of vital interaction that (individually or in fusion) exist on the thematic level. But it is also true, I would like to suggest, that the text, as a verbal construct, can modify the ways in which it establishes itself as a frame of reference and a system of contextualization, and that it can do so in general accordance with the themes it discusses and displays.

The most fundamental way in which the form can, then, mirror the themes of loss is through a denial of that activity of ordering that is automatically ascribed to everyday languages as well as to more conventional literary ones as their basic function: semantic reference.[6] In the terms of Charles William Morris's semiotics, the semantic dimension of the fictional text breaks down or becomes unstable. There results a shift to (again in Morris's terms) the pragmatic dimension of the text: its interaction with the reader, its *Leserappell;* one might also say, there occurs a shift from meaning to significance. The implied subjectivity of the text—both implied author and implied reader—creates whatever reference there is. As with all forms that the act of reading takes, this happens on the basis of the interaction between the text and the real reader, but only once that connection has been established as one that predates all concrete perception of meaning.

If this process, too, becomes unstable, there remains only verbal "play," or (again in Morris's terms) syntagmatic contextualization. The text only has the meaning of a purely formal contextualization of verbal elements; it does not appeal to the reader to construct some kind of more "real," more tangible meaning than its surface offers him, and it does not pretend that the verbal elements out of which it is made up have separate, semantic contents.

Language being the mixed thing that it is, it is almost impossible to conceive of texts that realize any of these possibilities in a pure manner. But it is possible to find texts that rely for their contextualization predominantly on one of these semiotic dimensions. And the basis of the predominantly "constructive" readings of modernist texts that were referred to above is (if I am not entirely mistaken) the view or axiom that they rely most importantly on the pragmatic dimension of the text; the *Leserappell* is so strong that the reader is drawn into the text, and his activity, in reading that text is the reconstruction of a "hidden" referent for the text—a referent, moreover, to which a degree or kind of reality is ascribed that tends to transcend that of our everyday world. By way of contrast, postmodernism is supposed to rely primarily on the syntagmatic dimension, revelling in pure verbal play and refusing both the reader's involvement in the text and the reconstruction of a referent.

But in texts like Gertrude Stein's portraits ("Van or Twenty Years After," for instance), like the dialogues in many of Hemingway's most reductionist short stories ("Cross-Country Snow," from *In Our Time,* appears to be a good specimen), or even like Sherwood Anderson's "Death in the Woods"—all of them texts one might regard as central to the modernist canon— the reader is denied precisely that involvement out of which he might derive the energy to reconstruct a referent for the text. This denial takes place through metafictional comment at the end of the Anderson story, through the hermetically closed cliché of dialogue phrases in Hemingway's, and through the extreme fragmentation of the entire discourse in Stein's; the technical means are different, but their ultimate effect is to throw the reader back onto the syntactic dimension. On the other hand, there occurs in many of those texts that are generally regarded as the central ones in anyone's version of a postmodernist canon the recovery of a true sense of facticity. The sense of history, which had crumbled in part under the pressure of the exaggerated demand for an overarching meta-physically guaranteed or relevant meaning, as it was made by many of the Modernist texts, is regained in bits and pieces, as fact, as episode, and as moment of suffering. And on a totally different level, postmodernism moves in the same di-rection of a reaffirmation of semantic reference: it regains that undoubted referentiality of metafictional comments that has bothered so many critics and led them to charge the post-modernists with writing in bad faith. What they have over-looked is, in my opinion, that within the entire "split" repertoire of modernism/postmodernism affirmation and negation di-alectically interact with one another and each functions as the other's enabling basis. To indict the deficiencies and arbitrar-inesses of language and of the mind makes sense only if, on some level or other, one can reliably do so, and if on that level, too, one can establish some idea, ideal, or utopia of the authentic—however tenuous and endangered such a utopia may be. And to search for a more authentic perception of reality, as well as for more authentic ways of verbalizing it, only makes sense if there is a well-grounded and well-developed notion and experience of alienation and inauthenticity. All I have been trying to argue is that modernism and postmodernism share a doubleness of vision and that they have developed a coherent, if highly diversified, repertoire of strategies to realize and cope with that vision.

3

Yours Faithfully, the Author

Maurice Couturier

I HAVE A COLLEAGUE at the university who finds himself in a strange predicament. He is a comparatively well-known specialist of a famous writer, and his small but fervent coterie of aficionados (should I say "aficionadas?") among his students often address him by that more famous name, no doubt as a tribute to his supreme act of impersonation. The same colleague, who, I hope, will never read these pages, is also cursed with a striking resemblance to a handsome and amiable political leader who is much better known in France than the aforementioned "famous writer." My colleague had never had to complain about this resemblance until a mentally disturbed girl of twenty-six accidentally crossed his path; she came up to him at the end of a cocktail party and warmly spoke a few endearing words, which my baffled colleague, who had never seen her before, failed to understand. It turned out that the girl had taken him for the amiable politician. After this first and (so far) only meeting, she even sent him a letter, addressed to something like "Ronald Smith" (a combination of the politician's first name and of my colleague's last name), and in the envelope there was only a visiting card with the girl's printed address and phone number.

I leave it to the imaginative reader to think up a psychologically, or poetically, relevant dénouement to the blossoming plot. In the meantime, I would like to investigate some of the maddening tricks that the postal system can play on you if you are not careful.

Here is a middle-aged woman, called Jane, who is terribly afraid of losing her good looks. Every morning, after rouging her cheeks, lining her lips and applying mascara to her eyes, she walks up to her mirror on the wall to check the value of her shares on the stockmarket. The rest of the day, she writes anonymous letters to people whose names she picked up from the telephone directory. Here is a sample:

Dear Mr. Quistgaard:
Although you do not know me, my name is Jane. I have seized your name from the telephone book in an attempt to enmesh you in my concerns.[1]

It goes on like this for two pages; the whole letter is quoted by Donald Barthelme in his weird book *Snow White.* Jane has apparently become terribly bored with her dumb mirror; she lacks "connection," as she lamely confesses. She is aware that in our modern, media-maniac world, people may feel that they are "overconnected"; what is actually lacking is genuine exchange between people who live "in the same universe of discourse" (p. 44). Television, the radio, and the telephone actually make it possible for people to live entirely on their own; they turn out isolates at the same rate as the Koreans and the Japanese turn out electronic components.

Now, you may ask, what is an isolate? In a 1971 article, Paul Watzlawick mentions an extraordinary experiment once undertaken by Frederic II: he took a few children and entrusted them to the care of well-meaning nurses who were supposed to look meticulously after their bodily cares without ever saying a word to them or exchanging with them in any way. The purpose of the experiment was to find out if the children would spontaneously speak Hebrew, Greek, or Latin. Needless to say, the experiment lamentably failed; the children died.[2] What did they die of? Obviously not of malnutrition. Not, either, of not learning to speak. More likely of not being allowed (or encouraged) to establish interpersonal relationships with the other children and the nurses; they were involved in a process of telegraphic communication, the ultimate source or sender being the unseen, inaccessible emperor, but they could not respond nor establish any other form of exchange.

This anecdote may help to understand what happened to little Miles in *The Turn of the Screw*.[3] His well-meaning but neurotic governess, acting upon the authority of his careless uncle, gradually isolates him and submits him to something like a double-bind, making him utterly incapable of interacting with her or the others. She is the representative of the inaccessible power and does her utmost to prevent Miles from communicating with the outside world. The trauma is the more tragic for the little boy as Miles is (or confesses to be) a purloiner of letters; he intercepts messages that are not addressed to him. For him, communication is not easy; it is a painful necessity and a tragic impossibility. The theft of the governess's "empty" letter precipitates a crisis; he is now a complete isolate, since he has no way of seeing himself and the world through somebody else's writing nor of acting (however perversely) upon other people. He dies of being an isolate, of not being allowed to, or capable of, exchanging or interacting.

Jane is somewhat like the governess. She singles out her victim, breaks into his "universe of discourse" (a phrase probably meant as a gentle thrust at structuralist orthodoxy), and pierces a hole in his "plenum": "Even a plenum, *cher maître*, can be penetrated" (p.45). Her words do not have a constative but a performative effect; they do not describe a state of things (Mr. Quistgaard losing his sanity), they produce it. Jane (who is also Tarzan's mate, as the book makes clear [p. 32], is a violent person in the story, like her model, the stepmother, because she is too narcissistic to exchange and interact; she takes pleasure in mailing nasty messages that the receivers will be in no position to answer, breaking their peace of mind and sending them upon a frustrating quest to discover her identity so as to put an end to the harassment. Like Humbert Humbert, in Nabokov's *Lolita* (1955), trying to track down his rival by leafing through the pages of hotel registers, Jane's victims will desperately struggle to identify her and to stop her from diluting their "theirness."

Jane's arrogance is somewhat belied, however, by the end of her letter: "You are, essentially, in my power. I suggest an unlisted number" (p. 46). The last sentence can be interpreted as a supreme insolence, a refined torture. If Mr. Quistgaard takes an unlisted number without moving homes he will (or may) continue to receive Jane's letters. If he does either of these things, then he will show that Jane was basically right about him and has completely taken control over him.

Jane may not be joking after all. By suggesting this solution to Mr. Quistgaard, she obliquely implies, perhaps, that she herself considers it a little shocking that any person can penetrate any other person's plenum provided the latter be listed in the telephone book. Being narcissistic, she can't help acutely m23sensing what it must feel like to receive such a letter. There is a teasing suggestion that she has actually been writing a letter to herself; she has a wonderful understanding of her addressee's feelings because she puts herself in his shoes. It is clear, therefore, that the plenum that is in danger of springing a leak is her own, not that of a problematical Mr. Quistgaard or Kierkegaard.

This anonymous letter is not of course like most anonymous letters we hear about (or receive). It is signed ("Jane"), but since the addressee is not known by the addressor, there is practically no danger that the addressor's last name will ever be identified. It is a mirror letter; Jane is not trying to work her revenge on somebody she knows or has reasons to complain about. She has no way of knowing what Mr. Quistgaard looks like; she only knows that since he is listed in the directory he is neither a bum nor an industrial mogul, and he must therefore be a middle-class citizen, with a wife, children, a comfortable house, and a car. As a result, she can only project her own feelings when she wants to imagine the addressee's reactions to her letter. That is how she paints up a kind of male version of herself—a mirror-image of herself, the vain and bossy stepmother of Snow White. This letter does not fit the definition of a letter offered by William Gass: "Since a letter is written in the absence of its recipient—indeed, because of that absence—it is like a soliloquy intended to be overheard."[4] Jane's letter is a soliloquy not intended to be overheard, not even by the dumb beasts that surround her in the jungle. She loves herself too much to be able to communicate and therefore will remain a fraud and a failure in comparison to Snow White, who inspires love with her beautiful body and esthetic pleasure with her poems.

The protagonist of Thomas Pynchon's *Crying of Lot 49*,[5] Oedipa (a male mirror-image of Oedipus, we presume) is also a very narcissistic person who is very much concerned with the problem of communication. It is not her fault, naturally, that she must go to San Narciso to execute the estate of her one-time lover Pierce Inverarity, but she could have selected another motel than "Echo Courts." The whole story begins with a letter from Metzger, her coexecutor from the law firm in charge of the estate, informing her of her good luck. The true source of this letter is Inverarity himself who put her into his will; the time gap between the writing of the original letter (the will) and its reception by Oedipa is due to the fact that Inverarity died months after the writing of it and that the will was found months after his death. Here we have a situation that approximates the one described by John Barth in *Letters:* "But every letter has two times, that of its writing and that of its reading, which may be so separated, even when the post office does its job, that very little of what obtained when the writer wrote will still when the reader reads."[6] The will is nothing but a letter from the dead. Little attention is paid to the wording, only the "signified" matters, as it were.

Oedipa is immediately transformed by Pierce's will. She leaves her muddled husband, Mucho, and her hometown, Kinneret (her kitchen, as it were), and travels south to an unknown city. The first and only letter she receives there is from her husband: "The letter itself had nothing much to say,"[7] but this very fact inspires her to have a good look at the envelope on which she reads a blurb put on by the government: "Report all obscene mail to your potsmaster" (p. 32). She doesn't realize the meaning of this blurb, which, considering the fact that she has just been unfaithful to her husband with an obscene male, Metzger, turns out to be quite appropriate. This inscription, plus the message from Kirby on the latrine wall at the Scope (p. 37), marks the beginning of her paranoid investigation of the Tristero system, which is going to expand dramatically until the "crying of lot 49" in the last page of the novel.

Her plenum has been penetrated by Pierce Inverarity's will (as translated or reported by Metzger's letter). She is now forced to consider the world around her as if it were suddenly a new world, a new plot. The muted horn, "a symbol she'd never seen before" (p. 37), now crops up everywhere, including in places that were familiar to her so far (San Francisco, for example). Pierce's will empties her world of all the things she had taken for granted, making her suddenly blind to them, and fills it with her paranoia.

The story, here again, is reminiscent of *The Turn of the Screw:* once the governess has seen (or thinks she has seen) the ghost of Quint (a pale, hatless replica of her employer in London), Bly becomes a different place altogether. The governess's paranoia, which gradually contaminates Mrs. Grose and the children, metamorphoses the place and makes it unrecognizable. The trigger is here again a letter, the letter within a letter from Miles's school announcing that the little boy has been dismissed for good. The letter was addressed to the governess's boss, but the latter forwarded it to her without even opening it, thereby confirming that she was fully in charge.

Jealousy (Jane), a dead love (Oedipa), and frustrated love (the governess) stir up an incredible energy that ignites letters, firing them up with intense metaphoricity. Love or the absence of love is a madness, like delirium tremens; it makes you metaphorize, an act that can be interpreted in two ways, depending where you stand, as Oedipa realizes: "The act of metaphor then was a thrust at truth and a lie, depending where you were: inside, safe, or outside, lost (p. 97). There are two ways to be safe, enjoying one's plenum, like Mr. Quistgaard before he received Jane's letter, or being a psychotic. Jane, Oedipa, and the governess are "simply" neurotics; they have their doubts all along. They wonder whether they are not making things up, mapping out a new world, or inventing a new reality of their own (little Flora's stylized boat, for example).

Oedipa, after her momentous discovery, suffers from the same delusion as Luzhin, in Nabokov's *Defense* (1964), who was so engrossed in chess that he finally came to view the world around him as a gigantic chessgame threatening to destroy him. Once Oedipa has heard the voice from the Shadow, she becomes acutely aware of the world's obstinate intention to communicate: "The ordered swirl of houses and

streets, from this high angle, sprang at her now with the same
unexpected, astonishing clarity as the circuit card had. Though
she knew even less about radios than about Southern Cali-
fornians, there were to both outward patterns a hieroglyphic
sense of concealed meaning, of an intent to communicate"
(pp. 15–16). The forged stamps, the W. A. S. T. E. inscrip-
tions, and the post horn signs that bombard her are the pal-
pable evidence of the world's intention to communicate. The
roar of the world gradually rises to a thunder and overwhelms
her. She naïvely thought, like all the disciples of Frege or
Wittgenstein, that only man could communicate, here and
now, and she suddenly discovers that a god-like figure, Tristero, has disseminated a tremendous amount of information
around the world that will eternally circulate and even expand.

Some critics have offered a religious interpretation of the
novel; they failed to realize, however, that the novel is the
confine of "Silent Tristero's Empire" (p. 128). The prime mover
of the plot is silent Inverarity impersonating Tristero. The
signs he scattered around him in his lifetime have outlasted
him, and now Oedipa is painstakingly trying to collect them
in order to make sense out of them and thereby to make
contact with the dead lover's intent: "He might have written
the testament only to harass a one-time mistress, so cynically
sure of being wiped out he could throw away all hope of
anything more. Bitterness could have run that deep in him.
She just didn't know. He might himself have discovered The
Tristero, and encrypted that in his will, buying into just enough
to be sure she'd find it. Or he might have tried to survive
death, as a paranoia; as a pure conspiracy against someone
he loved . . . Had something slipped through and Inverarity
by that much beaten death?" (p. 136). Tony Tanner may have
been ill advised when he stated that in this novel "the problem
is finally about America."[8] Inverarity's letter from the dead
has forced Oedipa to look into a financial and semiotic estate

that, otherwise, she would not have known existed or could exist; it has instituted her as a privileged decipherer/reader. The estate is apparently a metaphor for the work of art. Once it is completed (and especially when the artist has retired for good), it becomes the responsibility of the reader to produce and organize it. Among all the manipulations, "modes d'emploi," there are some that are more appealing, more relevant, than others; those, presumably but not necessarily, are closer to the author's intent as we can guess it! But there is always the danger that we may go astray. We stand at the receiving end of the communication chain and have no way to make contact with the prime source. Your arrogant structuralist (counting the present writer at some point in his career) or jubilant deconstructionist will tell you that the question is of no interest—the author is dead, thanks be to God!

I have a little imp at my side who reminds me that the author (let's say Nietzsche) killed God some time ago. What a paradox! Ever since the beginning of the eighteenth century, novelists have gamely been trying to slay, liquidate, rub out, and zap the author, to put him out of his misery. Samuel Richardson stumbled upon the epistolary form to execute the sacrifice; others after him developed the free indirect speech, the interior monologue, the narratorless text, and the collage. However, writing is such a thankless and unrewarding job that nobody would take such torturing pains to write books were it not to achieve authorship. The French writer Jean Guenot, commenting upon Danton's last words to his executioner ("Sanson, you must show my head to the people, it's worth it"), remarks: "Every writer who produces a book will become the author of his head. Or of his cock. He will need to show it; before or after his death, whichever."[9] The author has never been so frisky and robust than at the end of the nineteenth century. Balzac had to share some of his royalties with God and the good people of Paris, Angoulême, or Saumur

whom he greatly depended upon to concoct his novels; Joyce
owed a thinner slice to the Dubliners; Beckett and Nabokov
even less to Cosmopolis.

Naturally, the writer (especially the novelist) would like to
believe that once the book is out, he is out of the book, that
it is now the reader's business, not his own. Still he is painfully
aware that the reader will rifle the book to discover the author,
and this is precisely why he develops such elaborate strategies
to be out of it. Michel Butor once said, in answer to a question
about the privileges of being a painter: "Writing is, for me, a
kind of magic which is going to transform the entire world
into a kind of web. You see, there is for me a way to go further,
to do more than they [the painters]. Naturally, one must avoid
getting caught. There are people who catch me from time to
time, but there are times, too, when I succeed in going beyond
these limits or these frames without getting much caught."[10]
Jane and Inverarity are strong narcissistic figures, but they
don't want to get caught, just like Michel Butor; that is, they
refuse to be considered as vain, haughty, and cruel persons.
To achieve that, they overburden their readers with insoluble
enigmas and pitiless spite, forcing them to defend themselves
as best they can, in the hope that, in the process, these dazzled
lip-movers will forget to investigate the author's whereabouts
(a word that Lawrence Sterne reminds us, can strangely be
synonymous with "cock"!). Hence the appropriateness of the
anonymous letter as a metaphor for the novel.

Nabokov's last novel, *Look at the Harlequins!,* can be read
as a wonderful allegory of the author-reader merciless conflict. The first letter inserted in the book provides a counter-
example of what the author-narrator, let's call him McNab,
is trying to achieve in his novels. One day his wife, Iris, shows
him a letter she claims to have composed for the novel she
is currently writing, and she wants him, a professional writer,
to suggest a sequel to this letter. The letter, written in bad

Frenchy English, is from a Frenchman called Jules who is shamelessly begging his one-time mistress not to let him down, otherwise he will die of grief. McNab, who is also a good linguist, senses that the letter can't have been written by a Frenchman: " 'It is a Russian blackmailer knowing just enough English to translate into it the stalest Russian locutions.' "[11] Iris doesn't care about his linguistic lore, she only wants to know " 'what should happen next . . . Should this situation end in slapstick or tragedy?' " Cruelly, McNab answers, " 'In the wastepaper basket,' " (pp. 63–64). The letter fails to meet his own requirements as a piece of fiction. The trouble is, of course, that it is not fiction at all. Iris has just jilted a lieutenant Starov whom she had an affair with and who pesters her. McNab's refusal to answer her leads to tragedy, as Starov shoots Iris, in the next chapter, before shooting himself.

McNab's understandable mistake comes from not having recognized that his wife "had been transcribing an authentic letter" (p. 64). If he had been more thoughtful, he would have gathered that his remorseful (or disenchanted) wife, whom he had suspected before of being unfaithful to him, was begging for help and did not know whom to turn to. This is a typical communication failure. Iris, who did not know if her husband suspected anything, could not tell him the truth about this letter, so she transcribed it, erasing as it were the handwriting of Starov and appropriating the words. McNab, believing that she was the writer of this letter, advised her judiciously to strike out this letter (remember Ada's "Destroy and forget!"[12]) because it was unworthy of her as an author. At the same time, he was unwittingly paying tribute to her shrewdness, her capacity to lie or conceal her secret while exposing it. Iris is, therefore, a clever but ill-fated imitator of the minister in Poe's "Purloined Letter" (1845) who kept the stolen letter in the most conspicuous place to make sure it would not be found by the police.

Though a professional writer, McNab will make exactly the same mistake. He concedes, almost in the middle of the book, "In this memoir my wives and my books are interlaced monogrammatically like some sort of watermark or *ex libris* design" (p. 85). The story will show that this interlacing is more like an intermeddling. Whenever he wants to propose to marry a woman, he is compulsively urged to speak about his mental disorder, that is, his incapacity mentally "to switch from one direction to the other" (p. 4), to retrace his steps in his imagination. When he describes his predicament to Iris on a beach, she immediately understands that he wants to marry her. The second time, with Annette, he writes a letter in which he explains his illness, announcing that he will officially propose to her at her next visit and begging her (if she consents in advance) to wear a certain Florentine hat (an echo, no doubt of the sail episode in *Tristan and Isolde*). Silly Annette does come the following Friday, but without the hat; her attention was sidetracked at the last minute, she claims, by her father reading something about an ancestor of McNab. The latter wonders if she has actually read the whole letter (p. 107). The third time, with Louise, he explains during a party that he has a friend, let's call him Mr. Twidower, who is affected by a strange illness. Louise gets the message, although he had not officially made his proposal yet, and says: "Oh. I'm also going to marry you. Yes, of course, you idiot" (p. 182).

Each time, the novelist invents a more elaborate (and probably a less reliable) system of communication to make his proposal. The woman he loves is supposed to understand that his confession counts as a proposal. The exchange works like a potlatch, it seems: I give you something that is dear to me (the secret of my mental illness), and I expect you to reciprocate by giving yourself to me.

The fourth time, he borrows the technique used earlier by ill-starred Iris: he asks the woman he loves (referred to only as "you") to read a passage from his latest novel, *Ardis* (McNab's version of Nabokov's *Ada,* we assume), in which the mental illness of the protagonist (the same as his own) is described (pp. 231–32). While she is reading, he is out on a walk, reading mentally over her shoulder; but when he decides to turn back, physically, he has a mental breakdown. He regains consciousness at the hospital after weeks of paresis, but he has utterly forgotten his own name. The woman who was reading his novel when he collapsed discusses the protagonist in the third person, as did McNab with the addressee of Jules's letter: she has failed to understand that McNab wanted her to read that particular passage in order to tell her, obliquely (poetically?), about his illness, and therefore she doesn't say, as the novel ends, that she will marry him.

McNab has not managed to communicate to the woman he loves that he is ill and wants to marry her. But his failure is also, poetically, a success. *Ardis,* though it teems with autobiographical details, doesn't read as an autobiographical novel; the woman reader is not aware of communicating with the writer she may be in love with (she will never say so), but with the characters in the story who act as screens and prevent her from making contact with the author, as this comment indicates: "His mistake . . . his morbid mistake is quite simple. He has confused direction and duration. He speaks of space but he means time" (p. 252). She is so engrossed in her discussion of this character that she forgets the whole thing is McNab's invention. This is his marvellous achievement—this, his "most private book, soaked in reality," can fool even a lover (p. 234). McNab is baffled by this feat, because he is afraid that it "might be an unconscious imitation of another's unearthly art," that other being, as we know by now, none other than the author himself, Nabokov (p. 234).

Here we have a perfect example of the conflict opposing the writer to the author. McNab knows himself as a lover and a writer, not a very successful man in either parts. His mental breakdown takes place at the very moment when the woman he loves makes contact with the author through the book, in the physical absence of the writer who is taking a walk. Her response to the book is experienced by McNab as a tangential response, as Jurgen Ruesch would phrase it.[13] This kind of response can have serious psychopathic effects on children and presumably on vulnerable adults as well. The woman didn't jump from one system (fiction) to the other (reality) as McNab expected her to, and therefore she failed to answer his proferred question. They are not in the same universe of discourse, as Jane would put it, a paradoxical situation considering that he was the creator of the system he wanted her to walk out of. This episode amply proves that it is the reader, not the writer, who invents the author. The writer won't be an author unless his text can be purloined or appropriated by the reader, unless the reader projects the writer as a reversed image of himself.

In modernist and postmodernist fiction (and here I see no difference between James and Barthelme, Flaubert and Pynchon, Joyce and Nabokov), there are two systems of communication that function tangentially:

In *Look at the Harlequins!* the situation is even more complex. McNab's writee is the woman who may become his fourth wife, and since she has failed to get the message while reading *Ardis*, McNab must now spell things out for her. He writes his autobiography, hoping that this time he will get through to her. Actually, as we realize, he is desperately trying to rub out the tangent that separates the two systems, to make the writer and the author coincide in order to beat schizophrenia. The difficulty, of course, is that this feat could be achieved only if writee and reader coincide too, and there is no way he can make sure of that. See what happens when Lacan's "barre" starts to swivel on its invisible axis!

Tangentiality (though it appears as a curse to weak-minded McNab) is the goal that writers like James, Barthelme, Pynchon, and Nabokov try to achieve. It is what allows the writer to become an author, that is to say, a godlike, inaccessible figure, somewhat like Bill, the chief of the dwarfs in *Snow White*, who refused to be touched, to interact with people, and had to be put to death for this.[14] It is achieved when the novel constitutes a plenum, as it were, when its meaning is undecidable, (see Kurt Gödel's theorem and Roland Barthes' analyses), that is to say when the reader must himself be an "auctor," an "increaser," someone who penetrates this plenum with the wedge of his own words and of his own letters. The plenum is akin to Hawthorne's scarlet letter, the tangent that separates and interconnects the sinner, the lover, and the poet on one side, and the censors, the puritans, and the sectarians on the other. It is an emptiness, of course, but it doesn't matter so long as nobody knows it!

Before I conclude this essay, I would like to mention that my colleague who received the disturbed girl's visiting card is also a "promising" novelist. In one of his novels there is an interesting anecdote about stamps: an old Pole who lives in America and who has collected stamps all his life decides to visit his ancestors' homeland before his death. Unfortunately he has no money, except his monthly social security check. So he decides to sell his best stamp collection to dispatch himself to Poland by surface mail on the *Queen Elizabeth II*. A new life begins for him when, in Warsaw, he realizes that his social security check converted into zlotys makes him a millionaire.[15]

Paper money, too, can turn aching dreams into blissful reality, as Malcolm Bradbury has shown in his latest novel, *Rates of Exchange* (1983).

The old man in the story ended up marrying a young barmaid, by the way!

4

A Room of One's Own

The Author and the Reader in the Text

Heide Ziegler

THE POSTMODERNIST NOVEL prefers narrative strategies of spatialization over those that produce a temporal effect. Hence the question of borderlines demarcating the realm of the text's self-sufficiency becomes increasingly important. This question should not be confused with the deconstructive concern with the margins of the text.[1] It is not, basically, a question of the permeability of fictional texts, by which means critical discourse can enter and overtake the fictional text, deconstructing its very premise, fictionality. In fact, the question of border-lines, or the claim to self-sufficiency, may be seen as a defense strategy on the part of postmodernist authors on behalf of the fictional text. Of course, one of the pathways into the text that eroded its seemingly stable fictional status was the author's making his reflections upon the narrative process as such part of the text. Particularly the novel as a medley genre has always permitted the author as well as the reader to intrude into the text, even as early as in Cervantes' *Don Quixote,* but only on pain of denying their own real ontological status: when they enter the text, author and reader become fictional characters within the text. The reflection upon this permutation from author or reader to character, however, can genuinely be called an "intertext" in that it absorbs the ontological difference between author, text, and reader into the concept of universal "text."[2] Intertextuality is the logical outcome of the historical development of the novel as a genre that tampers with, and attempts to seduce, reality.

The recent need felt by postmodernist authors to redefine the borderlines of the fictional text in order to reconstitute its special status cannot be seen as a naive return to the origins of the novel, since it was precisely the novel as fictional genre that established the conditions for its own demise. Instead, this impulse has to be seen as an endorsement of the tacit assumption that the novel can only survive by overreaching itself. Thus, it is a clearly recognizable trait of the postmodernist novel that instead of excluding the author and the reader from the text it attempts totally to inscribe them; not in order to refine the real author or the real reader out of existence, but in order to make them appear superfluous through their over-determination within the text. If the author-reader relationship can be seen ideally, not as a condition or a consequence of the text, but as the text itself, then the temporal threat represented by intertextuality can in effect be brought to a halt.

As stated above, the novel's ontological tension between author and reader on the one hand and the text on the other hand became evident with the rise of the novel itself. It was a problem for Cervantes, whose *Don Quixote* Thomas Mann has called a novel that comprises the world, that is, a novel that attempts to deal with reality by totally inscribing it into the text. In his essay "Meerfahrt mit 'Don Quijote'" ["Sea-Voyage with *Don Quixote*"], Mann nevertheless argues that the ending of Cervantes' novel is unsatisfactory. The fact that Don Quixote recovers from his insanity before he dies, rejecting his former idealism as folly, is all too sobering, since it is precisely this folly that the reader has become so fond of. The novel has transcended its original purpose—to vilify the adventure novels of the time—and created a character more admirable than any of his predecessors. In fact, Don Quixote has become so admirable that, according to Mann, his author has become jealous of him. Cervantes pretends to have Don Quixote die at the end of the novel in order to spare him any demeaning literary transformations at the hands of other authors. But the true reason, says Mann, is that Cervantes himself is so fond of his own character that he wants to keep him to himself: "Das ist ein Literaturtod aus Eifersucht - aber diese Eifersucht freilich bezeugt auch wieder die innige und stolz abwehrende Verbundenheit des Dichters mit seinem ewig merkwürdigen Geistesgeschöpf, ein tiefes Gefühl, nicht weniger ernst, weil es sich in scherzhaften literarischen Vorkehrungen gegen fremde Wiedererweckungsversuche äußert."[3] Cervantes is quite justified in assuming that he needs to save Don Quixote from future literary resurrections, since he himself created the conditions for this threat to his character's integrity. In the second part of Cervantes' novel, Don Quixote and Sancho Pansa have transcended the roles of characters they played in the first part. Their ontological status becomes questionable after they begin to encounter the readers of the first part of the book, who discuss Don Quixote and Sancho Pansa's past adventures with them. The question arises whether these readers treat Don Quixote and Sancho Pansa as the fictional characters of the first part of Cervantes' *Don Quixote,* or as the real characters they encounter, characters who underwent all those adventures and thus, in a sense, wrote them. In other words, in the second part of the novel Don Quixote, besides being a character, has become his own author, claiming the role of Cervantes himself. Cervantes himself is reduced to the figure of the fictive author and narrator, Cide Hamete Benengeli, who steps in to relate the second part of the novel. Thus, Cervantes willingly diminishes his own claim to fame, transferring it to his character, in the hopes that this character will take it upon himself to carry his author along into immortality. In this Cervantes expects Don Quixote to achieve an impossible feat: to transcend the death he has prescribed for him. The example of Cervantes' *Don Quixote* can serve to demonstrate how from the very outset the novel has thematized the relationship author-text-reader with the aim of overcoming its inherent ontological barriers.

Not surprisingly, the ultimate impossibility of this endeavor reveals itself in the ending of the novel. Don Quixote's death can be seen as a symbol of the flagging of the arrogated ontological independence of the imagination. In his study *The Chapter in Fiction,* Philip Stevick deals with the problem of a novel's ending as it relates to the division into chapters. Stevick contends that the Western mind habitually thinks in linear fashion. Thus, the artificial interruption of a linear, that is, causally structured story induced by the book's division into chapters creates a shock in the reader and thus forces him to constitute his own imaginative patterns that the following chapter will either reinforce or call into question.[4] However, in treating the ending of a novel simply like the ending of its last chapter, Stevick misses its ontological, if not its narrative, implications. Stevick's theory posits the possibility of an open ending for each and every novel since nothing will prevent the reader from constituting an unlimited number of imaginative patterns once he has reached the last line of the text. However, since at the ending of a novel both the author and the reader have to leave the fictional world, they need to justify their former roles as author or reader rather than prolong them in their imaginations; for in the face of everyday requirements both the role as author and as reader must appear artificial. The solution would be for the text itself to supply this justification, either by becoming increasingly self-sufficient so as to appear to reject the author's as well as the reader's imaginative participation in its own development, or by absorbing the roles of author and reader into the text to the point where the reflection upon the artificiality of those roles in the realm of reality becomes the *raison d'être* for the text itself.

In 1982 Robert Coover published *Spanking the Maid,* a text subtitled *A Novel.* Judged by its length, however, *Spanking the Maid* is a novelette, not a novel. Thus the subtitle calls attention to itself. *Spanking the Maid* presents us with something unexpected or novel, which pretends, moreover, to be chosen at random: *a* novel. Yet at first sight nothing in Coover's novel justifies the reader in expecting something unexpected or random. The structure of the text contradicts this expectation, just as its lacking bulk contradicts the pretentiousness of the subtitle. *Spanking the Maid* consists of a series of short chapters, involving two characters, the master and the maid, who daily repeat the same ritual: the master spanks the maid. This ritual is invoked whenever the maid inadvertently makes a mistake. Gradually, these mistakes take on a life of their own: a blanket, perfectly spread, appears to crumple itself. The apparently random develops an unexpected logic by which it perpetuates itself and thereby acquires the status of necessity. As a result, the master needs to spend more and more time studying manuals to teach him the perfect technique of spanking, for his ideal is the perfection of his power, mirrored in and justified by the perfection of the maid's daily chores. Yet, as he unsuccessfully tries to raise her to the level of this ideal, he in turn becomes dependent on her mistakes, and by implication on her existence, as the precondition of his own power: "Sometimes, especially late in the day like this, watching the weals emerge from the blank page of her soul's ingress like secret writing, he finds himself searching it for something, he doesn't know what exactly, a message of sorts, the revelation of a mystery in the spreading flush, in the pout and quiver of her cheeks, the repressed stutter of the little explosions of wind, the . . . dew-bejeweled hieroglyphs of crosshatched stripes."[5]

Master and maid are like God and man, or like author and reader, and for all of them the day of creation is drawing to a close. For while the text repeats the same scene—spanking the maid—with few, if any variations, the time of day for the action changes from morning to late in the day. As night approaches, the master, not having been able to achieve his ideal, begins to look for the "mystery" that will explain to him why he ever had to spank the maid in the first place. In like manner, God might be looking at the imprints He has left in the human soul, treating them as "hieroglyphs" that may bear a message for Him. And the author looks at the weals he has left on the "blank page" of the reader's naked behind, since these traces are like "secret writing," revealing to him something he did not put there.

Spanking the Maid becomes an extended metaphor for the relationship between author and reader, and it thematizes their mutual dependence to the point of excluding all other concerns—just as the necessity of domination and submission will eventually infiltrate every experience of master and maid and change it into a pretext for the repeated ritual of attempting to perfect their relationship. As a consequence, Coover's text becomes increasingly hermetic and its values radically ambivalent. For example, the bedroom of the master, the locale of the novel's action, is separated from the garden by nothing but a glass door, and the garden is always in sight. But neither master nor maid ever enter the garden, which could, or perhaps should, be read as a metaphor for life, so that it becomes either the garden of paradise lost or the imaginary garden of forbidden lust. The bedroom on this side of the glass door thus becomes the realm of reality where a daily ritual of pain is performed that represents the *conditio humana*.

As a result of existing in a circumscribed place, lust has become perverted into pain, but then both lust and pain cannot ever exist except when under the pressure of limitation. The exclusiveness of the bedroom represents the rationale as well as the dilemma of the text; it is the locus of the author-reader relationship. Since there is no alternative to this relationship, executed in the form of perverse ritual, the form of perverse ritual is rendered the only genuine value the text contains. Paradoxically, for Coover the novel as genre has to become hermetic in order to survive.

The hermetic relationship between author and reader as the ideal form of the text attains an almost absolute, existential pitch in Maurice Blanchot's *récit, La folie du jour. La folie du jour* is the story of a man gone blind after an accident who, instead of experiencing eternal darkness, is confronted with the sensation of unlimited daylight. Unlimited daylight, however, is "blinding," maddening. Thus the metaphorical not the real blindness drives the narrator into a state of insanity, because unlimited daylight can be as little defined by real objects as it in turn defines them. It, too, is insane, since sanity implies limitations: "A la longue, je fus convaincu que je voyais face à face la folie du jour; telle était la vérité: la lumière devenait folle, la clarté avait perdu tout bon sens; elle m'assaillait déraisonnablement, sans règle, sans but."[6] Ernst Cassirer, in his study *Philosophy of Symbolic Forms,* describes how the experience of transition from darkness to daylight necessitates man's positing of values. In effect, this transition consists of the experience of being born (in French *voir le jour*). According to Cassirer, all creativity myths show that man originally attributed to daylight a positive value, to darkness a negative one. In other words: in privileging the new stage, life, man becomes dependent on daylight in order to impose order upon chaos and cope with reality. Blanchot's narrator enters yet another stage of existence when he understands that he is called upon to become an author. The transition is marked by daylight's changing from a necessary condition of life to its sole condition. Unqualified existence, however, equals insanity. The daylight whose insanity the narrator has to face is the unlimited imagination that through ecstasy—the abovementioned "accident"—has stepped out of the reality of qualifying facts. The unlimited imagination can no longer define facts, just as the unlimited daylight can no longer define objects. When the narrator of Blanchot's *récit* turns from character to author, the story of his life begins to disappear. Its very structure dissolves, since structure depends on the facts or objects it attempts to structure. At the end of the *récit* the reader discovers that the whole story was a quotation, the narrator's attempt to explain to his doctors his former life and the reason for his blindness. In the penultimate paragraph the narrator repeats the exact beginning of the text. That was the beginning of the *text,* the doctors, being critics, say critically; what about the facts? The author's unlimited imagination has made it impossible for him to detect and relate facts, which are defined by the categories of time and space; he can only live by repeating himself, by continuously quoting his own story. But since the form of self-quotation represents a meaningless form of intertextuality—a text that continuously quotes nothing but itself constitutes no relationship between texts—Blanchot implicitly rejects the notion of intertextuality. Like Coover's *Spanking the Maid,* Blanchots's *La folie du jour* establishes itself as a self-sufficient text.

However, if Blanchot's text rejects literary critics, it does—like Coover's text—take the reader into account. After the narrator is blinded, that is, after he has become an author, the only person he still "sees" behind the backs of the doctors is the female silhouette of the Law, who represents the reader. This Law defies all expectations of liability; she concedes all the power to the narrator, yet only as long as she remains for him the Law. As in Coover's novel, the reader in Blanchot's *récit* is female and, also as in Coover's novel, the relationship between author and reader is a matter of erotics and power.

The female voice of the Law pretends to adore the narrator, but he is not permitted to ask anything of her; and although she grants him the right to be everywhere (as author), this only means that he may not ask for a fixed place in her (the reader's) life. In fact, she plays with him, by quoting him, whenever she feels like it. She will suddenly cry out, "Ah, je vois le jour, ah, Dieux,"[7] turning his existential predicament into a joke. Since the limitless daylight of the imagination that constitutes the author's blindness dissolves the borderlines of his own story, turning his life into an endless quote, he becomes a ready prey for the reader. Like an insatiable mistress, she can ask him to devote his whole being to her. Thus, living or dying no longer makes any difference to the narrator— "j'éprouve à vivre un plaisir sans limites et j'aurai à mourir une satisfaction sans limites"[8]—as long as he is able to fulfill her requirement that he be famous. Thus, he surrenders to the madness of the day.

If the metaphor of a perverse erotic relationship between male author and female reader could serve Robert Coover and Maurice Blanchot to lock both the author and the reader into the text, John Barth and Italo Calvino reject the idea of the pressure exerted by the borderlines of the text for the idea of a convergence of the identical concerns of author and reader, who gravitate towards each other in a love relationship that excludes all other concerns from the text, relegating them to a secondary order of importance. For Barth this convergence between author and reader develops from their mutual understanding that their relationship ought to be a consummate metaphor, or a metaphorical consummation. Consequently Barth attempts to turn into metaphor every element and aspect of his fiction, "the particular genre, the mode and medium, the very process of narration—even the fact of the artifact itself."[9]

A metaphor connects two realms of referentiality without ever quite letting the mystery of the borderline between those two realms become the logic of their connection. Author and reader represent these two realms. The fictional text as metaphor allows their relationship to constitute itself, which would otherwise be impossible because of the necessary time gap involved between writing and reading; no two persons can be author and reader of the same text at the same time. Writing and reading are by definition solitary preoccupations, yet the text as metaphor can link, through the metaphorical leap, the mutual desire of author and reader. In Barth's "Dunyazadiad," the first of the three novellas that comprise the metaphorically structured novel *Chimera,* which resembles the tripartite mythic monster of that name, the author-reader relationship is explained as such a love relationship. Here, as the author, Barth can encounter Scheherazade, his favorite storyteller, from the distance of the future, after he has discovered the magic word. Delighted, he tells her that he is an avid reader of her stories, only to discover that she has not as yet told these stories. Thus, from being her reader, Barth turns into the author by daily telling her one of the stories contained in *The Thousand and One Nights.* At night, Scheherazade then tells these stories to Shahryar. So, from being the listener of the stories, she turns into their well-known author. This game of give-and-take, taking place across the centuries, is a metaphor for love, and Barth tells Scheherazade "that writing and reading, or telling and listening, were literally ways of making love" (p. 32). Barth's choice of the word "literally" is revealing as well as misleading. For in describing the way Barth and Scheherazade make love, the word retains those connotations that relate lovemaking to the written word. Only in the realm of the written word, that is, within Barth's text, can this love take place. The author never actually makes love to Scheherazade, although he admits being jealous of Shahryar. But since Barth cannot forget that the condition of his encounter with Scheherazade—of their mutual roles as author and reader—is dependent on the fact that he is visiting her from the future, he cannot plead for "actual," but only for "literal," ways of making love. However, if lovemaking between author and reader is possible only metaphorically, even within the fictional text, then love demands that fictions be more important than reality: "Fictions, maybe—but truer than fact," (p. 53). Barth's defense strategy against the disruption of the writer-reader or teller-listener relationship is, therefore, to place the fictional text at the top of a hierarchy of texts.

The central metaphor that interrelates all the metaphorical levels of Barth's "Dunyazadiad" is its leitmotif: "It's as if—as if the key to the treasure *is* the treasure!" (p. 8). We can interpret the love relationship between author and reader, Barth and Scheherazade, as the treasure for which the text is the key, since their love can only take place with the help of the text. Yet, actually turning the key would reveal the fact that the treasure does not really exist; thus nothing but holding the key and not turning it will keep reality at bay. Holding the key means telling stories and listening to them, since telling stories and listening to them can take place at the same time—in contrast to writing and reading. The suspense created by holding the key without turning it is comparable to the suspense created in the teller and the listener by a story that is still being told or a love that is not yet consummated. Of course, Scheherazade in turn tells her stories to the king, not to Barth, but the true listener of her stories, who is comparable to Barth in that she cannot enter into an actual love relationship with Scheherazade, is Dunyazade, Scheherazade's little sister, whose sole role throughout the thousand and one nights will be to ask Scheherazade for the continuation of the present story-in-progress each time after the king has made love to her. In calling his novella "Dunyazadiad," Barth calls upon Dunyazade to help him justify, through her own reduced function, his ability to talk and listen to Scheherazade, but not to make love to her.

However, although the situation of telling and listening seems to be the most appropriate metaphor for a love relationship within the fictional text, the text's leitmotif of the key to the treasure that *is* the treasure nevertheless privileges the relationship between author and reader. Not because the greater tension between author and reader, caused by the fact that they function in their roles at different times, is nevertheless overcome by Barth's text, but because the real author and the real reader are now becoming dispensable. The authorial device of having Barth meet Scheherazade in the past and Scheherazade dependent on a future reader for the telling of her stories propels both of them out of their real environment into the realm of the imagination. Thus overcoming the barriers of time, Barth's "Dunyazadiad" is a perfect example for the employment of the narrative strategies of spatialization in order to achieve the self-sufficiency of the text, its independence from reality.

If, for Barth, the actor in the process of the spatialization of the text is the author, this actor is represented by the reader in Italo Calvino's novel *Se una notte d'inverno un viaggiatore*. Unlike Coover, Blanchot, and Barth, Calvino at first sight does not seem to establish an erotic relationship between the author and the reader, but between two readers, one male and the other female. Their communication begins in the bookstore, when both readers attempt to return a defective copy of Calvino's present novel. Since both readers at this point intrude into this very novel, they will never be able to find a complete copy of *Se una notte d'inverno un viaggiatore* as it must have existed before they became part of it. But their conjoined search for such a copy leads them to other fragments of the novel, which turn up in strange places, and it finally leads them to one another. Thus, Calvino at first sight seems to have written the story of those two readers, treating them like characters in a novel. But it is decisive that their role as readers remains primary. For only as readers do they search for the rest of Calvino's novel, not in order to meet one another; and although the two readers decide to marry at the end of the novel, it is the story they want to bring to a happy ending, not their relationship. In spite of their love they retain that loneliness that is the distinguishing feature of the genuine reader. And since this loneliness also distinguishes the genuine author, a relationship is also being established between author and reader, a relationship depending on a mutual ideal projection that can totally dispense with the real existence of the author and the reader. Thus, in Calvino's novel the editor of a publishing house who daily has to cope with real authors maintains that "gli autori veri restano quelli che per lui erano solo un nome sulla copertina, una parola che faceva tutt' uno col titolo, autori che avevano la stessa realtà dei loro personaggi e dei luoghi nominati nei libri, che esistevano e non esistevano allo stesso tempo, come quei personaggi e quei paesi."[10] True authors exist only for the reader or, to be more precise, they only exist during the act of reading. Traditionally, the author is believed to guarantee the "real" ontological status of the text through the fact of his own existence; his name on the title page of the book is meant to refer to him as a person. Calvino attempts to question this tradition. His novel fragments not only pretend to be written by various different authors, but they turn out to have not even been written by those authors by whom they pretend to be written (which, of course, is indeed the case). They either turn out to be translations, the originals of which have been lost, or they have been confused with other novels. The real author is thus continuously withheld from his readers, until the readers begin to react with withdrawal symptoms, having become addicted to the idea of author. Metaphorically, the reader becomes the traveler on a winter's night who can never reach his destination—just as the dependent clause, the novel's title, will never be embraced in any syntactical structure including a main clause. Even though the marriage between male and female reader seems to supply the novel with a conventional ending, the last scene still dramatizes the desire of the reader for the author as his unattainable idea. Both readers lie in bed, each one reading a novel. The female reader is tired and would like to turn off the light. "Ancora un momento," says the male reader, "sto per finire *Se una notte d'inverno un viaggiatore* di Italo Calvino."[11]

In contrast to Stevick's theory, the ending of the postmodernist novel is no longer an open ending. On the contrary, it establishes the circular structure of the novel. Just as the ending of Calvino's novel takes up its own title page, Barth's *Chimera,* the last novella of which is entitled "Bellerophoniad," ends with the words "It's a beastly fiction, ill-proportioned, full of longeurs, lumps, lacunae, a kind of monstrous mixed metaphor— . . . It's no *Bellerophoniad.* It's a ."[12] The word that needs to be substituted is, of course, *Chimera,* the title of the book. Blanchot's narrator also ends by quoting the beginning of his own story, while Coover repeats the hermetic structure of his novel in each of its sections. The circular structure of these postmodernist novels is a metaphor for their self-sufficiency. These novels attempt to resist what Jacques Derrida calls the process of *débordement,* an overflowing of the text that erodes the notions of beginning and ending, of title and margins, and ultimately of a realm of referentiality outside of the text. Derrida wants to liberate the text in order that its meaning be triumphant.[13] For him the process of *débordement* becomes an homage to life itself; it signifies life's triumph over death, since death appears to be inherent in every self-contained structure. However, from its very inception the genre of the novel has been in danger of losing the very meaning Derrida wants to liberate, precisely by disregarding the function of its borderlines as epistemological barriers. Gradually, the novel's borderlines have come to mark nothing but the locus where the Other, that which is not the text, could infiltrate the text and endanger any meaning that depended on the fictionality of the text as its precondition.

The self-sufficiency to which postmodernist fictions aspire does not imply the denial of facts or a refusal to incorporate them within their borderlines. But it aims to subsume facts under the head of fictionality. And in order to ensure the special status necessary for fiction to justify this subsumption of facts, the fictional text can no longer rely on its immanent aesthetic value. In a world where texts tend to be commentaries on one another, the postmodernist novel attempts to regain an independent status by fictionalizing the author-reader relationship to the point where the factual relationship between author and reader becomes irrelevant. This fictionalization, as a permutation of the relationship from actual interdependence to a mode of self-sufficiency, is achieved by changing the temporal sequence of writing and reading into the spatial concept of an erotic relationship between author and reader. And this form of spatialization once more supplies the novel with the ideal necessary to overreach itself.

5

Figure and Ground in Modern American Poetry

Ellman Crasnow

IN 1935 ROBERT FROST REPLIED to the *Amherst Student,* a college newspaper that had sent him greetings for his sixtieth birthday. Moving with qualified pessimism from his own age to the age in general, he claimed that "there is at least so much good in the world that it admits of form and the making of form." And he offered a diagram for this consolation: "The background is hugeness and confusion shading away from where we stand into black and utter chaos; and against the background any small man-made figure of order and concentration."[1] Such sentiments, in their defensiveness, suggest what might be called the Worringer wing of modernism. But Frost's irony in this letter resists easy classification; he is so knowing about the terms on which he will cheer himself up. And part of this knowingness resides in his schematic diagram: a basic representation of basic representation, a figure set against a ground. Yet the abstraction remains full of emotive affect as political reaction merges into metaphysical anxiety. It is also a peculiarly American diagram, in which the relations of figure and ground can be seen as modelling or mediating a larger set of relations between person and environment, settlement and wilderness, and other paired terms. As such it is almost a cliché in American culture, most notably developed in the nineteenth century by Emerson and Dickinson. I am going to assume familiarity with this tradition and to concentrate instead on showing how implications drawn from figure and ground may illuminate our reading of some modernist and postmodernist texts.

It is already clear that we are dealing with an analogy between the visual and the cognitive. The analogy, moreover, is made in and through a written text whose relations with both the visual and the cognitive may not be unproblematic, and that may thus constitute a critical third term. But I begin with the terminology of figure and ground in Gestalt accounts of the psychology of perception. The Gestalt school described the structuring of visual stimuli through psychological activity—an activity located in so-called "brain fields," whose pattern-making decisions could be generalized into certain laws; for example, laws of symmetry, of proximity, and of "good continuation." It is on the basis of such laws, according to Gestalt theory, that the distinction of figure from ground, as well as more complex schematizing and resultant human action, can take place.[2] Nor need the schematizing confine itself to visual fields: there exists a Gestalt interpretation of the syllogism in terms of restructured wholes, comparable to a perceptual process.[3] What is noteworthy in Gestalt theory is that configurations are actively and intentionally made, not given, and also that there are occasions when the distinction of figure from ground may be unclear. Ambiguous diagrams illustrate the latter point. For example, a symmetrical vase turns into twin facing profiles through a figure-ground reversal.

Gestalt psychology has not worn well. Its laws were never quantified; its brain fields have passed into the limbo of psychologistic speculation. One relevant critique is that of Piaget, who as it were historicizes the Gestalt laws on a genetic basis, following his studies of child development. He thus challenges the Gestalt tendency to completeness and closure: "So there is considerably more in a system of reasoning than a 'recentring' (*Umzentrierung*); there is a general decentralisation, which means a dissolution or melting down of static perceptual forms in favour of operational mobility, and consequently there is the possibility of constructing an infinite number of new structures which may be perceptible or may exceed the limits of all true perception."[4] This passage, with its stress on mobility and decentering, recalls Jacques Derrida's critique of structuralism;[5] and, indeed, Piaget later cites Gestalt as "the most spectacular form of psychological structuralism"—a structuralism inadmissibly "pure" and "detached from the subject."[6] It would be absurd to claim Piaget for deconstruction, but the coincidence of quasi-visual terminology in his and Derrida's critiques is striking. Both are dealing with schematized norms, systems of orientation; and both (though for different reasons) suggest a shift of emphasis away from the achieved structure of arrangement, towards the process between arrangements or towards that which the arrangement excludes. I shall try later to show an analogous decentering in literary texts.

Figure, of course, takes on a range of special meanings when applied to texts. The full range of these meanings may not be immediately apparent, but they are to a remarkable extent stored in the etymology of the term, which I shall trace through a classic work of scholarship: Erich Auerbach's essay on *"Figura,"* published in 1944 during his Turkish exile, and collected in *Scenes from the Drama of European Literature.*[7] The Latin *figura* originally meant "plastic form," something shaped or made—again an implication of intentional activity. But here the activity may be suspect. *Figura* comes from the same stem as the verb *fingere,* which can mean to form or to shape, to represent in thought or to imagine, but also to contrive, to pretend, or to feign. Its participle *fictus* means fictitious or false. We thus have a problematic link between figuration, representation, and fictionality. In addition, *figura* suffers a semantic shift through the Greek influence on Roman education. Greek, with its wider scientific and rhetorical vocabulary, is rich in concepts of form that must now be accommodated in Latin. *Figura* comes to cover many formal concepts, including the inflected and categorized forms of grammar and rhetoric— hence our "figures of speech." More complexly, it must deal with the division between, on the one hand, the form that "informs" matter, expressed in Greek by *eidos* or *morphē* and on the other hand, form that is merely a perceived shape, the Greek *schēma.* Our *figura*—which had always referred to out- ward shape—was used to translate *schēma,* while the Latin *forma* was used for *eidos* (this presumably is why we speak of Platonic Forms and not Platonic Figures). *Forma* and *figura* thus seem to provide, respectively, the idealist and materialist implications of form. But the distinction is not so tidy, for *figura* must also accommodate the Greek *typos,* as type of the universal or the exemplary, and so acquires its own idealist functions. There is thus a paradox within the Classical use of figure. And the early Christian Church adds a further com- plication; the pagan rhetorical figure that might transform or deceive becomes the Christian signifier, the *figura* of this world that passeth away (as in 1 Cor. 7:31), as opposed to a divine and imperishable essence. To elicit that essence requires a hermeneutic unveiling. Figures, metaphorically associated with shadows or clouds, can hide or obscure. But they can also mediate between mundane history and divine truth through what we would now call typology, that extraordinary pro- motional exercise whereby the pre-Christian Bible is dubbed an "Old" Testament and made to prefigure the New. This system of prefigurative types, and its secular adaptation, is of course familiar to Americanists through the Puritan tradition and its aftermath.

The concept of figure thus seems to differ from itself in both meaning and value, oscillating between universal and particular or between positive and negative. If one is worried by this oscillation one looks for something to fix the figure, to close the play of its difference, to hold it down: that is to say, one looks for a ground, "a hard bottom and rocks in place," as Thoreau puts it. This use of ground as a support or *"point d'appui"*[8] for figure can be seen in three stages. First, in the visual or Gestalt sense, ground is that from which figure stands out or diverges; it is necessary but secondary, not the point of attention. Second, ground is a structural foundation for the figure/ground ensemble, as, for instance, a musical ground bass. And third, ground is an essential justification for figure. We can describe this in terms of logic, as in "the grounds for an argument," but ultimately it's a metaphysical position. One modern version is Martin Heidegger's essay on "The Origin of the Work of Art,"[9] in which ground preserves an undisclosed aspect of being, to be revealed only when the artwork opens up a clearing through which the closed earth on which it is grounded can appear. The necessary conflict between closed and open is composed precisely through figure or Gestalt. I shall not try to list the many forms of modern primitivism that rely on a position like Heidegger's. But he has something more to offer us. He deals with the same question of turning Greek into Latin that we found in Auerbach, but for him it is a kind of fall or dissociation of sensibility. Authenticity, for Heidegger, resides only in Greek—and, of course, in German; so that latinization is a loss of his privileged holism, "the basic Greek experience of the Being of beings," and the beginning of "the rootlessness of Western thought" (p. 23). Derrida, in turn, has used this argument to trace the bias in Heidegger's metaphors of "basic experience"—*Grun-*

derfahrung or ground experience—and "rootlessness"—*Bodenlosigkeit* or bottomlessness. He shows that translation, for Heidegger, has ungrounded language; the terms may seem similar, but they are only phantom doubles, feeble simulacra, setting out over a bottomless void, *bodenlos*.[10]

Derrida differs from Heidegger in accepting this abyss without prelapsarian nostalgia. He and Heidegger can serve to suggest two opposed attitudes to ground and grounding: on the one hand, that which is originary and essential, which may be veiled but which is ontologically secure and, on the other, that which is fictionally or figurally constructed to hold off the realization of groundlessness in the abyss. The negativity and directionlessness of this latter phase may lead to the positing of figure as a means of orientation that is lacking in the ground, a move that is well caught in the Frost passage with which I began. Another way in which Frost will cope with the abyss is by internalizing it:

> They cannot scare me with their empty spaces
> Between stars—on stars where no human race is.
> I have it in me so much nearer home
> To scare myself with my own desert places.[11]

This in turn reflects the post-Romantic position in which subjectivity or identity is itself a ground.

In turning now to literary texts I want to begin with some minimal examples of figuration, a stroke or line, a first trace against the ground. Any line already divides a space, serves as a figure, with all the figural problems of ambiguity, intention, justification. This dividing activity is especially evident in outline or boundary. In one famous American *topos*, a human figure traces the shoreline, between land and sea.[12] Here, in terms of our discussion, the line may appear as "found" rather than intentionally shaped, and the artifice of figure can be assimilated to the ground of nature. A. R. Ammons plays this game in "Corsons Inlet." His speaker seems liberated, released from the geometrical "binds/ of thought" into the natural, flowing "blends of sight." And this privileging of natural traces is extended to poetic speech itself:

> you can find
> in my sayings
>> swerves of action
>> like the inlet's cutting edge:
>> there are dunes of motion.[13]

This may sound like a beautiful confidence trick, in which intentionality is shuffled away. But one of the pleasures of reading such a poem is to watch it undermine its own apparent naturalism. Its very figure on the page is a subtly deliberate spacing of words, lines, blanks, and precise indicators of rhythm; in fact, this artlessness has the artifice of figural shape written all over it.

Wallace Stevens takes the topic further in "Stars at Tallapoosa." Again we find an organic ploy:

> Wading the sea-lines, moist and ever-mingling,
> Mounting the earth-lines, long and lax, lethargic.[14]

But our awareness that simply to nominate a "line" is already to assert a figure is here sharpened by the appearance of a third field, the night sky, those interstellar spaces that were a desert for Frost's speaker—but not for Stevens's, who boldly triangulates the void, drawing imaginary lines as if charting constellations:

> The lines are straight and swift between the stars.
> The night is not the cradle that they cry,
> The criers, undulating the deep-oceaned phrase.
> The lines are much too dark and much too sharp. (P. 71)

Now the organic undulations of ocean are set within an altogether different and crisper diction. The lines make a figure that is not dependent on the night sky, not cradled in it, but that rather figures a fictive ground, a cat's cradle of lines stretched over the abyss. The abyss is in one sense covered by this figure—and yet not covered, in so far as we recall the link between figuring and feigning. It is an example of what J. Hillis Miller calls "the self-deconstruction of rhetoric."[15]

A late poem of Ammons, "The Arc Inside and Out," is especially poignant in its figural strategies. The speaker at first proceeds by decreation, a stripping away or emptying out in order to arrive at a pure figure, "the distilled / form." This is the negative way, but there is also a positive, a figural inclusiveness that tries to assimilate even the void in order to arrive at a total ground, "plenitude / brought to center and extent." These alternatives can't be resolved; they are simply "two ways to dream," says the speaker, who goes on to reduce them to the minimalism of the line:

> ultimately, either
> way, which is our peace, the little
> arc-line appears, inside which is nothing,
> outside which is nothing.[16]

The arc is like an ambiguous figure in a perception diagram. Is it concave or convex? Is it walling in or walling out, as Frost's "Mending Wall" inquires?[17] The differential privileging of inside and outside comes to be seen as just another figuration, ultimately unstable.

There is a contrary modernist drive towards stability that is expressed by reading texts in terms of visual syntheses. This is the doctrine of spatial form, associated especially with Joseph Frank.[18] My purpose here is not to rehearse the controversies but to remark that spatial form itself can be described as a ground; both in the structural sense of foundation and organization and as an ideal that grounds writing in stasis. The text becomes a figure that bodies forth or shadows forth this ideal. We might remind ourselves that spatial form and an interest in myth flourished simultaneously in postwar criticism. Frank himself correlated spatial form with a mythic sense of timeless pattern and cited Auerbach's work on Christian typology as a unified system analogous to what the moderns achieved in formal terms (p. 209). But one need not go this far to take the point of spatial pattern as a ground. The pattern, of course, can vary. One of the most powerful arrangements is axial, as in Ralph Waldo Emerson's topography, where man "is placed in the centre of beings, and a ray of relation passes from every other being to him."[19] But such a Ptolemaic imagination isn't indispensable. Any fixed vantage point may secure the prospect, and in turn prompt the sort of parody that John Ashbery offers in "The Skaters" :

> I am cozily ensconced in the balcony of my face
> Looking out over the whole darn countryside, a beacon
>   of satisfaction
> I am. I'll not trade places with a king.[20]

Now, the major Western pictorial mode of spatial organization has been perspective. And perspective also has a long history as a conceptual metaphor. Kant uses it as the sign of a purely heuristic device, and it recurs in Nietzsche's polemic against absolute truth. Against this relativizing approach to perspective we can set Thoreau's more positive metaphor: "I sit here this fourth of June, looking out on men and nature from this that I call my perspective window, through which all things are seen in their true relations."[21] Ashbery carries on this interplay of the visual and the cognitive, and perspective reappears in his pictorial poems, but unimpressively: "a weak instrument though / necessary."[22] This is not because Ashbery rejects its figural artifice—he is the last writer to worry about artifice—but because any single orientation fixes the relation of figure and ground, and this is inadmissible in a poetry that reminds us that "there is / No common vantage point, no point of view / Like the 'I' in a novel" (p. 56). This mention of the novel brings me to my next point. No poet since Browning has used narrative as thoughtfully as Ashbery. He says, in an article on Saul Steinberg, "The act of storytelling alone is of any consequence; what is said gets said anyway, and manner is the only possible conjugation of matter.[23] Notice that it is the act or manner of telling that interests Ashbery. And his is not a determinate narrative. It involves a movement of figure and ground, both separately and in their relations. The reasons for this are worth noting. What, in a text, serves to distinguish figure and ground in the way that visual cues do for a painting? Part of the answer surely lies in the linguistic function of deixis: "Deixis involves the use of spatial (and temporal) terms . . . which can be fully understood only if the hearer reconstructs the position or viewpoint of the speaker. . . . They are also in some sense gestural, pointing to (and indexing) elements, hence their name 'deictics' from Greek *deiktos* able to show directly.' "[24]

This is particularly clear in Roman Jakobson's study of shifters.[25] Jakobson explains that shifters combine the semiotic functions of symbol and index. For example, the personal pronoun "I" indicates both the subject of an utterance (by the conventional symbolism of language) and the person who utters (by an index of reference). But we have already seen in Ashbery that the "I" is in doubt, like other vantage points; thus not only is this means of relating figure and ground at risk, but the very agency of such relating is indeterminate. We can be misled into fixing the figure of an agent by assuming reference to a separately existing identity; Ashbery's conversational tone can foster this illusion, as can his fondness for what Jakobson calls phatic functions, those apparently redundant speech acts that serve to establish a social link; one

of them ("as you know") has even become the title for an
Ashbery volume. But, despite this social tone, existential identity is never really in question for a textualized speaker; as
one of them plaintively remarks, "I am only a transparent
diagram, of manners and / Private words with the certainty
of being about to fall."[26] When such falls occur they produce
the characteristic decentering movement of Ashbery's verse:

> That's why I quit and took up writing poetry instead.
> It's clean, it's relaxing, it doesn't squirt juice all over
> Something you were certain of a minute ago and now your own face
> Is a stranger and no one can tell you it's true. Hey, stupid![27]

The face of this "I" loses certainty both as target and as index
of identity. This, combined with the pronominal drift, produces an almost visceral torsion as the orientation of deixis is
subverted.

I want to turn finally to the more complex schemata in which
our figure becomes a human figure in a setting. John Dixon
Hunt describes "the figures shown in the landscape" as "the
artist's surrogates"; or, he explains, they may be surrogates
for the projected feelings of the observer.[28] And this surrogation applies to literature; think of how the tentative entrant
to a Gothic enclave acts as a surrogate for the enquiring reader.
In landscape texts, surrogation presents the extensional version of our figure/ground relationship; that is to say, it raises
not just representational but existential issues.[29] If Kenneth
Clark is correct in describing the development of landscape
painting as "a cycle in which the human spirit attempted . . .
to create a harmony with its environment,"[30] then we must
distinguish a negative, belated phase of that cycle, a mood
like that described by Rilke when he wrote: "For let it be
confessed: landscape is foreign to us, and we are fearfully
alone among trees which blossom and by streams which flow.
Alone with the dead one is not nearly so defenceless as when

alone with trees."[31] This feeling is not uncommon in modernist writing; it represents, precisely, a loss of ground. Stevens's poem "A Lot of People Bathing in a Stream" emphasizes the problem of reintegration by changing the element of "ground" from earth to water—water, the alien element, in which the human figure is not at home. For all that, the bulk of this poem is a success story. The figures are flooded in color and light, those great unifiers of landscape. They cross the boundary between land and water and dwell in their new element as in naked intimacy. But their refracted figures are now unrecognizable, "angular anonymids / Gulping for shape among the reeds." The poem is in part a fable of dissolution, like the masthead chapter in *Moby-Dick,* though the mood remains comic and the dangers are only implied. But the serious desire for a native ground can be seen in the final stanza, as the scene abruptly shifts indoors:

> How good it was at home again at night
> To prepare for bed, in the frame of the house, and move
> Round the rooms, which do not ever seem to change.[32]

This retreat signals a nostalgia for earlier, unproblematic integrations, and a more stable grounding.

Such nostalgia is less vulnerably evident in the postmodernist Ashbery. If landscape involves a complex investigation of figure and ground, he too can be described as a landscape poet, though not in a typological sense. Ashbery is antipathetic to the symbolist tradition, and offers no "types and symbols of Eternity." But if we go back behind the Romantics to their predecessors we find a more relevant model in the ideal or heroic landscapes of seventeenth and eighteenth century poetry. These, as described by Jeffry Spencer, are "essentially allegorical . . . equivalences on a mythic or metaphoric level of certain contemporary preoccupations, anxieties, and desires."[33] Ashbery certainly offers something like these "equivalences," and I would distinguish two stages in his procedure. The first is structural. Ashbery produces something like a prospect poem *manqué*, in which the achieved view never quite arrives; instead, we are always on the way to or from configuration, as if in a Piagetian dissolution:

> the signature of disgust and decay
> On an otherwise concerned but unmoved, specially obtruded hill,
> Flatness of what remains
> And modelling of what fled.[34]

The Gestalt is typically still in process of formation, or already breaking down. And the effect varies from comedy to an Audenesque foreboding and cultural resonance. The second stage includes the first, developing from structure to sign. Allegory enters through a string of cultural codes, commonly jammed together in an overcrowded and vertiginous succession:

> "Up
> The lazy river, how happy we could be?"
> How will it end? That geranium glow
> Over Anaheim's had the riot act read to it by the
> Etna-size firecracker that exploded last minute into
> A *carte du Tendre* in whose lower right-hand corner
> (Hard by the jock-itch sand-trap that skirts
> The asparagus patch of algolagnic *nuits blanches*) Amadis
> Is cozening the Princesse de Cléves into a midnight
> > micturition spree.[35]

Here the opening and closing intertexts, popular song and *Carte du Tendre,* interact to cancel any single grounding. And the *Carte* itself is a stylized spatial allegory, embedded as a *mise en abyme* of its context. In seventeenth century *précieux* culture it was an amatory progress chart, all witty abstraction: the River of Inclination, the Lake of Indifference, the Sea of Unfriendliness, and so on. This excessively idealized figure here suffers the indignity of apparent materialization into a ground, a setting for some rather sleazy action. The organized map of *tendresse* is made to explode into novel *dis*organizations. And the point of change is not located in any pictorially significant part of the picture—just the apparent accident of a corner. The trick is repeated in "For John Clare," another landscape *manqué*, in which Romantic interchange notably fails: "As for Jenny Wren, she cares, hopping about on her little twig like she was tryin' to tell us somethin', but that's just it, she couldn't even if she wanted to—dumb bird."[36] But even this uneasy prospect closes with a new energy ballooning out of what, by pictorial standards, must be the least likely location: "Meanwhile the whole history of probabilities is coming to life, starting in the upper left-hand corner, like a sail (p. 36). To describe background in these terms is to rob it of the power of illusion, as the setting for any pictured scene. And yet it is precisely in disillusion that the invigorating shift occurs, as if disillusion were exemplary for postmodernist representation.[37]

Part 2
Applied Clinometrics

6

The Exile of Binx Bolling

Walker Percy's *Moviegoer*

Claude Richard

THE MOVIEGOER IS A NOVEL of exile on two counts: first because of the complex relationship that Binx, the narrator-protagonist, sustains with the real and because of the sense of his development in the completed fiction as evoked by the aorists of his present tense narrative; and again, in a double manner, by means of the narration itself: any narration is exile, for the real that it contrives to evoke is absent. Binx's narrative is furthermore produced from a "para-bolic" speech that its etymology characterizes as always liable to fall or glide by the intended meaning, to dualize itself through its inability to make the closure of the sign adhere to its referent.

As in *The Charterhouse of Parma,* Binx's narrative offers the reader of his "confessions"[1] a choice of mediate or immediate[2] readings: the immediate reading given by the man who is very much in the world (p. 54), who has no idea of the breach

Translated from the French by Carolyn Grim Williams and Marc Chénetier.

between fiction and the real, will contrast with the mediate reading of the exile who lives in the gap that opens when he "sticks himself into the world" (p. 54). He who lives in the mediate must somehow find the niche of the free spirit and ungainly body in a calibrated world.

Tolerance of the real thus implies finesse and detour.

Exile

The Real

The real is not merely relative, quantum or even random, it is also precarious. Its status is doubtful, its identification uncertain. For someone interested in *physis* who wondered about means of determining it, who studied *The Expanding Universe* and its answers to questions concerning the fundamentals ("I read only 'fundamental' books,") and "sought to understand the universe" (p. 69) by removing himself from it, the real is not self-evident.

Supposing he manages, by sheer will, to rid himself of the universe, he will not so easily be rid of himself: "a memorable night. The only difficulty was that though the universe had been disposed of, I myself was left over" (p. 70). "I" will always be the remainder. Today, outside of the subject, the real no longer exists, unless as a remainder or even waste.

The presence of a remainder is the symptom of a deficiency, an unidentifiable deficiency. The real is caught up in a "turning, reversible structure, a structure of ever-imminent reversion, where one never knows what is the remainder of the other".[3] Binx is tormented both by the real *and* its absence.[4]

The foreword demonstrates this: everything here is *fiction*, there is no "resemblance to real persons." Any resemblance to the real would be fortuitous: here again, in Binx's narration, the real is absent, with only one exception ("Every character, except movie stars, and every event without exception are fictitious"): the stars who display "a resplendent reality" (p. 16) characteristic of movie stars only ("their peculiar reality," p. 17).

Let us not for all that conclude that there exists an *arché* of the real that would provide the artificial or imaginary basis for a relationship of binary opposition. These stars should not be confused with real persons or real actors: "When movie stars are mentioned, it is not the person of the actor that is meant, but the character he projects on the screen" ("To the reader," unpaginated). Movie star and film character: here is a double persona, the fiction of a fiction. The only real is that which is twice fictitious.

A mode of association between the real and its alleged icon[5] thus emerges in which the real easily takes on the fluidity or volatility of fiction (Scottie's death) while the simulacrum that it suggests by free association ("It reminds me of a movie," p. 4) takes on the solidity[6] that characterizes the real.[7]

This routed real that deserts the mind and forces Binx into ontological exile ("The world is lost to you, the world and the people in it, and there remains only you and the world and you no more able to be in the world than Banquo's ghost," (p. 120) reemerges almost capriciously at the heart of disaster and malady. Kate reminds us that access to reality is bought at the price of the other's death: "Everyone pretended that our lives until that moment had been every bit as real as the moment itself and that the future must be real too, when the truth was that our reality had been purchased only by Lyell's death" (p. 81). The complicity of the real and the accidental is already becoming apparent: "Have you noticed that only in time of illness or disaster or death are people real?" (p. 81).

All quests are quests of the real[8]: they have crossed or will cross the path of Pat Pabst's: "[He] was in Mexico looking for the Real Right Thing" (p. 169). Must novelistic heroes always put the R in real, then, Binx wonders ("Or—do what a hero in a novel would do: . . . he is just in from . . . Sambuco where he has found the Real Right Thing" (p. 199). In this manner, they reendow the real with specificity, reify and objectify it over and against the proliferation of flashing, undulating signs that bear witness to its volatility or fluidity.

If a real exists, if there is an *arché* of reality, it can only manifest itself in its anteriority and loss: "A time past, a time so terrible and splendid in its arch-reality" (p. 210). The real is always in the past tense. In the now, the real is no more. It is impossibility made present.

For Binx, the real is to be rediscovered in the fictitious and the completed ("I accept my exile," p. 89). There is no more reality in and of itself, no more reality without an image or a memory. The real depends on its representation as strictly as the remainder does on its principal. The real could therefore be what the image left over.

In any case, what Binx, a hero of modernity, has discovered is that in order to signify, the real is not sufficient in and of itself: without the image (the film as mask and exposure) that authenticates it, the real is empty ("the emptiness . . . will expand until it evacuates the entire neighborhood") or remains conjectural ("Nowadays when a person lives somewhere, in a neighborhood, the place is not certified for him," p. 63). Even if simulacra have not quite established their precession, they bail out the real in order to guarantee its temporary existence.

Both identity and locality, these symptoms of the real, rely on simulacra: "But if he sees a movie which shows his very neighborhood, it becomes possible for him to live at least, as a person who is Somewhere and not Anywhere" (p. 63).

The movie theater is the place where, during the projection, absence is exorcised, where space and time see their authenticity certified, and where, through motion, the threat of metaphysical drifting is delayed ("cut loose metaphysically speaking," p. 75).

Space and time are discovered thanks to a film[9] and taste like it: "Yet it was in the Tivoli that I first discovered place and time, tasted it like okra. It was during a release of *Red River*" (p. 75). If a causal series remains, it is modeled on an inverted vector that leads to the real, or rather to a perfect simulation of the real where the signs of a hyperreality are substituted.[10]

This is what Binx, a resident of Gentilly, has suspected in his four years of principled and convinced exile, years devoted to a quiet longing for alterity, a peaceful passion for the elsewhere, a becoming other.

Exile

Adolescent, Binx played all the roles and spoke all the languages ("I lived in the hope of pleasing him by hitting upon just the right sour-senseless rejoinder," p. 35) to penetrate the inner sanctum, the fraternity of fraternities (a series of Greek letters). Walter lets him—locks him—in the circle: "I was *in*" (p. 36). Only Walter can therefore understand the real meaning of the stay in Gentilly: "What are you doing with yourself *out there* in Gentilly?" (p. 39).

In the outsideness of Gentilly, this elsewhere of gentility ("us . . . gentlefolk" says Aunt Emily, p. 222), Binx devotes himself to his metaphorical Jewishness or, as the theosophical Aunt Edna puts it, to his reincarnated Jewishness (p. 89), but, in any event, Jewishness as experienced by the exile: "We share the same exile. I am more Jewish than the Jews I know. They are more at home than I am" (p. 89). Binx's Jewishness is of a transcendent nature; neither political, nor historical, nor religious, it is the pure Jewishness of otherness and exile.

Gentilly and the Champs-Élysées[11] (as Aunt Emily, whose traditional naivety is blended with penetrating trickery, understood very well) represent for Binx privileged places where exile behavior is permissible: "Shrug, turn on one's heel and leave." Leave, i.e., go to the elsewhere of the future without yet being in the here and now. Be between, be two. "One may simply default. Pass" (p. 220). To pass is to play dead, to be in the dummy's chair, that is to simulate a lack and therefore fail to be, to speak, or to act. Rediscover the elsewhere that manifests itself in the lack; then, reject the alienation of plenitude. To lack is to be absent, but it is also to miss something. It is to recognize, thereby, the other signified by its absence. Or again, "to default," failing to be but also to appear: exile as contumacy. Intimations of flight, through speech. Presence of an absent. Being as contumacious appearance. Being double. Being here and there. The subject and its double. The subject and its simulacrum. Its simulacrum on trial. Always guilty, always judged—by the other within me.

Sit down ("How does he sit?"), then read ("How does he read *The Charterhouse of Parma?*"): as a bus rider this means to place oneself in the mediate ("mediately graceful and aware of it?", p. 214), being struck by the curse of duality invented by romanticism: "He is a romantic . . . he will defeat himself, jump ten miles ahead of himself" (pp. 215–16). This is the portrait of the film enthusiast or, rather, the moviegoer: "He is a moviegoer, though of course he does not go to movies" (p. 216).

A "moviegoer" is he who is always beside himself (p. 228), ahead of himself: "He will . . . scare the wits out of some girl with his great choking silences or having her, jump another ten miles beyond both of them and end up flying to the islands" (p. 216).

The "moviegoer" is the man divided by the fact that his desire never coincides with its object: "He has just begun to suffer from it, this miserable trick the romantic plays upon himself, of setting just beyond his reach the very thing he prizes" (p. 216). The "moviegoer" is defined as he who goes to movement, he who goes out of himself and stabilized reality, he who exiles himself radically, a "seeker" (p. 13) dedicated to the horizontal quest.

Willy-nilly, Crusoe was an exile, a "moviegoer". The quest will begin again, in the solitude of the islands (p. 216) where the discovery of otherness originates in the inscribed trace on the pagelike ground. Any exile is Crusoe bending over the image ("print") of the same ("foot") that is an other (Friday): "When a man awakes to the possibility of a search . . . he is like Robinson Crusoe seeing the footprint on the beach" (p. 89).

A footprint is not only the sign of the presence of the absent other but also primal writing, a trace of the otherness by which the subject marks his presence in the world and his desire to represent himself in the other-of-the-sign.

This mysterious, absent double, this Friday that all writing is, is the means of any subject's representation of his duality, his exile among the simulacra of writing—of the letter traced in the dirt (or on the facade of a currency exchange bureau).

From the start, Binx called himself the prey of letters. From the first sentence, he claims to be the recipient of a message ("I got a note from my aunt, " p. 3) that carries a belief in the potential earnestness of utterances: "She wants to have one of her serious talks" (p. 3).[12]

Exile was precisely an attempt on his part to flee such a faith in language, a peaceable plan for self-removal and, more notably, a systematic deviation of signifiers from their supposed models: Gentilly housed its business in a pseudo-bank, a building whose facade bears an inscription ("iron scrolls over the windows," p. 72) made from cast-iron letters—a gold-plated "gothic" display, which this sophist flaunts as an arbitrary but financially rewarding image. This simulacrum, under whose sign the voluntary exile nourished by the nomadism of *Arabia Deserta* (p. 69) places himself, aims—a pure paradox—at signifying stability: "Here," the letters proclaim, "is good old-fashioned stability" (p. 72). Is this a deceitful proclamation? Pure simulation? Literal representation (the written text) is the arbitrary double of an absent real believed to be perceived through the grid of letters: "Looking through the gold lettering of our window" (p. 117). Here is a striking image of the exile represented by any passage through the radical procession of speech.

The Exile of Language

To narrate is to lean toward referential illusion, to feign belief in the sign's grasp of the referent, to effect a coincidence, along the euphoric axis of the narrative[13]; in other words, to attempt an effect of linguistic absence. To narrate in the present is to try and effect the coincidence of narration and fiction, an effort in which the referential illusion is minimally born of the absence of such textual markers as would all too crudely point to the gap between language and its referent, language and its time. It consists in erasing the narrative markers of alterity in order to have us believe in the perfect referentiality of the signifier. Past tenses are markers of that sort and among them is the preterite, the tense of the completed past, often called the definite past, the use of which cannot but express distance from the time of words, doomed to forging parables with parabolic tools. Furthermore, language cannot totally rid itself of its mimetic function and mimesis is part of the parabolic.

In order to speak the unspeakable, Binx, who no longer even believes in approximate univocity (an idea dear to Aunt Emily who has "been assuming that between us words mean roughly the same thing," p. 222), breaks up a dead language, grated threadbare by conventional referentiality, and he espouses comparison as one does religion. Language always says something else because it needs to compare. To compare, to point to similarities, is to underline, by means of an antiphrase of sorts, the differences between objects that resemble one another. The other can only resemble me because he is other: "You are so much like your father and yet so different" (p. 154). Same does not compare with same. Language resembles the real because it is like it, comparable to it; in other words, language is not reality. Speaking—narrating—is letting the wind blow, the wind of "chef menteur," the wind of desire (p. 227) that ascertains the existence of the other on which it depends.

Binx's linguistic mode is the mode of comparison—a language full of *as* and *like*, full of metaphors that under the pretense of expressing identity will in truth express the inadequacy, the difference between the object and what purports to express it, in short will express nothing but the radical exile of language.

Among the words that come from elsewhere ("wanderjahr," "spiel," "malaise," and "sac au lait"), among the crafty shifts of signifiers ("wonder-wander," pp. 41, 55, 69), among the henceforth mute signs ("Now the only sign is that all the signs in the world make no difference," p. 145)[14], among the women whose "becoming" is "becoming-dog" ("I'[11] be dog," Sharon answers obstinately, pp. 118, 133), in the absence of a god that has neither head nor tail (p. 145) and who consequently invites us to openly practice palindrome (p. 131), in the general drift and slide of words over the things they are supposed to designate, Binx expresses the exile of any narrator whose narration can express no more than the powerlessness of language: "It is impossible to say" (p. 235). With these words, the narrative proper closes. The rest is epilogue, metaspeech (pp. 187–91).

Binx, a narrator conscious of his role, will indeed let his narration exile itself from itself and from its original realistic goal. A narrative with objective pretenses, addressed to a random and indifferent recipient (the reader), turns into an address to Rory Calhoun.

Rory is a movie star, neither man nor god, hero nor centaur. The narrative, simultaneously incantation (p. 106), confession, and denial (p. 199), addressed to the heroic recipient, divine or mythical, escapes the order of narratives. As petition, incantation, offering, or confession, it postulates another function of language that shifts from evocation to invocation. Binx's narration flees toward a narrative elsewhere, toward a simulacrum-addressee whose reality is entirely made up of fiction.

As exhaustion of signs (p. 145), impossible evocation (p. 235), or invocation addressed to a figure of absence, Binx's speech incessantly expresses the imminent death of language. It is enunciation. In *The Moviegoer*, the intrusions of the definite past never cease to remind us of the temporal exile of a narration in the present that would consequently like to make the time of an action and the time of enunciation coincide. The narration will nevertheless always signify its exile to that which it evokes or brings together and even the present tense will be haunted by the ghosts of an anteriority: "I remember," "It reminds me." The second and third paragraphs of the novel thus betray the duality of a narrative that yearns to evoke a rediscovered coextensivity of the verb and its tense: "I manage. . . . My home is. . . . I am a model . . . (pp. 5–6). Acting, having, and being are the semiotic trinity of referential illusion. But the powerful aorist will not be forgotten; as a narrative in the present tense, *The Moviegoer* is shot through with reminiscences in the preterite that question the alleged oneness of speech and give it away as inevitably nostalgic.

Nostalgia, that "characteristic mode of repetition" (p. 170) is the repetition of precedence amidst difference and thus reestablishes the empire of the double.

Narration is always an exile.

Its utterance is incomplete because it can only express resemblance and not identity. At the idea of the "sad little analogies" to which speech (that of the doctors) is reduced, Binx is so anguished that he loses his words ("unspeakably depressed," p. 154). Language is the prisoner of analogy and the emblem ("and again my father disappears into the old emblem," p. 153), of the symbol (p. 37) and the sign (p. 145).

It is, in other words, not only that today the wind blows from "chef menteur." Binx's narration in fact progresses on the sharp edge of the signifier; it is a narration between two chasms produced by someone who balances words (English or foreign), moving along the tightrope of language. "'Tightrope' is an expression Kate used when she was sick the first time. . . . It seemed that they (not just she but everybody) had become aware of the abyss that yawned at their feet, " (pp. 110–11). Verbal tightrope walking corresponds to the quest for existential balance. "Tonight," says the last paragraph of Kate's diary—another narrative with no addressee except the double of the self—"will tell the *story*—will the new freedom work—if not, no more tightropes for me, thank you" (p. 110). Telling a story is walking the tightrope of language.

The narration opens onto a referential abyss, a vacuum that awaits "certification" by the image or the word. Binx's father, romantic among the romantics, went from words to the things they evoked: "I remember when my father built the lodge. Before he had read the works of Fabre and he got the idea of taking up a fascinating hobby. He bought a telescope and showed up the horsehead nebula in Orion." Reality is the image of a nebula perceived through a telescope. "After he read Browning . . . (he) saw himself in need of a world of men" (p. 91); reality lies in the power of words to produce desire.

For Binx's father, saying preceded being. All meaning was anterior. Exile from all that is in order, at any cost.

The Homeland-Family

That from which Binx tore himself is that from which any exile retires—that which stands for his homeland: homeland-mother, homeland-father, homeland-aunt and uncle, the mental and physical territory to which "he belongs after all" (p. 26).

The sense, and even more so the meaning, of Binx's exile cannot be understood without a preliminary exploration of the homeland-family he has left.

The Homeland-Mother

The mother is apprehended in the serene activities of her preparing meals, in her dedication to the commonplace (p. 142). The ordinary is her only passion. But its practice is not simple; it is a choice (p. 151) based on a marvelous instinct (p. 149), a constant discipline of insertion into the everyday.

The art of the commonplace originates from a maternal concept of time as defined by everydayness. If the day is a unit of time, if the oppressive quotidian emanating from the mother's world (p. 145) invades the realm of the real, events lose their "importance" (p. 153), things are stripped of their alleged grandeur, and life becomes a series of tactical moves designed to prevent emotional expenditure; "The one enterprise she has any use for: the canny management of the shocks of life." The homeland-mother is the place of the insignificant: "She settled for a general belittlement of everything, the good and the bad." Her rigorous discipline tracks down and reduces the meaning and the power to affect that all things possess: (Lonnie's) illness, (Duval's) death, God: "After Duval's death, she had wanted everything colloquial and easy, even God" (p. 142).

Insignificance as a life or survival plan is the very everydayness Binx must also escape: "Perhaps there was a time when everydayness was not too strong and one could break its grip by brute strength. Now nothing breaks it but disaster. . . . Nevertheless I vow: I'm a son of a bitch if I'll be defeated by the everydayness" (p. 145).

There are numerous strategies for evasion: the father's physical wanderings seem, at first glance, the best help for

Binx: "Any doings of my father, even his signature, is in the nature of a clue in my search"(p. 71).

The Homeland-Father

In his son's imagination, the father opposes the mother's temporal grid-laying with his own spatial wandering: "Off he went with a bottle of *Liebfraumilch* under one arm and *Wilhelm Meister* under the other," Aunt Emily tells him (p. 45). This wandering could signify the apprenticeship of the romantic adolescent, a likely educational program ("Now, I wander seriously," p. 69), an aristocratic tradition ("*wanderjahr*", p. 55) that could lead to a nomadic life ("One of my few recollections of him is his nighttime prowling," p. 85).

But, in fact, the father's wandering is never a search for nomadism. It is the bohemian mask for a quest of the transcendental, the desire for stabilized truth and meaning that will kill the father (all fathers?). The main lesson Binx learned from the paternal example is that romanticism and science are deadly drugs. The lesson is important enough to be noted in his diary, the only note he sees fit to show us: "Explore connection between romanticism and scientific objectivity" (p. 88).

A revealing notation indeed, as Binx suspects that the very foundation of romanticism could be comparable or even identical to that of science. This common basis must be a belief in the autonomous existence of the object, a belief basic to the concept of objectivity.[15] Science and romanticism thus belong to the same secret ideology—an irreversible faith in the nature of things (the question is not whether they are knowable or not), a recognition of the autonomous existence of objects with all the consequences that such beliefs entail (self-discipline, belief in progress, and therapeutic programs, p. 86). These are consequences of little import when considered in and of themselves, but every one of them betrays the perverse foundation of romantico-scientific faith. A fetishism of reality that brings along with it a fetishism of meaning, a dogged compulsion to give meaning to actions and things, "It was like he thought eating was not *important* enough. You see, with your father," the mother reminisces, "everything, every second had to be—Be what, Mother?—I don't know. Something" (p. 153).

Binx was thus caught between theories of time—a maternal theory of the emptiness of the day and a paternal theory of the intensity of the instant, two discourses that only contradict on the surface for both are but manifestations of a common postulate on the objective existence of time. They contribute to the construction of a generalized meaning of the universe[16], a construction that manifests itself a posteriori as an object distinct from the consciousness that thinks it up.

Homeland-Aunt

Theosophy and eschatology are the generalized, exhaustive, and faultless paths to understanding advocated by the two aunts Binx confronts, the two avuncular systems of thought he tries to flee.

The theosophic aunts. Theories of knowledge are handled wholesale by Aunt Edna and her ilk. Her "deep theosophical soul-glances" (p. 177) are but the symptoms of the hyper-theosophism of totality, characteristic of all aunts as a group. "Of my six living aunts, five are women of the loftiest theosophical pan-Brahman sentiments" (p. 108). There is violence in this threat of the "All."

Aunt Emily. On the other hand is Aunt Emily, no less of a danger in spite of appearances. She is Binx's "great" aunt as one were "high" priest. If her form of religion is, in its theological pluralism, closer to ecumenism than to her sisters' theosophism ("My aunt likes to say she is Episcopalian by emotion, Greek by nature, and Buddhist by choice," p. 23), this is because her more dangerous imagination cannot be satisfied with the revelation of God's nature and man's unification with the divinity and must go beyond this ideology. In the presence of Aunt emily, Binx feels the awful prurience of ends: "My neck begins to prickle with a dreadful-but-not-unpleasant eschatological prickling" (p. 50).

Such is the supreme threat—the seductions of the eschatological, the paternal ghosts of hidden meaning wandering through our actions and our familiar places. The motherland wherefrom Binx has exiled himself is first of all that which is symbolized by Aunt Emily, Binx's true adversary, the only system of thought capable of obstructing his becoming. It is the power of an eschatological mentality invading the whole territory, playing on the predetermined sense of the future in order to imprison the present: "Everyone pretended that our lives until that moment had been every bit as real as the moment itself and that the future must be real too" (p. 81).

Terrifying is Aunt Emily's power, devastating the power of her words. The faculty for metaphorization of the Southern woman (p. 108), her capacity for naming ("She calls me . . . a limb of Satan"), the art with which she hyperbolizes the ordinary ("She calls me . . . the last and sorriest scion of a noble stock," p. 26), the fecundity with which she produces speech ("She summons me for one of her 'talks'," p. 27), in short, the threat represented by the discourse of the Southern aunt can be assessed in its effects. By listening to her, the exile "in a split second [has] forgotten everything, the years in Gentilly, even [his] search" (p. 26).

Aunt Emily, as her manifest belief in the capacity of language to produce the real through image indicates, shares the same philosophy as another great Southerner, more fragile and moving, but nonetheless formidable: Blanche Dubois. The latter's language is a device that metaphorizes at all costs; a device for agrandizing, abstracting, and masking; a hyperbolic system generating meaning in the presumed emptiness of Stanley's apartment. As such, it is only a defense against a supposedly hostile reality. Aunt Emily's own process of metaphorization, which may be defensive at the deepest level, nonetheless appears as the aggressive elaboration of a world by means of deliberate transformation, transfiguration, and "transmogrification" meant to generate a substitutive real essentially defined by the stable meaning of the figures produced.

Aunt Emily's language is a mythifying agent.[17] Dissatisfied with a real whose unity escapes her, she uses comparative copulas no longer to indicate difference indirectly but in order to implement the metamorphosis of images required by her ideology. Memory provides the self-image she desires ("It is as their favorite and fondest darling that she still appears in her own recollection, the female sport of a fierce old warrior gens," p. 26) and her environment undergoes the mythifying effects of her language. One by one, Jules, the man whose insertion in his world is most harmonious (p. 30), then Sam Yerger, and finally Mercer, who lost his sense of identity in the affair (p. 49) will find themselves transfigured by her discourse.

Mercer is transformed into the mythical figure of the faithful Sambo: "Mercer she still sees as the old retainer." Jules, in spite of the end of an heroic era, is metamorphosized into "the Creole Cato, the last of the heroes." Aunt Emily transforms and transfigures (p. 49) and she passes on to Kate this petrifying power, an unnamable sickness of which she must rid herself: "In her long nightmare, this our friendship now falls victim to the grisly transmogrification by which she unfailingly turns everything she touches to horror" (p. 63). Aunt Emily, who holds the heroization of her family to be less important than the metaphorical process itself, is well aware of this: "All the stray bits and pieces of the past, all that is feckless and gray about people, she pulls together into the unmistakable visage of the heroic or the craven, the noble or the ignoble" (p. 49).

Closer to Blanche's than it may seem, her discourse is the generator of an inhabitable real: "So strong is she that sometimes the person and the past are in fact transfigured by her" (p. 49). After all, Blanche's discourse had successfully transformed Mitch into a "gentleman caller."

The reality Aunt Emily manages to create in the masked terror of its absence appears as a panic-stricken need for code in the great prosopopoeia (pp. 219–23) where her anguish of emptiness is watermarked: "I have been assuming that . . . among certain people, gentlefolk I don't mind calling them, there exists a set of meanings held in common" (p. 222).

This "deck" of meanings, as one would speak of a "deck of cards," this code, is not merely the code of Southern gentility. It is a universal code ("universal sentiments," p. 108) that will make possible the survival of the last fetish to which Aunt Emily and the world she stands for are fiercely attached. This ultimate—and therefore primary—fetish is "meaning": "For her too, the fabric is dissolving but for her even the dissolving makes sense" (p. 54).

Emily and her world are devoured by the cancer of understanding: "She understands the chaos to come" (p. 54).

The unconscious, preying on the terror of an absence, pulls an admirable trick: one preserves meaning only because meaning is all there is. Held in the framework of meaning, the mind can immediately go back to weaving the fabric of its real, reconstructing systems of relationship, the crossing of threads that create the texture of the real and surreptitiously reinstate a "one." Listening to Emily and her likes, the fabric presently mends: "As I listen to Eddie speaking plausibly and at length of one thing and another . . . the fabric pulls together in one bright texture" (p. 18). Like Emily ("She pulls together," p. 49), Eddie, who belongs to her world, weaves a unique reality with picture-words. In the semidarkness of the porch, Binx the child had learned how the family members created the real; he can still hear "the echoes of porch talk on the long summer evenings when affairs were settled, mysteries solved, the unnamed named" (p. 153).

Emily and her family live in a world of naming, the naming by which one constructs a world in one's image. From such structures was exile necessary.

This whole world speaks the discourse of mastery: Binx's father disciplines his body and tries to control matter through science (p. 86); Walter organizes everything (p. 39); Aunt Emily plans out Kate's recovery (p. 28); the party itself, the carnival, in the hands of people like Walter, is the object of hierarchical organization (krewes); analysis and scientific research (as opposed to "search," p. 54) are so unanimously praised that Kate herself is ready to succumb. Binx, in such a world, has contracted the malady of understanding that postulates an end and a foundation to things. At that time, he was reading the "fundamental books." In such a world where quests are vertical because the truth is to be found up high (p. 69), people such as Harold Graebner believe in communication and use the postal service to send messages that only tell their naive faith in communication, as did these "long, sensitive, and articulate letters" (p. 87) that Binx has long since quit sending.[18]

In such a world, life has a precise meaning. We are on this earth to "make a contribution" (pp. 54, 101). In such a world, one "schemes," like Sam, out of innocence and goodness. Repressive plots are merely the consequence of a banal belief in the "natural," a piety and a grace that Aunt Emily claims (p. 222) her likes have inherited from the immediate in nature.

The lovers' discourse (p. 198), the idea of sin (p. 200), the cycle of ideas à la Paul Newman (p. 211), the Southern heritage (p. 223), beauty (p. 196), goodness, truth, nobility (p. 224), and especially the idea that one must have "a goal in life" (p. 226) are constructions, products of naming, artificial proliferations that forbid the approach of a certain reality and no longer have meaning for Binx.

The world that words and ideas gave Binx was a construction, an edifice, a chance and arbitrary structure produced through a calibration that calls itself public service: " Here is the public service truck with its tower, measuring the clearance under the oak limbs and cutting some wet drooping branches" (p. 62). At that point it is not surprising that Walter, who believes in "the meaning of symbols" should speak of a "caliber of men" (p. 37), just as ammunition fits into firearms! A calibrated world, the real on the mark, people in step—army or skaters (p. 78), these eternal letters offering cheap happiness (p. 7), such is the conventionalized reality in the discourse of constructors, particularly that of theosophists and teleologists. For the supreme edifice, the radical construction based on a signifier, is God and His accomplice, the concept of Nature[19]: "My unbelief was invincible from the beginning. I could never make head or tail of God. The proofs of God's existence may have been true for all I know, but it didn't make the slightest difference. If God himself had appeared to me, it would have changed nothing. In fact, I have only to hear the word *God* and a curtain comes down in my head" (p. 145).

God is a masking signifier, a great veil thrown over the mind. He is, among so many others, a signifier who thinks himself an idea, and ideas with their sidekicks the ideals are, in the final analysis, the visible structures of our alienation: "Having learned only to recognize *merde* when I see it, having inherited no more from my father than a good nose for *merde*, for every species of shit that flies [ideal volatility of that *merde!*], smelling *merde* from every quarter, living in fact in the very century of *merde*, the great shithouse [here comes the edifice!] of scientific humanism" (p. 228). Aunt Emily, emblem of all possible constructions, is a fervent believer in the products of idealism: "Katherine, you're perfectly right," she says to Kate, "Don't ever lose your ideals and your enthusiasm for ideas" (p. 194).

In this way does one die of an overdose ("I ran out and took four pills," Kate concludes, p. 194), an overdose of discourse, structures, and determinism.

"It is impossible to say why," (p. 235) Binx says at the end of his quest. Happy is the exile who has finally freed himself from causality. "Why" is the silliest question in the world because it plays in the hand of destiny, which requires determinism to annihilate the liberty of pleasure.[20]

What Binx learns from Kate is that no one is required to ponder the causes and effects of a reality that is purely accidental.

Of Chance and the Desert

The Education of an Exile

Ignorance, like pleasure, can be learned. Nothingness is a discipline, like nonsense. *The Moviegoer* is an example of a familiar genre, the *Bildungsroman,* a novel of the deprogramming of a young American adult. The axis of the moral and religious imagination is vertical; God is on high, like truth. This is the space of *research*—from bottom to top, toward transcendence or truth, invariably located in high places. These heights postulate fundamentals ("fundamental books"), beginnings and ends, subjects as distinct from objects ("I stood outside the universe"), the cognitive processes of the subjects below ("And sought to understand it"), and therefore completions ("the main goals of my search were reached"). Research is linked with the ideology of elevation: "The greatest success of this enterprise, which I called my vertical search . . . " (p. 69). Any vertical research can come to an end ("There I lay in my hotel with my search over," p. 70). The plurality of fundamental books is resolved in the singularity of the completion.[21]

The horizontalization of the quest (*search,* as strictly distinct from *research*), the refusal of ends and aims, the opening up to spiritual and bodily wanderings is only the happy result of a fertile negation ("Another idea occurred to me yesterday as I read about Khalil in the high plateau of the country of the Negd," p. 71). Thus is the "one" negated ("Because as you get deeper into the search, you unify. You understand more and more specimens by fewer formulae, " p. 82) for the greater glory of the difference that is always being renewed through movement: "I vowed that if I ever got out of this fix [sic!], I would pursue the search" (p. 11). "I have undertaken a different kind of search, a horizontal search" (p. 69).

As a quest with no aim or object, its own rotation constitutes its only self-justification: "A good rotation. A rotation I define as the experiencing of the new beyond the expectation of the experiencing of the new." Its success is defined through loss— loss of consciousness, loss of mastery, and loss of self. "For example, taking one's first trip to Taxco would not be a rotation, or no more than a very ordinary rotation; but getting lost on the way and discovering a hidden valley would be" (p. 144).

Horizontalization, an implicit rejection of the hierarchy of things (the high and low), sums up the education of the exile. Through it he reached the desert. This is not the desert of secret objects and myths of the novelist of exoticism, not the localized, modest and picturesque desert of romantic travelers, but rather the desert that offers itself up as emptiness, absence, a plenitude of non-being, or at the very least as scarcity of objects and meaning. The formerly voracious reader has now found out how to reduce his library to a single work pertaining to the desert: "My library is a single book, *Arabia Deserta*" (p. 78).

The exile's apprenticeship requires such passage through the desertification of the research field. Let Arabia Petraea give way to Arabia Deserta so that the love of the true seeker for the emptiness of deserts may bloom: "He [Mrs. de Marco's son] hates the desert. I am sorry to hear this because I would like it out there very much" (p. 74).

In the economy of Binx's narrative itself, the desert of *Arabia Deserta* lies in a strict binary opposition to the novel of place: "She conceals *Peyton Place;* I conceal *Arabia Deserta*" (p. 69).

The desert is the non-place where time and space—two conventions dispensed with by the exile's reading of *The Universe as I See It*—can no longer be hypostatized by the subject. Who will say, in the true desert, what distinguishes space from time and vertical from horizontal?

The heirs of Rupert Brooke and the unvanquished (p. 88) carry the burden of a double belief in full utterances and high-mindedness:

> On the program hundreds of the highest-minded people in our country, thoughtful and intelligent people, people with mature inquiring minds, state their personal credos. The two or three hundred I have heard so far were without exception admirable people. I doubt if any other country or any other time in history has produced such thoughtful and high-minded people, especially the women. And especially the South. I do believe the South has produced more high-minded women, women of universal sentiments, than any other section of the country except possibly New England in the last century (p. 108).

Thus are high mind and lofty views seen as perversions of altitude, a seduction of the universal and the metaphysics of the 'All' (p. 108).

Set against the high-mindedness of the men and women of the American elite, crises of absent-mindedness (pp. 89, 119), during which the real flashes before us, will enrich Binx's real quest, as per the lessons of Linda and Sharon. Binx prefers the revelations of "absent-minded girls" to the lessons of "high-minded women." When the mind is no longer there, the real reemerges. When the mind is absent—when the woman-dog absents herself ("M-hm—absently", p. 118), the becoming-being manifests itself.

Would-be realists, lose your minds!

The human wonder is not so much men's minds as women's behinds: "Sometimes she speaks of her derrière, sticks it out Beale Street style and gives it a slap and this makes me blush because it is a very good one, marvellously ample and mysterious and nothing to joke about" (p. 42).

Women's derrières are the other side of things, what lies beyond-the-mind, inaccessible to reason, the negation of hierarchies, and the last refuge of the wonderful, of the mysterious, and of the beautiful: "Her [Sharon's] bottom is so beautiful that once as she crossed the room to the cooler, I felt my eyes smart with tears of gratitude" (p. 65).

By what cultural aberration, Binx wonders, did men come to value the "silly turned heads" of the girls of America at the expense of "their fine big bottoms" (p. 123). This is where the ideology of elevation and the vertical imagination lead.

In the face of culture, history, and science's totalitarianism, in face of the fetishism of the word-message, there remains only one solution: "tear it up" (p. 88). "It": at first reading, this is the henceforth vain reply to Harold's letter. On second reading, it is the so-called expletive "it" ("a word not necessary to the sense," according to Webster's dictionary), a signifier in the hole where the 'All' gets swallowed up: the exile sees that he must tear up, in an expletive way, intransitively; tearing up as heuristic method.

Simulacra

Such a gesture leaves room for the pure simulacra of money and the movies. As a sophist of the modern world, Binx distinguishes himself in the primary talent of the sophist, his "natural" gift for making money, and the satisfaction this talent gives him (p. 71). Better yet, money is a deep and uncynical joy (p. 92), almost mystical: "Money is a better god than beauty" (p. 196).

Binx's taste for money is pure love. Money for him is never associated with wealth or the comfort and pleasures it can secure. The only value Binx assigns to money is substitutive. It represents a good defense against the dangerous seductions of beauty: "Ten years ago I pursued beauty and gave no thought to money. I listened to the lovely tunes of Mahler and felt a sickness in my very soul. Now I pursue money and on the whole I feel better" (p. 196).

Money does not relate to anything, is useless, and harbors no value; it is a pure object of desire in a psychological climate stripped of all greed, in a moral context from which value judgments have been banished. The money Binx acquires never means anything. It is by contrasting Sharon's attitude toward money that we may understand its moral insignificance in Binx's eyes. Her wariness (p. 96) toward the gift of money clearly means that, in her eyes, it has meaning and is invested with purchasing power (of objects or of subjects) that confers a moral value upon it.

This is not so for Binx and the sophists. Money represents nothing. It is pure arbitrariness, pure simulacrum. Money has no odor and no referent. It has nothing to do with the real.

Neither do movies; as pure fabrication of the pseudoreal, the movies also belong to the order of simulacra[22] but possess, in this order, the privileged and ambiguous place of the original thing. In fact, if there ever was a model or an original form, if ever there was in this world an anterior to any reproduction[23], this would be a cinematographic archetype or, better yet, an archetypal situation of confrontation between subject and simulacrum, the locus of this confrontation, a primordial in-between: "Back to the Loop where we dive into the Mother and Urwomb of all movie-houses—an Aztec mortuary of funeral urns and glyphs, thronged with the spirit presences of another day, William Powell and George Brent and Patsy Kelly and Charly Chase, the best friends of my childhood—and see a movie called *The Young Philadelphians*" (p. 211).

In the beginning (in the original form) was, therefore, the time of the cinematographic representation, the celebration of the missing ones whose spirit haunted the simulacrum.

Similarly, the image of the accident is another organizing principle of the novel. The first film mentioned in the story, on the edge of the associations of images, is a film about an accident, shown in a theater located there by mistake: "A theater in a new suburb. It was evident somebody had miscalculated . . . and here the theater, a pink stucco cube sitting out in a field all by itself. . . . The movie was about a man who lost his memory in an accident" (p. 4).

This self reflecting image places Binx's adventure under the sign of the accidental, the messenger of chance, that returns time and again as a leitmotiv throughout a mental journey that concludes on Binx's being wed to the spirit of the accidental.

Chance and Its Messenger: The Accident

Accident of the amnesic in the original movie (p. 4), the bacteriological accident in *Panic in the Streets* (p. 63), the subway accident related in *Reader's Digest* (p. 77), the western entitled *The Oxbow Incident* (p. 79); there are many metafictions in the novel dealing with the theme.

The narrative's territory is inscribed within a series of accidents. The narrative's setting, the South fallen prey to the demon of the analytical (p. 65), is in reality a setting dominated by the accidental. In this particular South the structures and constructions themselves ("You see that building yonder?") bear the seal of the accident: "That's Southern Life and Accident" (p. 196).[24]

The place occupied by automobiles ("the car is all-important," p. 121) in the fiction (Kate and Lyell's accident, Binx's Dodge sedan, the MG that is so soothing for the troubled soul—"the malaise" and the Ford responsible for Binx and Sharon's accident) underlines this constant presence of the accidental in a world where there is but a semblance of order: "When I first slid under the wheel to drive it, it seemed that everything was in order" (p. 121).

It is perhaps not unimportant to note that none of the multiple accidents that mark the narrative have deplorable or even unpleasant consequences. In the metafictions as in the fiction, the accident has the beneficial effect of turning the victim into a stranger (p. 5), guarantees the authenticity of the real (the "certification" of the neighborhood by *Panic in the Streets*), encourages communication between New Yorkers (the subway accident, p. 77) and is finally related to a windfall: "As luck would have it, no sooner do we cross Bay St. Louis and reach the beach drive than we are involved in an accident . . . . When I say luck would have it, I mean good luck" (p. 120).

As the text unfolds, the positive connotations of the accident are confirmed and make us easily accept the assimilation of the accident with birth, defined as a gift of life: "Your mother thought it was the accident [during which Kate's fiancé Lyell perishes] that still bothered you." "Did you expect me to tell her otherwise?" "That it did not bother you?" "*That it gave me my life.* That's my secret" (p. 58, my italics). This is Kate speaking, Kate who was literally born of the accidental death of her fiancé, who paid her reality with the death of the other, and for whom the real is the product of disaster ("Only in time of illness or disaster or death are people real" (p. 81). Kate cannot help appearing as the fertile spirit of the accidental when she admits with neither shame nor morbid pleasure that, for her, happiness and accidents are closely related; the happiest moment of her life happened right after the accident that cost her fiancé his life (p. 59).

This double birth to life and happiness points her out as the *genius tutelae* of the accidental. All that smacks of a contract ("She has broken her engagement with Walter," p. 66), that suggests stasis or stability (married life, p. 197), or that indicates health by the silence of the organs and the mind ("I feel fine when I am sick," p. 81), anything reminiscent of order (pp. 195–96), balance and seriousness ("Her own fashion of being serious: as an antic sort of seriousness, which is not seriousness at all but despair masquerading as seriousness," p. 81), anything that could make one believe in the permanence of the subject's identity ("I had discovered that a person does not have to *be* this or *be* that or be anything, not even oneself"), or in cause and effect sequence that controlled one's becoming (p. 114), anything that would deny deviation, gaps, unforeseen changes, or liberation (p. 115), that would lock contrasts into strict oppositions ("I know your old upside-down trick: when all is lost, when they despair of you, then it is, at this darkest hour, that you emerge as the gorgeous one," p. 172), or postulates a center ("I only wanted to—break out, or off, off dead center," p. 181); in a word, all that stands opposed to the wonders of chance ("wonderful", pp. 115–16) is alien to her.

Kate's love gravitates toward that which is detached ("What made you feel wonderful?" "It was the storm . . . The storm cut loose," p. 57), breaks the order of reasons (pp. 114–15) and compacts with destiny; it is partial to all that glides, like trains (p. 183), out of order and out of preestablished orders (p. 195). It is the disorder of events ("Something is going to happen," p. 211) insofar as events indicate the presence of the miracle and wonder of things.[25]

Submit to daily miracle, open body and soul to the surprises of becoming[26], however much structuring people may detest it, make reason recognize mystery. Wonderment is a rigorous discipline: "Not for five minutes will I be distracted from wonder" (p. 42).

To exile oneself is to learn to leave open "the great flood-gates of the wonder-world."[27] Binx will marry Kate, the spirit of true exile—the antidote of structure, a bird or horse (p. 115), forever to forsake constructions and remain open to the accidental ("What if I don't make it?" will be her last question, p. 241), forever to be associated with the positive power of the untimely, to an event that is as unpredictable and unnecessary as the wind.

Let the order of reasons die out; then shall the wind rise, and reaffirm its creative power in the chaos ("The Lord of

Misrule," p. 230) of desire. "Nothing remains but desire, and desire comes howling down Elysian Fields like a mistral" (p. 228).

Mistral: maestral: maïstre. Master.

Desire is the only master and no one ever discovered whither the Mistral wafted him.[28]

7

The Energy of an Absence

Perfection as Useful Fiction in the Novels of Gaddis and Sorrentino

Johan Thielemans

T HE SCENE IS NEW YORK, the date Christmas Eve
1949. At Esther's apartment a number of people have
gathered to meet a famous author.

Such is the subject of chapter 7, part 2 in William Gaddis's
Recognitions.[1] In style and treatment the text is different from
the preceding pages. There we have a normal distribution of
descriptive and narrative text versus dialogue, both clearly
controlled and organized by a distinct Gaddis voice. There
have already been interruptions of the narrator's voice by
dramatic dialogue where the text of the novel proper has been
traversed by beliefs and opinions, seemingly overheard, and
sometimes emanating from unidentified sources.

But in the party-scene the ratio of prose to dialogue is
drastically reversed. The interventions of the author are reduced to a strict minimum, and the text veers towards a pure
montage of spoken utterances. The effect striven for is of a
dual nature: the text wants to deal with chaos, by being chaotic

in itself. But a second reading of the same text reveals that the chaos is neatly organized and controlled by a few of the leading ideas governing the whole of the novel.

The main problem of the book concerns authenticity: are works of art genuine? are people real? is human contact and understanding possible? Each of these questions turns around the concepts of truth and falsehood. The novel makes the frightening suggestion that everything and everybody may be a fraud.

If this is so, one may ask, what is the value of life? Gaddis's answer to this pressing question is that in order to be valuable life needs both religion and beauty. In his scheme of things the artist has an extraordinary role to play. To be an artist means to communicate with higher values and to confer dignity on our day-to-day life, which would otherwise be merely ridiculous and despicable.

Given this analysis of the world, it will not surprise us to find that artists of different disciplines and with widely varying degrees of talent populate the pages of *The Recognitions*. To the characters in this novel it goes without saying that the past has produced undisputed masterpieces. This awareness is a first cut through the substance of our experiences: past and present confront each other as periods characterized by deeply different qualities. The artists of the past were able to produce objects with transcendental value, because the conditions of society were fundamentally different. The troubling question is whether or not present-day conditions make the production of valuable works of art possible. The biographies of the many artists illustrate their eagerness to reach the status of their admired models. Their longing to be part of the glorious tradition is their fate, as it constitutes the reason for their being unhappy, tormented, and ineffectual in this world. The true artists (Wyatt, the painter, and Stanley, the composer) suffer from being late, to borrow a term from Harold Bloom.

Indeed, the novel amply documents the amazement, the agony, and the delight of the clinamen.[2]

This historical cleavage is illustrated by the protagonist Wyatt, who refuses to be original, which, he says, is the curse of our century. Instead, he finds his true genius by painting in the style of the Flemish painters of the Middle Ages. To reach excellence in art the old masters observed a particular method of production. By mastering these techniques he reaches moments of great artistic power. A similar point of view is shared by Stanley, who models his own works on medieval forms. Both find something authentic by imitation.

Opposed to these two characters are a number of artists and critics who refuse the old standards and beliefs. They are fake and try vainly to give their lives meaning or shape by trying to establish some inner value. But they fail and are so many instances of an essential loss.

This general meditation on the nature of art and the quality of life lived by contemporary artists leads to a reflection on the state of language. The linguistic universe is similarly divided into two fields. One is felt to be a place where the word would have a full meaning, where the messages would have their full weight. The quality of such a language would be the expression of individuals who would be touched by grace. But examples of this type of linguistic utterance are absent. There is a strong suggestion that poets speak it, but in daily life the actual spoken words feel like parodies of the real thing or forgeries of a real value. Consequently the language of the dimension of the ideal is absent. The debased form is present everywhere. Also in this case there is the awareness of a past and a present: the language was excellent, once, but now it has turned into an instrument of ridicule.

Between Gaddis's views about painting and language there is an important difference: the quality of painting is discussed in the body of the work. The state of language, on the other hand, is made into the very material of the text. It is precisely in party scenes, such as the one at Esther's, that Gaddis makes the reader experience the effect of unauthentic lives on verbal performance.

The cast of the party comprises both the major protagonists and a large number of minor characters. Although Gaddis devotes seventy-eight pages to it, the party hardly advances the plot. We only learn that Wyatt pays a visit to his wife Esther, who cannot persuade him to stay with her. Stanley unsuccessfully tries to persuade the literary agent Agnes Deigh to join the Roman Catholic Church. Anselm, a failed author, takes a razor and decides to follow the recommendations of Matthew 19:12 literally; he castrates himself in the men's room of a subway station. The plot material concerning Wyatt and Stanley takes some seven pages, while Stanley's argument is part of the web of conversations, which forms the real texture of the chapter.

On the most superficial level the montage of snatches of conversation, sometimes reduced to one-liners, reads as a chaotic farandole of ironic remarks and quick comic vignettes. A more careful reading of the text reveals that the chaos is only apparent because Gaddis has organized his material around a fairly limited number of topics. They appear and disappear, suggesting a musical structure with its alternating themes and their development. The alternation is governed by contrast and surprise, giving the overall impression of a contrapuntal allegro, fully in tune with the music by Handel that is the loud and insistent background to the party's conversations. Pursuing the musical analogy further, we could say that the different themes are written in the key of hesitation and outrage.

The contrast between the themes is achieved by selecting subjects from a broad spectrum, ranging from the lofty (discussions on the meaning of art and the function of religion) to the banal (international tourism). Personal relations form another dominant topic, as the participants offer a fairly complete scale of possibilities, ranging from extramarital love to homosexual encounters and including a critic masturbating while observed by a lady friend. Some topics are used for comic effect and concern the media (Hollywood, television, and advertising), psychoanalysis, business deals, art galleries, and publishing firms.

Although these are disparate subjects, they are all embedded in one overall thought. They are signifiers with one signified: the decline of all values. This is immediately alluded to by the first lines of the chapter in which a tall lady remarks that a convent has been turned into a madhouse. The link between church and madhouse is the concept of loss. Every single item will later be seen to have been detracted from its original or true value.

The party scene is, then, a satire in which things are seen as they are, but also, at the same time, played off against our awareness of how things should be. "If we are (being historical creatures) fallen, we can begin our redemption by our subjection to satire, which helps us to discover and measure our fallenness or our concupiscence."[3] Such is Gerald Bruns' description of the proper intent of the satirical stance, and it applies fully to the text under consideration.

But Gaddis's text goes much further than simply poking some witty fun at the artistic circles of Greenwich Village. The very wording of the text generates meanings that take us beyond simple satire. The fragments of conversation are of a dual kind, if we take into account the sources from which they emanate. When the speaker is identified by a name, there is no problem. But sometimes the speaker is but vaguely indicated by a characteristic (such as, the tall lady) and in the more interesting cases the speaker is all but unidentified, as the author resorts to the use of indefinite pronouns. This syntax of vagueness becomes a signifier in its own right and points to a general loss of individuality. Depersonalization, which is a characteristic of the uncredited utterances, is a dynamic force, as it bounces back on the named characters and takes away much of their solidity. Different isolated questions, which apparently break the flow of the conversations, turn into focal points structuring the chaotic field, by thematising that very chaos. These are questions such as: "How do all these people know each other?" (p. 571), "What does *that* mean?" (p. 569, repeated p. 613), "Do we know half of what is happening to us?" (p. 623). Two further moments in the text are particularly meaningful. On page 607 the tall woman repeats four times to interlocutors who turn away from her, "Do you see what I meant?" The text itself answers this with three repetitions of the sentence. "That's what I hate," as if floating on air. To this disembodied voice "someone" (only identification) remarks, "Merry Christmas . . . If you'll pardon the expression." The introduction of *Christmas* is more than a simple joke. It highlights once more the devaluation of all positive concepts and suggests a reason for the absence of a meaningful center.

The same sense of hopelessness is evoked on page 626 when another montage of impersonal utterances points to the devalued character of any positive idea or emotion. "If you call that art" is followed by "If you call *this* living" and "If you call that love." This absence of meaning is experienced with a great degree of emotionality, which translates itself in psychological despair and the urge to commit suicide. The theme of suicide is hinted at in the opening lines of the chapter with a reference to the bandaged wrists of a girl. Later an unidentified speaker confesses to having tried to commit suicide twice in two weeks by taking sleeping pills (p. 569). The motive of sleeping pills is carried through the rest of the text as a kind of bitter running gag, as a child begs for sleeping pills from everyone present for her mother downstairs. The theme returns in a casual aside about the critic in the green wool shirt, in which we learn that his wife shot herself (p. 576).

Later we see a young man, Charles Dickens, looking for razor blades in the bathroom with an unmistakable intention. He is thwarted when Anselm confiscates the razor. Here the plot takes an ironic twist, because Anselm, following his own dictum that "you can't discuss absolutes in relative terms" (p. 630), decides to follow the example of Origen and castrates himself in order to reach the Kingdom of Heaven.[4] The actual phrasing of the scene is so ambiguous, that the act itself suggests the committing of suicide. Such are the darker hues, coloring what superficially looks like "pseudointellectual chitchat."[5]

The text makes us aware of the dichotomies full/empty and presence/absence of meaning. In both cases the first terms are implied and function as unformulated places of desire. In the text there is a suggestion of a way out of the dire predicament of contemporary man. Stanley, the composer of church music, explains to Agnes Deigh that the world is falling apart. The resulting fragments are self-sufficient, so that it is "almost impossible to pull them together into a whole" (p. 616). (This is, at the same time, an apt comment on the form of the chapter itself.) Stanley feels that "the whole" can be reached through a work of art. But art in itself is not sufficient; it should acknowledge the supremacy of religion. The Roman Catholic Church, Stanley feels, provided, in earlier times, the necessary center of life and experience, so that "meaning" was not problematic. He quotes Voltaire[6] to underline the fact that "even Voltaire could see that some transcendent judgment is necessary, because nothing is self-sufficient, even art, and when art isn't an expression of something higher . . . it breaks up into fragments that don't have any meaning" (p. 617).

If art does not accept to be subjected to a higher transcendental value, it becomes an end in itself, adopts the "fallacy of originality" (p. 632) and becomes, through its own self-sufficiency, another instrument in the general process of alienation. "When art tries to be a religion in itself." he concludes, it is ... "a religion of perfect form and beauty, but then it is all alone, not uniting people" (p. 632).

This general argument (which is both the real subject of this chapter and of the novel as a whole) finds its concrete shape in the text itself. The argument is not presented as a logical construct, but as an experience. The complaint about fragments is uttered in a fragmented text. The ultimate function of these fragments both proves and belies Stanley's point of view, because the reader experiences both the chaos and the underlying meaning, as the chaotic state of the text is itself a signifier. The text in its totality has become a sign and, as such, gives us the sensation of a vanishing position.

The same problem affects the actual language used, with its tension between the fallen word and the language of the absolute. The chapter consists of degenerated language, a fact that is marked by several stylistic devices. Much of the quoted dialogue consists of stock phrases and examples of dead, ritualized language. The dialogue itself is written as a close imitation of spoken language, full of false starts, repetitions, and interruptions of syntactical structures. The many hesitations are both mimetic and meaningful. All the time, a meaning is in the process of trying to be formulated. Language constantly attempts to say what remains unnamed. The words spoken are so many failures at communication. While this particular difficulty is more or less present throughout the whole chapter, and this both on the level of the interpretative relation of the reader to the text and on the level of the reciprocal communicative relation among the participants on the page, it is foregrounded through exaggeration on page 594, where a series of questions without answers moves towards the brink of a complete collapse of meaning. The quality of the actual language registered—Gaddis as "author" and source of the words has virtually disappeared from these pages—rehearses in itself the whole problem. The intellectual argument, culled in these words, is all about the necessity of perfection, but it is couched in a debased form of language illustrating the impossibility of the thing wished for. The mimetic aspect of the novel is in itself the object against which the novel constantly protests.

The Christmas party in *The Recognitions,* together with similar scenes in the novel, is seminal in that it presents a particular verbal technique, which Gaddis will elaborate upon in *JR* (1975). While in *The Recognitions* the party scene is still exceptional and only one of the styles Gaddis uses, in *JR* the spoken voice becomes the sole medium of the author. This *tour de force* in the manipulation of the information[7] yields a verbal object, which consists of trash. The linguistic material of the text is completely debased. Gaddis includes all the redundant words, all the imprecise *phrasings* characteristic of an undereducated verbal culture. The unchecked proliferation of the spoken word leads to, or is the manifestation of, a cheapened culture. Perhaps behind this spite for the spoken word there is the feeling that the "true" word can only be written down as the result of a moment of concentrated silence.

The effect of the painstaking imitation on the reader is of a complex order. The imitation yields both pleasure and frustration. The pleasure of the reader consists in his admiration for the dazzling ability of the author to record the many imperfections. The frustration proceeds from a thwarting of expectations about the form written language should have. It can do with a suggestion of imperfection (viz. the conventions of dialogue in plays), but it sees itself as an improved version of that imperfection. It is by neglecting this hierarchy that Gaddis's text acquires its unique character. It is also an aesthetic decision, which is not without its risks. The reaction of George Steiner is, in this respect, revealing. While in his case we have a critic who responds deeply to the problem of the state of our culture and is preoccupied with the disappearance of a particular form of highly coded and polished forms of discourse,[8] it is remarkable that he could not discern any quality in Gaddis's novel. He called it "unreadable"[9] precisely because the very verbal material fell outside the province of any rhetorical and stylistic standard Steiner might adhere to.

The very form of the text obliges us to reflect on the equality of the novel as a whole. This becomes an even trickier question as there is no denying that Gaddis holds in high esteem the very concept of a "perfect work of art." The making of such an object is the very ambition of each of the adult protagonists, and as such it is one of the major elements of the plot in *JR*. The ambitious scope of the novel can only mean that such is also Gaddis's ambition, but he prefers to attempt it through a paradoxical practice, which inevitably raises the question of whether such a lofty goal can be reached through a corrupt medium. It means that if we judge *JR* to be a major work of fiction, it is so despite the language it uses.

But where is the point in this process at which banality turns into art? The mimetic virtuoso performance by Gaddis goes beyond the mere registration of speech, which actually looks "recorded." The mirror is traversed because the utterances on the page stand in critical relation to the absent forms of language. The text is pervaded, not only on the plot level but also in the very substance of the words itself, by a thirst for the Other, for the realm of the beautiful, the perfect. The language on the page is eroded by entropy, but the novel as a whole longs for a language that is free from it.

This important tension between presence and absence, between *is* and *ought,* lends the text its real energy. The tension is not an act of external interpretation, but the result of the conscious position taken by the author towards the language on the page. Gaddis, as the implied author of the text, pretends to be totally absent. Consequently the novel consists solely of words spoken by characters. The one place where we could expect the Other to speak, namely the place explicitly occupied by the author, remains mute.

This chosen muteness opens the field of the text, but it would be wrong to think that the author is totally absent. The text is, rather, a veil behind which he hides, and he is most powerfully present as the orchestrator of the voices. Through careful montage he reaches his effects and meanings. If the text is said to be excellent, it is on this supralinguistic level. There the text exhibits an organization that the chaotic surface of the text tries to eradicate or obscure. There every accident of the text signifies irony, discrepancy, contrast, and contradiction. The fragmentation is only apparent and articulates itself in a complex argument on the level of the grammar of the novelistic form by exploiting a number of signifying techniques that draw on our full cognitive powers for decoding a text. On this level the felicities of invention are plenty, and it is by bringing these devices into play that the novel as a whole may claim a place in the pantheon of Perfection that has been the impassioned subject of the imperfect babble on the page.

A similar conflict between forms of language can be found in the writings of Gilbert Sorrentino. Having begun his publishing career as a poet, it is less surprising to find him concerned from the very outset by problems concerning the power of the word. This has attracted his attention to such a degree that in the debate about the preponderance of form and content, he clearly sides with language. In an interview several years ago he confessed that the subject matter of a poem is less important than "the quality of the language used."[10] This led to short poems containing "minimal amounts of situations, feeling, thought and imagery, expressed in a minimal vocabulary."[11]

Both in these poems and in his early novels, *The Sky Changes* (1966), *Steelwork* (1970), there is a recognizable author's voice. It shapes the sentences and the lines with care, controlling rhythm, pace, and structure. If we see any experimentation in these novels, it is with basic forms of the realistic novel. With his third novel, *Imaginative Qualities of Actual Things*[12] we see the first traces of a dramatic shift. The subject matter of the novel deals satirically with the artistic community in Greenwich Village, to which Sorrentino belonged in the sixties. One of his irritations concerns poor writing. He is angered by the ease with which the cliché takes over. A linguistic formula, through its repetition, is felt to steal the life from an actually lived experience. When on page 240 he writes "I don't know what to do, the scene mercifully fades before my eyes," he feels the urge to add in a footnote, "I am indebted for this phrase to the 9,000-odd writers who have used it before me."

The cliché remains a topic of concern throughout his novels. As author, a concept that implies a particular social position and a specific duty towards language, Sorrentino abhors formulas that point to a lack of linguistic awareness. But if we take into account the part played by clichés in the novel *Aberration of Starlight* (1980), we see that Sorrentino holds these high requirements as valid for himself and his colleagues, but for speakers from a different social class, clichés have a privileged meaning. In the linguistic life of the underprivileged they prove the ideal instruments for the expression of deeply felt emotions. As he feels a strong sympathy for the working class, to which his mother belonged, his acceptance of the cliché is a manifestation of his respect.

But when he changes social milieu, he becomes intransigent, and the stereotyped phrases are exposed as so many indications that the intellectual and artistic characters uttering them live in a world of pretense.

The parallel with Gaddis's convictions concerning the state of the language and the quality of life are obvious. But on a purely technical level Sorrentino formulates them differently. He is constantly, insistently present as the punishing, deflating commentator, so much so that the real protagonist of the novel becomes the impatient author himself.

Bad style will remain at the centre of Sorrentino's interest. It is again the subject of his massive novel *Mulligan Stew*.[13] This novel deals with the attempt of the author Anthony Lamont to write a novel. It is the record of a complete failure. The text presents itself as a collection of separate texts, emanating from different writing instances. There are chapters from published books, a diary, letters, a collection of poems, extracts from a notebook, lists of items, and an interview. There is, however, not one line that could be ascribed to the author of *Mulligan Stew*. By this strategy the place of "author" has been voided. Again the field of the text opens up, but this time it is written language that occupies it. The form of language is not fixed, as issuing from an ideal place, but instead all the written languages of the linguistic community invade the text. As there is no "true" language, spoken by the "author," there are only quoted instances. The fact that they are quoted impairs their referential capacity. The outside world is bracketed out. The novel is not about reality but about the way in which language is used. Each manner is found to be wanting, and every attempt inside the novel to produce literary excellence is shown to result in a ridiculous sham. The most striking example is offered by Lorna Flambeaux, a young poetess who sends her first collection, *The Sweat of Love*, to the protaganist Lamont.

Although in an appreciative letter to her Lamont claims that the book of verse has "just that exact, modern combination of candor and craft that has long been missing from our poetry," (p. 164) it is clear from the poems, included as another form of document from "outside" the novel, that they are appallingly crude, each exhibiting yet another form of bad poetry. Ironically, Lamont will later discover that although the "delightful and talented Miss Flambeaux" (p. 219) only writes in pornographic-exalted terms about lovemaking, she is in fact a respectable, shy young lady who is easily shocked.

Mulligan Stew is, then, a collection of examples of bad writing. As reader we are aware that the "absent" author, Sorrentino, has a double mind concerning the phenomenon of second-rate literature. There is a part in him that loathes the execrable ways of (ab)using language. But the mere size of the novel, combined with the absence of examples of the other, valuable type of language, oblige the reader to conclude that Sorrentino has a strange form of fascination with these forms, as he would otherwise not take so much trouble to convince us of his astonishing capacity for imitating bad styles. Indeed, if we raise the problem of appraisal, we once more are confronted with a paradoxical situation: the parodies are executed with such expertness that they form the fundamental reason why several critics have judged this anthology of bad writing to be a novel of exceptional quality.[14] But in what way is the trite material recuperated? Why is *Mulligan Stew* an alchemist's trick by which base material is turned into literary gold?

It is a question that fascinates Sorrentino so strongly that it becomes the motivation for the composition of later texts. In *Mulligan Stew* there is still a fairly straightforward answer for explaining our appreciation; the poems by Lorna Flambeaux would, issuing from a real Miss Flambeaux, be dismissed out of hand. But in the context of the novel they are a signifier and as such create indirectly the character of Miss Flambeaux. The context, then, is decisive for the value we ascribe to literary texts, not to their intrinsic worth. The boundaries between perfect and imperfect language become blurred.

The later novel *Crystal Vision* (1982) offers a related meditation on the problem of the status and function of a perfect language. The novel consists of seventy-six short chapters (one chapter for each of the cards from the tarot pack). In each of these a character tries to tell an anecdote to his friends in a cafe or on a streetcorner in Brooklyn. The subject matter is a repetition of the situation of the earlier, realistic novel *Steelwork* (1970). The stories concern crippled, dead lives. But the reader's attention is constantly deflected towards the medium, and the substance becomes wholly secondary. Each monologue is interrupted by remarks of a critical nature by the listeners. This excessive awareness of form prevents them from paying attention to the psychological misery and needs of their fellow human beings. Care for the words functions as an alienating force. As such *Crystal Vision* offers the negative face of the idealistic approach to writing.

Sorrentino's most recent novel *Blue Pastoral* (1983) takes the discussion one step further. It is a kind of road novel and echoes Sorrentino's first novel, *The Sky Changes*. Both novels describe a trip through the United States (from New York to San Francisco via New Orleans) and use the same itinerary. Such a procedure shows dramatically that Sorrentino gradually considers plot merely as a starting point from which to work. But he is not a storyteller. Neither is he an analyzer of characters; he is an adventurer of language. The plot is minimal. Serge Gavotte, possessor of a piano, buys a cart and takes his family (his wife Helen and his son Zimmerman) on a trip through the States, looking for the perfect musical phrase. He finds it in San Francisco, on the last page of the book, and the last line, appropriately, is a musical notation. The blurb to the book suggests the moral lesson that the quest is futile, and Gavotte could have found the same phrase by staying in New York, pounding his piano. Of course the journey, not the destination, is the point. But what is the nature of the journey? The text consists of sixty-three chapters, each of them composed in a different style. We remember how the *persona* of the different characters made the different specimens acceptable in *Mulligan Stew*. In *Blue Pastoral* there is no fictional Lamont at work. Here are many narrative stretches that can only be traced back to Sorrentino himself. He has provided us with a real anatomy of bad styles. *"Blue Pastoral* is a kind of catalogue,"* John O'Brien has commented, "of the ways in which already corrupted language proliferates itself, ending in utter chaos."[15] This judgement is essentially correct but not complete. Of course, many chapters are satirical. Prime examples are the political speech by congressman Glubit (chapter 13), the babble at a gala cocktail party (chapter 25), and Father Donald Debris and S. J. on sex (chapter 36). In each case a mentality is exposed through exaggeration.

Parodies are the most conventional forms of language manipulation, and they display the imitative powers of the author. But, as the Gavotte family travels through the United States, the different languages, from regional speech to idiolects, traverse the text until the text turns into a linguistic map of America.

There is a comic effect, present in many other chapters, that is more characteristic of Sorrentino's enterprise. Here the author looks for particular types of distortion of the standard written language to produce yet another witty version of English. In chapter 2, the words of Dr. Ciccareli are transcribed in the idiom of the comic immigrant familiar from Chico Marx (this example partakes of all categories at once: ethnic stereotype, satire, and spelling). The novel-within-the-novel, entitled "La Musique et les mauvaises herbes," reads as a too-literal translation from the French. In these cases the reader easily perceives how two linguistic systems interfere with each other.

There are still different types of distortions, arrived at by imposing on the language purely arbitrary rules, so that the resulting text reads as a puzzle. Misspellings force the reader to bring into play his perspicacity, as the decoding of the printed words appeals to an underlying correct, intelligible version. In chapter 14, Serge Gavotte and Representative Glubit speak a scrambled version of English.[16] Some chapters are generated by mechanical rules: in chapter 48, Sorrentino pretends to give a list of New Orleans Jassorchestras. The real jazzbands have extraordinary names, but in the novel he combines this element with the French colonial background of the town, so that Sorrentino, by a shortcut, arrives at the names of French avant-garde writers, yielding such denominations as Mickey Butor and the Time Passers or Fats Gide with the Baton Rouge Boys (p. 225). Similar applications of arbitrary rules generate the last chaotic chapter, in which the text collapses under an avalanche of interfunction signs. The text itself consists of fragments from a full text.[17] Finally, language is reduced to isolated words, and at that point the text stops and a few notes on a bar conclude the novel. When language has completely vanished, a purity from another dimension takes over. Through these techniques Sorrentino tries to reduce the referential qualities of language, and tries to make an object in which language itself is the center of attention. Each variety of style, including the parodies, are as many text machines that operate by obeying a different set of rules.

Whatever the result of such an activity, the tension between language that adequately expresses a content and varieties of language that fall short of doing so (and which are by definition ridiculous) remains the creative principle. If we place the novels in the wider context of Sorrentino's complete literary oeuvre, we can even see how this tension structures and unifies his poems and novels. Sorrentino has been strongly influenced by William Carlos Williams. From him Sorrentino inherited a demanding aesthetic of the novel. "It is the novel, of itself, that must have form," he has written, "and if it be honestly made we find, not the meaning of life, but a revelation of its actuality. We are . . . directed to an essence, the observation of which leads to the freeing of our own imagination and to our arrival at the only 'truth' that fiction possesses."[18]

This austere programme looks very difficult to square with Sorrentino's actual output. The high standard invoked does not immediately call to mind the activities of an anarchic arch-joker. It seems much easier to apply to his poetry. There we meet with an author who tries to put in simple words simple, recognizable experiences. He puts them carefully together, so that he finds it possible to regard them as artifacts for which not meaning but form is the essential feature.[19] The difference between his poems and novels is so vast that his output has a schizophrenic feel. We are tempted to say that as a poet he moves in the field of the pure; his language wants to be personal and perfect; it is clearly Sorrentino speaking. But in the novels he prefers to disappear, and this vanishing act allows a very important transgression. It allows him to get out from under the rule of the pure language, which functions as a kind of linguistic superego. Sorrentino becomes creative by sinning, because whatever the nature of his critical rebuke, there is no denying that he is fascinated by the diverse forms of language. A debased form of language provides him with exceptional occasions for showing his dazzling talent at imitation and invention. The sinful connotation of this verbal activity, which is often linked with sinful sexual practices, gives it an unlimited energy. The opposition between the hierarchy of high and low is overcome by the simple but significant fact of the appearance of pleasure: pleasure in the reader for such a demonstration of uncommon virtuosity. The distinction between pure and impure has all but lost its validity, as we have moved to the exhilarating possibilities of the distortion of a codified language. It is not the adventures of the characters but the adventures of language itself that are breathtaking.

This discussion of the novels of Gaddis and Sorrentino has revealed a span of tension, conflict, and frustration outside the traditional fictional categories of character, plot, and motivation. The verbal substance has been violently cut into two territories. The words in the world—the realm that can be done justice by painstaking mimesis—are found to be debased and devalued. They emanate from a wounded society, and they show limited and stunted forms of consciousness.

In their descriptive and imitative function, they are passive elements. Through the awareness of a different language, though, with the accompanying concepts of a different psychological life and a different set of social values, the words on the page become energized. Their presence is wished to be an absence, while what is absent hovers over the text as a wished-for presence. The absent language functions as a point of view beyond and above the world of actual words. The felt presence-through-absence gives rise to an automatic, unformulated but experienced radical criticism. The language of the novel is never at rest, satisfied with itself (as the prose of Saul Bellow, for instance, certainly is). The written text consists only of the words that are possible, a state of affairs that is accompanied by the painful feeling that in fact only the word of the Other should do. As long as the Other—as superego, as model, as perfection—does not speak, there is no reason for satisfaction. But this insight is paradoxical, because it does not lead to frustrated silence. It functions as the conceptual precondition to set the textual machine in motion. Dissatisfaction turns out to be a powerful fuel, because it allows for such a rich and varied meditation on language and reality that the resulting texts are immense (as the lengths of *The Recognitions, JR, Mulligan Stew,* and *Blue Pastoral* testify).

In Gaddis's novels the critique of the abuse of language leads to a moral and political point. The entropic state of the language is shown to be our daily condition, but the characters in his two novels protest passionately against this state of affairs by cultivating the ambition to escape from the cheap universe of the commonplace through art. The event of the appearance of a perfect work is felt, as it is in a long Neo-Platonic tradition, to have a redeeming power.

Sorrentino starts from a similar position, but in the course of his works the problem changes character. He severs more radically the tie between language and reality. His texts gradually lose some of their complexity by abandoning the illusion of dealing with rounded characters. The tension between pure and impure is rearticulated in paradoxical terms. The realm of the pure language (the language of poetry, the language of full meaning) functions initially as a yardstick. But, by imitating the varieties of debased language, Sorrentino discovers a field with riches all its own. The protean act by which the author vanishes behind a virtually endless number of personae yields such intense pleasure that the attraction of the language of the Other wanes. The concepts *pure* and *impure* get divorced from the pair *quality* and *trash*. The attraction of the second term in these pairs is enhanced by the connotation of dealing with something forbidden. The texts have the vitality of sin.

Sorrentino has discovered that the appearance of pleasure, erupting from a paradox, is the key to value and quality. He risks staying outside the realm of perfect language, confident that out there it is also possible to be a "great" author.

If Sorrentino has, in tune with the literary theories of the time, maintained that fiction is first and foremost an object made out of language, his struggle with the verbal material has brought him to the point at which he forges new languages—never *his* language, but always languages that look borrowed or contrived. If he builds, in the tradition of the great fictional authors, his own universe, then it is a universe made wholly of words.

In their practice both Gaddis and Sorrentino have clearly shown that the hierarchical difference between pure and impure language has been a useful fiction. It has been a major feature in the writing of several postmodern authors. It is present in Thomas Pynchon and in the short stories of Donald Barthelme. This shows the seminal importance of the party scenes in Gaddis's *Recognitions*. In them a typical American sensibility has been touched upon; to the present day it proves a major stimulating force.

8

Between Latency and Knowledge

Figures of Preinitiation in Nabokov and Balthus

Pierre Gault

ALL HAPPY FAMILIES are more or less dissimilar, all unhappy ones are more or less alike."[1]

Ada begins thus, and what does it matter that Tolstoy's quotation is shamelessly reversed? The arbitrary mechanism of the two symmetrical formulae imprints a compelling movement inscribing the book in the "already-read," dooming writing to endless repetition, and condemning the text to the status of palimpsest.

The deviation that the narrator assumes with affected innocence as a postulate strikes the book a priori with conditional originality. From this, perhaps, stems the impression one has constantly when reading Nabokov, of being caught between the intoxication of a discovery and the poignant emotion of rediscovery. We are continually close to the commonplace, with the feeling of being struck at our most intimate.

The narrator of *A Russian Beauty*[2] lays claim to the necessary recourse to the commonplace in the following short description of Olga's childhood:

> Her childhood passed festively, securely and gaily, as was the custom in our country since the days of old. A sunbeam falling on the cover of a "Bibliothèque Rose" volume at the family estate, the classical hoar-frost of the Saint Petersburg public gardens . . . A supply of memories, such as these, comprised her sole dowry when she left Russia in the spring of 1919. Everything happened in full accord with the style of the period. Her mother died of typhus, her brother was executed by the firing squad. All these are *ready-made formulae*, of course, the usual dreary small talk, but it all did happen, there is no other way of saying it, and it's no use turning up your nose. (P. 13)

For the purpose of our study, we shall single out in this passage the affirmation of an incapacity to tell the real in any other way than with clichés. Here, in the context of the Russian Revolution, the impossibility of escaping from an iconography is assumed as a precondition to Olga's own history, and any idiosyncratic inflection can only be added to these "ready-made formulae."

The principle Nabokov assumes here seems to be valid for the whole of his work and could be read as a metaphor for his own writing. What is in keeping with what he calls "the style of the period" can indeed apply to his own style: "There is no other way of saying it." The unspeakable, the horror, the most extreme pathos do not escape the cliché. It is perhaps even in this way that the excessive is best expressed in so far as the cliché is palimpsest, the commonplace expression of all sufferings experienced and erased and the eternally renewed expression of this suffering. (This is doubtless why the most authentic expression of a profound emotion, be it inspired by love or death, is first of all inflected in the commonplace; next come the lyrical variations.) Nabokov's writing is an endless exploration of this dimension of the "ready-said," these "ready-made formulae" that always leave us wondering whether they figurate the world or reconstruct it. In this study I intend to explore the use Nabokov makes of what could be defined linguistically as preconstructed structures. I intend to deal here with a whole facet of language that is characterized by preestablished grammatical constructions imprinting on discourse an order such that any inflection or any break will inevitably be seen as a deviation from the norm. We are not as concerned with wrongly oversimplifying a branch of linguistics on which relatively little has been written as with investigating what is at stake in manipulations that undermine syntactical order or call into question the stability of set-phrases.

Remaining true to the warning to the reader hidden in the fake quotation from Tolstoy, we will thus attempt to pick out of Nabokov's discourse figures that display, in a single formulation, the mark of preestablished order and the deviation that generates turmoil.

The violation of order, which can be read in the willful distortion of the text, shows simultaneously the need for the quotation and the necessity to extricate oneself from it. It is in the "nictating" quality (to use one of Nabokov's favorite adjectives) that characterizes this paradoxical position of Nabokov's writing that we will seek to determine what is at stake in the repetitive transgressions of the codes that are usual in his work.

In *Ada,* Ada and Van take advantage of the nocturnal burning of a barn that has mobilized the inhabitants of Ardis Hall, and they find themselves lovers for the first time. The next morning, Van, who is the first down to the dining room, awaits his young friend whose appearance is hailed by the narrator (the elderly Van) in a short description: "She wore—though not in collusion with him—black shorts, a white jersey, and sneakers. Her hair was drawn back from her big round brow and thickly pigtailed. The rose of a rash under her lower lip glistened with glycerine through the patchily dabbed on powder. She was too pale to be really pretty. She carried a book of verse" (p. 101).

The first line is hardly drawn when Nabokov detains his reader for a moment, long enough to point out—all the while denying it—the existence of a complicity. By removing all responsibility from the protagonists, he obviously assumes that there must be collusion elsewhere than in the diegesis, and at the same time he invites the reader to turn away from the referent in order to acknowledge more compromising games.

The warning occurs before a brief listing of clothes in which the message of amorous disorder is delivered in three terms: "black shorts, a white jersey, and sneakers." The idea that governs the list obviously defies the laws of logic. The description is made neither from top to bottom $(1-2-3)$ nor from bottom to top $(3-2-1)$ according to the laws of mathematics or of anatomy. On the contrary, an anarchical distribution is offered $(2-1-3)$. Van's gaze first rests (in theory) on the black shorts (site of turmoil), which mark and mask Ada's sex. Then, after a short passage on the white sweater, it vanishes shamefully or stealthily on the "sneakers," opportunely preferred to possible "tennis shoes."

Nabokov offers here an exercise in "reading-writing"[3] that calls into question the laws of the arithmetical progression in series 1 with the added bonus of the debunking of logic and the advent of amorous disorder.

The best way to celebrate this disorder is to conform to the eternal rituals and play the poet's part. The brief portrait shows off its heavily mimetic alliterations and, in case the reader has not understood, Nabokov has Ada carry a book of verse, a blatant symbol of the endeavor. The portrait of Ada, the sonnet to Ada, or the ode to Ada already exist in another book, just as Olga's childhood is already inscribed in the Comtesse de Ségur's books. Everything has already been said elsewhere, and Van can only offer his own variation of the set figure: She wore . . . The hair . . . The rose . . . The start of each verse dictates the clichés of the genre to the poem, whether the beloved's name be Laura or Ada.

Oddly enough, the content of the poem does not meet expectations. The structure may lead the discourse to set sites, but the song does not possess the necessary stress and the sweetheart is not the prettiest. Ada's portrait contains an almost ungrateful presence of childhood redoubled in an awkward way by the too ostentatious alliterations: "her hair was drawn back from her big round brow and thickly pigtailed." It is a child's face that is described in this short sentence. The braid that pulls back the hair, leaving the forehead bare, produces an effect of pathos that is probably due to the smooth and integral exhibition of this face, claiming attention for the unattractiveness of the large forehead, which does not comply with the canons of feminine grace. The pathos, in fact, probably stems from this deviation. We expect that Ada, changed by her experience during the night, might show some sign of complicity. On the contrary, it is childhood that emerges, exacerbated, as if the passage rite has only emphasized the juvenile features, accentuating the fact that Ada belongs to a period of latency on the verge of preinitiation. The referential detail pointing most directly towards childhood is, of course, Ada's hairstyle, a guarantee of innocence, which places her in the category of "pigtailed little girls."

Let us pause for a brief theoretical clarification, long enough to study more closely the braid exhibited at the end of the sentence in a surprising expression. "Pigtail" is a set-phrase[4] whose constituent process can be conjectured. The word springs from a comparison and is made up, lexicalized, by the integration of its two components when the hyphen disappears; in this process the pig and its tail, which inspired the poetic word game, have disappeared completely. The possibility of transforming the noun into an adjective, the word *pigtailed*, confirms the absorption of the original metaphor into the lexicon by the integration of the noun in a grammatical construction, a recategorization as linguists would say. And yet it is perhaps the excessive nature of this grammaticalization that sets us thinking. The adjective "pigtailed" is commonly used (especially as an epithet). But the addition of the adverb "thickly" appears to "saturate" in an embarrassing fashion the construction that is already very much on show with the use of "pigtailed" as an attribute. The pig was mentioned a great deal in the preceding chapter, in which Van, the narrator, attempts to recall with an elderly Ada the moment when "for the first time (she) might have suspected (he) was also a sick pig or horse" (p. 91). Thus, the set phrase "pigtail" undergoes reactivation through a rather suspect grammaticalization and also through the interplay of indexical signs. The poetic process that originated the word, lost when the word gained a denotative function, is insidiously encountered in the playful juxtaposition of thick, pig, and tail.

The image of innocence given by the character and sustained by a superficial reading is thus brutally threatened by the almost vulgar forthrightness of a new isotopy. The question is obviously one of deciding to whom this shocking vulgarity should be ascribed—if indeed vulgarity there be. Essentially, undoubtedly to the reader, who could have been content with the referent and not have given way to the perversity of a linguistic readjusting. Nabokov usually functions in this way. As Maurice Couturier points out in a recent article on eroticism in American literature, "he invented literary devices to give his reader the impression that the fantasy was all his"; this obviously leads to a definition of the two accomplices of writing that is very compromising for the reader: "Nothing is described by the narrator, everything is reconstructed by the eavesdropping reader."[5]

We shall not, however, be contented with this acknowledgment of an undeniably ludic intent in our particular example. Let us come back to the way in which we have seen innocence established and called into question in the single expression intuitively fixing the ludic in the referential order. It is in fact the reader who is assigned the task of deciphering the word game. Nabokov expects him to become the accomplice of the elderly Van who tells his own story. But the turmoil can only spring up if the reader readjusts and reascribes to Van, still a child almost, the gaze that rests on his young friend. Emotion can only arise from this readjusting, and we must consider the exceptional quality of the game offered us.

The vehement display of thick, pig, and tail, which outlines behind the naive portrait of Ada an imagery as explicit as pornographic graffiti, is inscribed on the canvas like the erased but indelible marks of a palimpsest. From the very figure of innocence springs an acknowledgment of desire so brutal it can only be expressed with reprobation. The adverb "dirtily" will appear after the short portrait, lost between "freely" and "delightfully," taking part in the orgasmic scanning of the three adverbs, but present as the semantic mainspring. Thus, Nabokov's tour de force consists in having the reader rediscover the turmoil of the first initiatory steps, beyond the amused acknowledgment of a word game.

The source would seem to be the figure linguists call the set-phrase: when reactivated, it allows the intimate juxtaposition of an apparently referential, anecdotal order and a metaphoric disorder that is in no way explicity indicated as being a trope. We might see in this figure a degree zero of the metaphor[6] the absorption of which in the order of discourse is particularly designated as the privileged site of a staging of initiation, or rather of the preinitiatory moment, that period of tension towards a sensed knowledge still strongly marked and even contained in acquired structures. Thus the set-phrase, the figure par *excellence* of an order of discourse that also designates an existential order, might especially lend itself to a representation of deviation, of disorder, of emotion. The fact that the figure is not explicitly marked as such but requires the optional reactivation by the reader might stimulate the character's state of mind. The character is himself confusedly aware of the simultaneous presence of complementary and antagonistic forces both vehement and diffuse. Nabokov's text is full of these strategies in which reader and character, manipulated by the narrator, are initiated side by side, Eleusinian companions, the former reactivating by his reading the erased mark of his own initiatory emotions reincarnated by the latter.

We could quote numerous examples here, from the set-phrase, revived by a fanciful slip, in which Ada explains to her uncle who asks what she was doing during the nocturnal fire that she was "fast ablaze in her bedroom," to this paranomasis that Van himself undertakes to complete, effectively transforming "striped" into "stripped:" "She wore the striped teeshirt which in his lone fantasies he especially liked to peel off her twisting torso" (p. 64).

The intent can immediately be seen to be more openly ludic than in the example we studied at length. But what skill in the juxtaposition of the moment when desire confusedly springs up and of the fantasy that figurates it! In order to better delimit the specificity of what we defined as a figure buried in diegesis, we will offer some brief contrasting remarks inspired by the striking kinship between our short sentence and a passage from John Fowles' *Collector*. Fowles, also a lover of pigtails, lets his narrator describe the first meeting with Miranda: "I saw her several times too. I stood right behind her once in a queue at the public library down Crossfield Street. She didn't look at me once, but I watched the back of her head and her hair in a long pigtail coming down almost to her waist, sometimes in front, sometimes at the back."[7]

In this fleeting vision of the girl who will become his prisoner, the butterfly collector multiplies around the object of his desire the signs of order and of interdiction. The queue, chosen site of a one-way meeting, allows access to a public place, the temple of knowledge; the unbearable intimacy created by the desired and dreaded promiscuity is as it were sterilized by the implicit presence of others and the pretext of the meeting, access to collective knowledge. Theoretically, there is no room for any kind of intimacy.

The narrator's mania for writing down in his notebook his observations in the slightest detail leads him to mention the name of the street, a detail that apparently authenticates the story by situating it in a fictitious geography and perhaps provides the reader with the first sign of turmoil coming from this field to be crossed. As with Ada, the braid points to childhood and confers on the scene a juvenile quality that splashes the voyeur, clearing him as did the pretext of the chance meeting earlier. The length of the braid has been judiciously calculated by Fowles in such a way that it does not reach the waist, that compromising site where femininity diverges from childhood. It is, however, a supple vector, describing the back and front of the young woman's body, miming by proxy forbidden caresses. The character's exhibition is clearly to be seen in the disappearance of possessive adjectives, which tends to neutralize the desired forbidden body: the "her" of "her waist" which appeared, seemingly erroneously, at the end of her braid is swiftly cancelled out in a very stiff expression in which the sex and the buttocks have become "in front" and "at the back." Thus the pig and its tail are energetically censored here. The reader's task consists in discovering the character's neurosis, transmitted through a beam of indexical signs; to recognize what is at stake in the description, he has to acknowledge the isotopy queue/pig/tail once more buried in the referent. We cannot fail to be struck by the similarity of the two approaches, which both aim at the reactivation of a set-phrase and, under cover of a discourse on order, propose the emergence of amorous disorder.

In order to gain access to the narrator's disorder, the reader has to become the accomplice of Fowles' rhetorical strategies and finally has to reconstruct a turmoil that he cannot easily claim for his own. The reconstruction has in fact taken place at the expense of two formal operations during which emotion is lost to the benefit of an aesthetic reading in which the ludic loses its initiatory functions.

Fowles' technique appears to be the result of what Gérard Genette calls a diegetic metaphor[8], one inscribed in the referent but which no explicit sign happens to display as a trope. Genette quotes the example Hitchcock gives of a train entering a tunnel at the moment when the hero lies down on his lady friend. Staying in the realm of railways while coming back to Nabokov, we find the same metaphor used to express the confusion felt by Van and Ada when they take each other's hands for the first time: "On very still afternoons, one could hear the pre-tunnel toot of the two-two to Toulouse from the hill, where that exchange can be localized" (p. 85).

The advantage of such a metaphor is that it allows the establishment of a complicity between narrator and reader, leading up to the feelings the character experiences confusedly but could in no way recognize clearly enough to express them. In other words, the diegetic metaphor permits the expression of that which is inexpressible for the character, so long as this inexpressible is the object of an intertext sufficiently coded for the reader to recognize it at once. This is no doubt why Nabokov jokingly suggests strong Freudian imagery (the train in the tunnel) in a frenzy of onomatopoeia. Plainly this type of metaphor ensures complicity with the reader but condemns him to the already-known. The initiatory power of the reading is obviously diminished and the character loses some of his depth. For Nabokov, such a strategy is certainly to be read as a playful diversion, and we find here the usual derision of everything in any way connected with Freudianism. The situation is rather different for a faithful Freudian like D. H. Lawrence. Lawrence's landscape is strewn with diegetic metaphors, which the reader has to decipher in order to understand what the characters can only express with expressionist gestures or action. Thus the reader is always one step ahead of the character, and by the time the character has confusedly grasped the nature of his crisis, the diagnosis has long been established. We must obviously place Lawrence in his time and recognize the didactic quality of a writing that aims at having a reader who is often ignorant of the Freudian intertext discover a logic patiently secreted by the diegesis itself.

However, the presence of this handicap, in which the character always lags behind the reader, partly defuses emotion to the advantage of the aesthetic and formal satisfaction that can be found in Fowles' fragment. Playing on the same figure and using the same harmonies, it does not create the profound turmoil that Nabokov's concision manages to produce. Fowles' characters are the object of a coherent, distanciated discourse. The set phrase *pigtail* leads to a laborious reanimation where emotion is lost to technique. On the other hand, the close symbiosis between referent and metaphor that Nabokov offers not only brings the narrator and the reader suddenly back to the very site of initiation, but it also inverts the handicap. We might even think that the advantage goes to the character who possesses such an intense degree of emotion that reader and narrator can only exhaust themselves in their endeavour to reformulate and rediscover it.

Before proceeding with the study of the figure we have just outlined as a privileged site of intense exchange, let us consider its theoretical properties. We may define it as a set-phrase reactivated in both a radical and discreet way. One of the main characteristics of a cliché is that figurative meaning has been, so to speak, congealed to the detriment of other possible meanings. The reactivation therefore consists in reviving one or more lost meanings, which at once puts into question the univocal nature of discourse. In Nabokov's work we often find the brutal superposition of the familiar, the referential (defined by the set-phrase) and of an excessive dimension questioning the familiar while being inscribed in it. The tension it provokes results from the adjunction of the extreme and the familiar in an oxymoronic relation of *inscribed excess*.

Visiting the recent exhibition of Balthus's works in Paris, I had the feeling that there existed between Nabokov and the painter a striking kinship, a kinship that seemed intuitively to go beyond the common taste of both artists for transitory stages and young girls caught at the disturbing moment of prematurity.

In his attempt to define the status of the referent in the logic of the Surrealists, Antonin Artaud (in an article devoted to Balthus) underlines what he calls "a fundamental discredit cast on appearances." "If it does not deny the existence of objects," Artaud says, "the surrealist world disorganizes them; in its conception of things it promulgates first of all a divorce between the unlimited and reason. We can find no difference between the world of dreams and that of applied reason."[9]

What is important is this indifference, the divorce that deprives the referent of its referential value by setting the sign free from its denotative function.

Balthus, on the contrary, chooses to reinvest the object with its familiar function. As Artaud says, "he recreates the world of appearances" and the type of reading he defines confirms what we have underlined in Nabokov's writing. "In one word, Balthus starts from the familiar; there are in his painting universally recognizable elements and aspects; but the 'recognizable', in its turn, has a meaning that not everybody can reach or recognize either."

A precious definition indeed of the painter's manner that accounts with perfect lucidity for this promiscuity of the familiar and the unutterable that probably generates the impressive tension at the source of emotion. What overwhelms in Balthus's painting is the feeling that an intense symbolism, perhaps the answer to all our nonformulated questions to which there is no answer, is at hand, inscribed within the intimacy of the prosaic. It is indeed what we have recognized in the little portrait by Nabokov: "Her hair was drawn back from her big round brow and thickly pigtailed."

A first reading smoothly defines itself, justified by familiar denotations and precoded connotations, and that reading might prove sufficient. It only delineates what Artaud called "the recognizable." As for the meaning of that "recognizable that not everybody can reach," it lies within the submerged metaphor that upsets the stable and illusory notion of innocence by grafting onto it the dimension of desire. Referent and metaphor are thus knotted in an oxymoronic relation that the surrealist rupture would not have allowed.

To put it differently, we might say that the divorce between the object and its transposition in the surrealist metaphor completely disjoins the two axes of our reading. The syntagmatic and metonymic order of the referential discourse disappears in favour of the paradigmatic and metaphoric, as the consequence of a postulate of incompatibility.

In Balthus and Nabokov, on the contrary, the metonymic is ceaselessly threatened with metaphorisation but retains its rights. Emotion is probably due to this constant menace that provokes a continual repetition of the crossing of the two axes; the impossible answer that haunts us is there, close by, hidden within the familiar, and the text ceaselessly exhibits its trace.

I do not have the feeling, having required Roman Jakobson's assistance, that I am indulging in a particular taste for jargon or that I withdraw from the immediate pleasure secreted by the works of both artists. Balthus and Nabokov are obviously theoreticians of language, adepts of metafiction. But in the same way that their metaphors are inscribed in the referent, their theoretical reflection lies in the diegesis itself.

I have just mentioned the axes organizing the juxtaposition of two readings. Their network scores Balthus's paintings with perfectly readable rigor. A strict geometry of skirting-boards and wainscoting, borders of carpets and tablecloths, angles of walls, pillars and mantels of fireplaces, and stiff furniture. *The Patience* (*La Patience*), *The Children* (*Les Enfants*), *The Fortune Teller* (*La Tireuse de Cartes*), and many others show this interplay of vertical and horizontal lines. A stable orderly world both stiff and reassuring is thus defined, softened by a few curves (the paunch of a vase, the oval of a looking-glass, or the curvaceous leg of a bench). Then, brutally, a diagonal, a slant, or the secant stiffness of an arm disturb the ordering of this right-angled world. In *The Children* it is the broken line of the kneeling girl's body in the foreground of the painting. In the portraits of Thérèse, *Girl with the Cat* (*Jeune Fille au Chat*) or *Thérèse Dreaming* (*Thérèse rêvant*), it is the sharp angle of the elbows raised behind the head or the upraised leg, the foot resting on the straw of a stiff bench, displaying at the center of the painting the isthmus of white pants. In *The Patience* or *Happy Days* (*Les Beaux Jours*), it is the diagonal of the girl's body. The same network can be recognized in a brief excerpt from *Bend Sinister*, which could be used to describe a Balthus painting: "Between the pillars of the porch, geometrical sunlight touched your reddish brown bobbed hair, your plump neck, the vaccination mark on your sunburnt arm."[10] Such is the perfectly formal staging of the narrator's desire, displaced on the slanting ray that caresses the girl.

As the adjective "geometrical" incites us to do, it is tempting to see here, inscribed in the diegesis (even if the scene is purely imaginary), a graphical illustration of the discursive figure under examination. The slanting vector which points to the narrator's confusion finds the cause of its trajectory in the space that separates the vertical pillars of the porch. It is thus in the very structure that symbolizes order here that the secant challenging this order has its origin. A figurative counterpoint to the linguistic operation that we have defined as "reactivation of a set-phrase", it juxtaposes, thanks to that beam of sunlight, a vision of childhood and innocence and the brutal irruption of desire. We may remark, in addition, that the beam finally hits the little vaccination scar, another set site, where, for the last time, order and disorder are confronted, this mark being the "letter" of childhood and a staging of desire, this discreet displacement making the body accessible.

Nabokov's text is interspersed with "genre paintings"; the narrative breaks off, making a temporary halt on a brief intimist scene. We could look for captions to Balthus's paintings in *Ada*. Thus, for such-and-such a portrait of Thérèse there is this evocation of Ada in which Van attempts to define ravishment: "Ravishment—because of her pale voluptuous impermissible skin, her hair, her legs, her angular movements . . . the sudden black stare of her wide-set eyes, the rustic nudity under her dress" (p. 52).

As in Balthus's work, the features that characterize the girl are both familiar and neutral, at the same time specific, intimate, and perfectly conventional. Ada, Thérèse, and the others are interchangeable in a common symbolic system that springs, however, from a moment of intimacy. Once again we find this promiscuity of the anecdotal and the symbolic that gives the reader the impression of being faced with a scene of initiation, the outcome of which concerns him and disturbs him. Should we seek to find out what is at stake in the awkwardness of the angular movements or in these eyes set too far apart (by which standard?) and gazing intensely, fixedly, openly on life and death?

The discreet and disturbing presence of death also appears in the next caption, which might apply to the *Girl at the Washstand* (*Jeune Fille à sa toilette*): "Next morning he happened to catch sight of her washing her face and arms over an old-fashioned basin on a rococo stand, her hair knotted on the top of her head, her nightgown twisted around her waist like a clumsy corolle out of which issued her slim back, rib-shaded on the near side" (p. 53).

For the opaque mirror of the *Nude by a Fireplace* (*Nu à la Cheminée*) whose discreet obliqueness breaks the regular network of verticals and horizontals, leading the reader to some unreadable reflection, Nabokov has substituted the tenuous shade of the ribs, implicit slanting streaks on Ada's side, suggested in a strangely neutral formula; "the near side." The definite article, when we have expected a possessive, cuts off the detail from the diegetic intimacy of the scene, drawing the reader towards a dark dimension that bears the mark of mortality. Oddly enough, an uncommon compound adjective, "rib-shaded," evokes this surprising emergence of the mortal order. Nabokov once more chooses a preconstructed structure to introduce the element that comes to question the smooth emotion of the anecdotal. The "genre-painting" *Ada at the Washstand,* common site of the discourse of intimacy, has discreetly taken on a dramatic valency.

On the other hand, the anecdotal is explicitly erased in this other snapshot in which we see Ada literally invade the space of the table, like the girl, in Balthus's *The Patience,* engaged in studying the cards. There is the same dialogue between the body and the stiffness of the chair, the same angular elbow: "Ada was sitting straight, incurving her supple spine in her chair, then as the dream of adventure (or whatever she was relating) reached a climax, bending over the place . . . and suddenly all elbows, sprawling forward, invading the table" (p. 54).

If we compare the staging of these two pictures we find that the same complex of flat surfaces and vertical lines serves as a support for the expression of sensual vitality. But the pretext narrative is put between parentheses. The narrative we must reconstruct may be contained in the cards; "spine" and "elbows," places where the skeleton sticks out under the flesh, are its paradigms.

Thus the thematic and formal parallel between Nabokov and Balthus leads us to recognize common global strategies. They both go in for "genre scenes," both explore the commonplace, and both move away from it, drawing the reader into a confused and disturbing symbolic system in which words full of inexpressible meaning, such as desire, death, and fate, are indiscriminately juxtaposed.

Studying this likeness more closely, it seems we can go even further and define more surprising convergences of the written and the pictorial. Looking at the scenes Balthus depicts often gives the impression that a sequence of ordinary, familiar life has been arrested for a moment, fixed in a movement, ready to resume its course. This intuition comes from the fact that the chosen movement is nearly always transient, intermediary, and rarely settled in temporary comfort. The sleeping girl depicted in *Thérèse dreaming* (*Thérèse rêvant*) cannot sleep in a position that can only be a transition between possible states: waking and sleeping, life and death. The girl who is reading in *The Children* (*Les Enfants*) cannot stay for long in an angular position already called into question by the curious supple nature of her legs. A strange malaise is communicated by such suspended immobility, by a referential world on the verge of tipping over that leads the reader-spectator towards a disturbed, interrogative dimension which the precariousness of the chosen gesture does not contribute to dedramatize. There is the same awkward discrepancy between what could be a "cliché" (meaning "snapshot" here) and what a judiciously shifted grouping presents as a photo that went wrong. Thus, the three sisters are grouped in a curious way around the sofa in the center of the picture.

We come close to a stereotype here; these are scenes in which we could figure. One could almost speak of "hollow paintings," because it is so easy to invest them with memories of our own childhood, of our own existence. And yet the act of identification always fails or always swerves towards a disquieting vertigo; the spectator is swept into the gulf that opens up between the known and the unknown. Nearly all of Balthus's paintings have reassuringly banal titles: *The Drawing Room* (*Le Salon*), *The Bedroom* (*La Chambre*), *The Window* (*La*

Fenêtre), *The Children* (*Les Enfants*), *The Three Sisters* (*Les Trois Soeurs*), *Cathy washing* (*Cathy à sa toilette*), or *Happy Days* (*Les Beaux Jours*). We can recognize in them the places and the characters of a peaceful middle-class existence, often explicitly connotated by the presence of nineteenth-century furniture in the Louis-Philippe or Second Empire style. The similarity between the title of the painting and what it represents is generally obvious. What we see in this picture *really* is a drawing room, with a sofa, wainscoting, and a piano; another picture *really* does represent a young woman washing.

The title and the picture function in tautological reciprocity; the former refers back unambiguously to the latter in denotative univocity, and the latter confirms the definition with an example sufficiently stereotyped to provide the expected referent.

It is precisely this stability of the denotative that Magritte attempts to call into question when he decides to accompany the representation of a pipe on a blackboard by the title *This is not a pipe*. In his study on Magritte, the title of which is the title of the painting, Michel Foucault backs up the justification given by the painter for the apparent inadequacy between title and painting. "The titles are chosen in such a way," Magritte says, "That they prevent my paintings from being placed in a familiar region that the automatisms of the mind would not fail to create in order to escape anxiety."[11]

Faithful in this to a surrealist idea of discrepancy, Magritte facing the real world, chooses to postulate an anxiety articulated on a questioning of the denotative function. By refusing the reader-spectator the comfort of a familiar certainty, he thus wishes to create an essential turmoil, a radical destabilizing, the prerequisite of any interpretation of his work. I quote Magritte because Balthus's aim seems basically similar to his. Balthus chooses to create anxiety by staking on a feigned resemblance, for there is no doubt that this picture is not a drawing room, that these children are not exactly "children."

The radical difference that Magritte assumes as a postulate is hidden here in the familiar, a recognized familiar, but one that takes nobody in. What is at stake in Balthus's paintings is to be found elsewhere than in what they seem to depict. And yet, probably, the commonplaces that we recognize in his paintings provide the components of an anxiety that is less theoretical than in Magritte's work but that may be more striking because it catches us at the heart of the familiar. This may be so much so that the apparent adequacy of the title to the picture increases anxiety instead of removing it, constrasting Magritte's honest insincerity with the perversity of feigned consent: "this is a drawing room," "this is a child"; yet the illusion is short lived and the order of the world assured by denotative belief is rapidly disturbed by the uneasy awareness that we are not dealing with a drawing room and that the child on the painting is not quite a little girl.

Thus the difference between the represented object and the required reading is announced in two radically different ways, which very distinctly remind us of the acknowledged distinction between buried metaphor and displayed metaphor. Magritte announces a discrepancy; Balthus undermines the referential order from inside, positing its common sites without a priori calling their existence into question.

In order to be convinced we only have to study how, in *The Drawing Room (Le Salon)*, a symbolic reading can be superposed onto the order of the familiar, following a strategy very close to Nabokov's. In *The Drawing Room,* the piano takes up the right-hand side of the painting, next to a heavy sofa made of black wood covered with velvet. A very young girl lies asleep on this sofa, her head completely occupying one of the corners of the piece of furniture and her left arm following the curve of the back of the sofa. In the foreground another young girl is kneeling, like the girl in *The Children,* and is reading a book she has placed on a carpet. There is the same stiffness of position; we might say she is crawling. We see the same strange sensuality of the leg, which a short skirt uncovers to mid-thigh.

The girl who is half-sitting, half-lying on the sofa is perfectly integrated with the structure of the furniture, so much so that she preserves the contour. The furniture is stiff and gloomy and its curved legs are of a particularly disturbing black that intensifies the child's own bare leg on the left of the picture. We are not sure whether we should understand that a mortal order subjugates the sleeping girl or whether she is the one who reanimates the set-phrase of a middle-class order by inscribing the bright red color of her jacket in the angle of the sofa.

The content of her dreams is no doubt to be found in the book the girl is reading, a familiar accessory in Balthus's pictures, diverting the character's gaze towards a different place, pointing out to the reader-spectator that the meaning is to be found elsewhere than in the scene depicted.

A score, the double of the book, remains open on the piano, as if the story of the two little girls were to be congealed a moment, for the duration of some mystery or other. Just as mysterious is our strange impression that a third person is present in the picture and yet absent from the scene; a silhouette, as if badly erased, vaguely appears, half-hidden by the dark mass of the piano. The picture is painted on a canvas on which another picture we can hardly distinguish might have been previously painted. The inverted question mark of the spiral that holds up the keyboard does not manage to strike such a palimpsest with insignificance.

The score, left open at some letter to some Elise, and the question represented by the spiral contest the order denotated and connotated by the drawing-room furniture.

Something, we feel, escapes us, as if the moment that has been grasped were stretched between the adherences to childhood and the felt presence of another order in the intermediate period preceding all initiation.

9

"An Exact Precession"

Leonardo, Gertrude, and Guy Davenport's *Da Vinci's Bicycle*

Nancy Blake

. . . dire
ce qui est, on
ne le peut pas,
mais le redire sans répit.

—*André du Bouchet*[1]

FOR SOME OF US at least, it is true that space and time are not opposites; nor are they absolutes, but rather they are arbitrary definitions of a multidimensional reality, what we call metaphors. Since Einstein's demonstration in 1905, most of us recognize what some of us knew all along, that between what is named "future" and "past" there exists an interval whose extension in time depends on the distance in space between an event and its observer. The present is not limited to a moment in time. To gain time, increase space. The farsighted have every advantage.

Guy Davenport's collection *Da Vinci's Bicycle* persistently displaces the realms of space and time so that the words recur with an effect of *Unheimlichkeit*. What he is saying is at once excessively familiar and excessively strange. It is familiar because his writing depends on writing—other people's, what we call quotation, or reference. Gertrude Stein, one of Davenport's favorite voices, liked to say that there is no such thing as repetition. For Davenport, there is no such thing as quotation. Even the illustrations accompanying the texts in *Da Vinci's Bicycle* are "derived" and "acknowledged." They are taken from other drawings or, often, from photographs; they are copies of copies—the same and different.

Guy Davenport's text follows the trail marked by other texts, by human thought. Texts always following the same curves in the landscape may eventually wear a path. Perhaps. Davenport's project may then seem to be to render homage to the spirits of his predecessors and so to renew their vital force, and ours. This is Gertrude Stein speaking through Davenport: "He [Apollinaire] could see the modern because he loved all that had lasted from before. You see Cézanne by loving Poussin and you see Poussin by loving Pompeii and you see Pompeii by loving Cnossos. What the hell comes before Cnossos if this sentence is to be a long one?"[2] Yet this supposition, like all those one can make, in the context of Davenport's book is only as true as it is false. For, rather than tell, the text demonstrates that the loss of a reference is not of any real importance. All that counts is the loss of balance, the upsetting of equilibrium that allows one to take another step, the loss of equilibrium that means life.

This is Leonardo Da Vinci speaking without any help from Davenport:

> Contemplate this flame and ponder its beauty,
> close your eyes, then look: what you saw of it

was not; what it was
is no more . . .

What is it that regenerates that which unceasingly dies of
engendering?[3]

"I think, therefore I was," yet am. The same and different.
The world is a metaphor for the world and Davenport's text
is fittingly able to turn itself "leisurely inside out and back
again, like candlesmoke in a still room."[4]

At this point it may be useful to note that what Stein called,
in a voluntarily unoriginal way, "the question of identity," is
traditionally, at least since Heraclites, mixed up with the notion (which is arbitrary, but nonetheless bothersome) of time.
Yesterday's identity invalidates today's being. The *Unheimlich*
is perhaps nothing more than the feeling of inauthenticity
one has when faced with a past self. On the other hand, if
one postulates an identity in time, this identity can only exist
on some sort of general level roughly equivalent to the similarity between one individual and another. The narrator of
"The Antiquities of Elis" is interested in rhythms. Time becomes timing: "It was Herakleitos who said that some things
are too slow to see, such as the growth of grass, and some too
fast, like the arrow's flight. All things, I have often thought,
are dancing to their own music. A Lydian song is soon over,
but the music to which the zodiac is turning requires twelve
times three thousand years to close its harmony, if we may
follow the calculations of Pythagoras, and the rhythms of time
for a child are so much slower than for a man that we have
lived for centuries before our beards arrive" (p. 137).

One of the leitmotifs of Stein's *Geographical History of America*
is the phrase "these are simple ideas."[5] It is a fact, however,
that nothing is less simple for the mind to grasp than the idea
of simplicity. Our thinking always comes up against the im-

probable character of any identity, i.e., the improbability of reality.

One simple aphorism governs all of Leonardo's thought: "*Col tempo ogni cosa va variando*" (With time, everything changes). Thanks to a perspicacity worthy of Stein, Leonardo leads us to the brink of the unthinkable. In his apparent cliché is expressed the experience of the inconceivable: the same body is not always the same. And space itself is not a trustworthy container for being. Vehicles for time, space, and the objects seen in it are always in movement, always the momentarily possible result of an infinite series of relationships. From Brunelleschi to Piero della Francesca, a world *certo ed abitabile*, based upon linear perspective, had excluded the dimension of time.

The faces painted by Leonardo, like his blades of grass, are crossroads for transient forces. The nature of these forces is a mystery, the velocity with which they travel, stupendous. As you blink, the world is transformed: "Contemplate this flame and ponder its beauty, close your eyes, then look." The mystery of the Mona Lisa is in the illusive quality of the air at dusk, humid and dulled by a vapor through which the daylight can no longer penetrate. This atmosphere erases the outlines of the face while it accentuates the relief, as if a portrait were a landscape. So the Mona Lisa is not the painting of a woman, but rather that of a certain quality in the air, a certain harmony in the universe, represented by means of a human figure. Leonardo's lesson is interwoven through all the pages of Davenport's book: "You must understand, Beckett said, that Joyce came to see that the fall of a leaf is as grievous as the fall of man."[6]

The artist is a spider in the midst of the intricate web of temporality. It is only if time is understood as "being-there" (*dasein*), Heidegger pointed out, that the traditional phrase concerning time can be meaningful: time is the principle of individuation.[7] Leonardo said the same thing differently:

The water of the rivers that you touch:
last of the waters that were,
first of the waters that will be:
                    present tense.[8]

In his *Philosophy of Experience,* William James, who has several walk-on parts in *Da Vinci's Bicycle,* evokes the "essentially provisional and therefore unreal character of everything that is empirical and finite." Present experience is insufficient and therefore unreal, not only because it is present, but by definition. It is no use trying to add up all past and future existences, in a Proustian effort to transcend time; the whole is never equal to the sum of its parts. The real is something like "a unilateral being whose mirror reflection does not exist," according to Ernst Mach. Davenport quotes the Dogon myth that explains creation, not as the perfect reflection of God, but rather as the mischief of Ogo who was searching for a twin. "The real," says Clement Rosset, "is that which has no double."[9] "Space and time were still the same thing, unsorted. So before God extended time or space from his mind, Ogo began to create the world. His steps became time, his steps measured off space. You can see the road he took in the rainbow: *To see creation!*"[10]

All thought is an endless wandering between tautology and deviation. Therefore: "A rose is a rose is a rose is a rose." In Stein's succinct theory of reality and of writing, the notion of the referential is irrelevant. What can you say about the real? If we follow Stein's logic, once we have named it we have gone about as far as we are likely to go, which is, in fact, quite a distance.

What is being? Philosophy asks the question that myth articulates: "In the beginning, he said, there existed God and nothing. God, Amma, was rolled up in himself like an egg. He was *amma talu gunnu,* a tight knot of being, Nothing else was. Only Amma. He was a collarbone made of four collarbones and he was round."[11] The question of being is not one to respond to binary logic. Leonardo dealt with it in terms of power and unbalance: "Force is what I call a spiritual power—unbodily and invisible, which comes into being like a brief life in bodies, every time that accidental violence brings them outside of their natural rest and being."[12] All that counts is the upsetting of equilibrium that allows the body to take another step forward, the lack of balance that is being.

What Leonardo, Stein, Picasso, and Wilbur Wright have in common, besides their "genius," is, of course, that they were all, whether they knew it or not, Pythagoreans, materialists. Davenport's text celebrates force and light as the matter they so unbelievably are: "Bitumen of Judea dissolves in oil of lavender in greater or lesser densities of saturation according to its exposure to light, and thus Joseph Nicéphore Niepce in the year of Thomas Jefferson's death photographed his barnyard at Châlon-sur-Saône. Hours of light streaming through a pinhole onto pewter soaked asphalt into lavender in mechanical imitation of light focused on a retina by the lens of an eye."[13] The universe in which we live and write is an infinity of relationships. The light enabling us to apprehend the real changes what we see as we see it. A problem for contemporary physics: how to measure the effect of a photon emitted in order to enable the observer to see his experiment. An element for a future text by Guy Davenport: the correspondence between Albert Einstein and Niels Bohr. Einstein: "When a mouse looks at the world, the world does not change." Bohr: "Yes it does, a little."

Existence is literally a movement out of the self. Writing, the act of writing, carries on a necessary relationship with the absence of being. It is, no doubt, an imaginary mirror for the temptation we all feel to reconstruct the image of a fictive identity. But also, and more importantly, writing is a response to an absence closely related to the *Unheimlich* that threatens all perception, all thought: "It says in the pages of Mach that the mind is nothing but a continuity of consciousness. It is not itself a thing, it is its contents, like an eye and what it sees, a hand and what it holds. Mach's continuity, like Heraklit's river, defines itself by its flow."[14]

When Gertrude Stein wondered what was the use of being born a little boy if you were going to grow up to be a man, she was not questioning causality, not really.[15] She was simply saying that when we look at our own life, we might as well be schizophrenic, because we are looking at the history of another. This is the refrain of the whole of *Da Vinci's Bicycle*. Yet the most disturbing piece is perhaps the final one, "A Field of Snow on a Slope of the Rosenberg," which reveals the fact that the act of writing is not as safe as it has seemed to be. At times the distance necessary to appreciate metaphor collapses. Then Nijinsky is not like a horse, he is one.

All the other texts in the collection used a collage of voices to illustrate the web of relationships that link perceptions. This one unveils the genius of psychosis: the power and anguish of coming face to face with the real. "I wander out every afternoon, the same way, and have my walk. Every day now for twenty-seven years. Could I once have written books? Once drifted across Europe in a balloon? Once been a butler in Silesia? Was I once a boy?"[16]

Guy Davenport's art is a grammar for languages with de-clensions: Toledo, Ohio is a form of Toledo, Spain; time is an aspect of space, being of nothingness, force of light. "And of life we can ask but continuity. That, as I explain to my doctors, is my neurosis, I have been, I am, I shall be, for awhile, but off and on, like a firefly."[17] Order and chance are not opposites certainly; perhaps they are absolutes, but only if the word absolute is sidetracked by a literal translator so that it read "without solution." Heraclites, for whom the opposition of contraries is harmony not suppression or reduction of dif-ference, but rather infinite coaction, irreducible contrast, would be an ideal reader for *Da Vinci's Bicycle*.

The unbelievable juxtapositions of Davenport's texts and collages may indeed seem to deserve Wallace Stevens' term of "necessary fictions." But more than this, as works of art, their message is one that tells us all we know and all we need to know about reality itself. For what is the only universal characteristic of reality?—its singular unexpectedness.[18]

10

On the Pertinaciousness of the Father, the Son, and the Subject

The Case of Donald Barthelme

Régis Durand

> *Many fathers are blameless in all ways, and these fathers are either sacred relics people are touched with to heal incurable illnesses, or texts to be studied, generation after generation, to determine how this idiosyncrasy may be maximized. Text-fathers are usually bound in blue.*
>
> *The father's voice is an instrument of the most terrible pertinaciousness.*
>
> —*Donald Barthelme,* The Dead Father

ANDRÉ GREEN ONCE OBSERVED that there "seem[ed] to be a sort of *avoidance* on the part of psychoanalysis with regard to contemporary literature."[1] The "psychoanalyst critic," Green goes on to say, finds it easier to work on classic texts because they are "doubly bound," and therefore accessible to an interpretive gesture of a logical kind: "The strict observance of the order of integration of the planes is conducive to the proposed deciphering process; scriptural characteristics point to preconscious representations which, in turn, make it possible, with the help of traces found in the written text, to deduce the unconscious fantasy" (p. 28).

I have tried elsewhere to characterize this process of unveiling and deciphering as essentially *modernistic* and to specify, in opposition to it, Lacan's contribution to a postmodernist version of the dramaturgy of the subject. An essential part of this contribution touches on the question of *aphanisis,* to which I return later.[2]

It is generally agreed that modernism marked if not the disappearance, at least the overthrow or the severe qualification of "the old-fashioned subject." Through irony, multiple points of view, and disjunction, the illusion of a stable all-encompassing subject vanishes. The question that must now be posed (and that many contemporary texts do pose) is whether a literary text can exist on the scattered remnants of the old-fashioned "unary" subject, or on no subject at all.

Jean Baudrillard is the only one, to my knowledge, to consider the implications of such an eventuality. In *Simulacres et Simulations* (1981) he was already heralding the "coming of the age of disappearance," the "apathetic disappearance of the subject." In *Les Stratégies Fatales* (1983), Baudrillard describes the triumph of the object, enigmatic and "fatal"—a triumph that comes about because the object belongs to the order of the accomplished, of that which cannot be escaped, whereas the power of the subject came from "the promise of its accomplishment." In other words, a theory of the subject, in Baudrillard's view, can only be that of a subject whole and powerful. If the subject is to be seen as divided or caught in a process of effacement it might as well be discarded altogether as a useless artifact and make room for the triumphant self-sufficiency of the object:

The subject, the metaphysics of the subject, were beautiful only in its pride, its arbitrariness, its untiring drive to power, its transcendence as the subject of power, of history, or in the dramaturgy of its alienation. Outside of that, it is nothing but a miserable wreck, grappling with its own desire or its own image, unable to command a coherent representation of the universe, and sacrificing itself to no avail on the dead corpse of history in order to try and resuscitate it.[3]

In spite of all his disclaimers, his careful reminders that his "nihilism" is free of all pathos and affects, there is something profoundly romantic in Baudrillard's elegy to the subject: if it cannot be triumphant, let it vanish altogether, and let the object reign supreme in its place. This is not "disappearance purely and simply," far from it. Enough fury is left (even it is the *Furie des Verschwindens* Baudrillard calls up at one point), enough of the mythic energy that is the driving force behind nihilism, to contradict or perhaps simply to *animate* the developments about indifference, simulacra, or the "glaciation" of meaning.

Baudrillard is of particular interest because he dramatizes very vividly some of the contradictions we encounter when we try to reconsider the question of the subject in contemporary texts. Baudrillard radicalizes the widespread experience of a dissolution of the subject in its erstwhile stable form. But when it does not appear in Baudrillard's apocalyptic version, this experience can be traced in two current attitudes—both of which have in common the conflict between the desire to do away with the old-fashioned subject, which has become inadequate to contemporary experience, and the necessity to maintain or reestablish enough of *a* subject for some sort of identification to take place, for some sort of story to be told.

The first of these two positions could be said to displace the question of the subject of/in the text to that of the subject of reading, while the second attempts to put forward a new theory of the subject compatible with the experience of loss and disappearance.

The first may take different forms, but all converge on the attempt to save the idea of a coherent powerful subject. If this subject is no longer to be found in the text (in the characters, the narrator, or even the author), it may still be found in the reader, in the subject of the act of reading. Thus all the various avatars of the so-called "reader-response" criticism posit, explicitly or implicitly, a powerful, coherent subject who redeems the elusive, labile, or dispersed nature of the subject in the text. Similarly, most versions of "deconstructive" criticism imply a very strong fantasy of mastery: that of a subject who projects him/herself as investigator, as decipherer; a redeemer, a "purveyor of truth" indeed. Thus, the dramaturgy of the subject that may seem to be missing in contemporary fiction has, in fact, in many cases been merely displaced. And the success in recent years of reader-response as well as deconstructive criticism (especially in their American versions) can be largely attributed to the new lease on life they confer on the subject—an imaginary gratification of a powerful kind.

In apparent opposition to this, there would seem to be all the discourses on indeterminacy, the "aleatory" nature of meaning and interpretation. But just as the subject of reading was seen to compensate for the effacement of the subject of/ in the text, similarly, the "negative capability" so often appealed to in connection with contemporary writing appears as the devil's share, the part surrendered to darkness so that elsewhere reason and totality can triumph. Thus we read article after article, fiercely academic peans to uncertainty and indeterminacy. What we have here is nothing but the new critical *doxa*, the catchwords and incantations of the day in the service of the same critical imaginary and its fantasy of total intelligibility and total control.[4]

The second position is the only one that has, in my view, attempted to deal with the question of the post-Freudian subject with some degree of plausibility. Instead of merely positing the disappearance of the "old-fashioned subject" (which only leads, as we have seen, to its return in various disguises), Lacan's version of the subject is predicated from the start on its division. The subject, Lacan suggests, is "born divided." It is a passage, a "pulsation"; not an all-powerful imaginary authority but a mere *effect*. Whereas the modernist subject could be described as essentially *epiphanic* (i.e., it always tended, through various crises and ordeals, toward some sort of revelation, of heightened awareness), the Lacanian subject is *aphanisic*. Emergence is always followed by a second beat, a loss, a disappearance. In *The Seminar XI* (*The Four Fundamental Concepts of Psychoanalysis*), Lacan has given several precise descriptions of this process. Here is one example: "The subject appears first in the Other, in so far as the first signifier, the unary signifier, emerges in the field of the Other and represents the subject for another signifier, which other signifier has as its effect the *aphanisis* of the subject. Hence the division of the subject—when the subject appears somewhere as meaning, he is manifested elsewhere as "fading", as "disappearance."[5]

The subject is no longer a stable construct. It is not, in other words, of the order of the sign ("which represents something for someone") but of the signifier ("which represents a subject for another signifier"); it is, before all, a tension between its realization and its disappearance, a "subjectification" more than a stable subject.

There is a sense in which the reader of some contemporary texts finds himself in a position analogous to that of the impermanent subject just sketched out. In the work of reading, says Roland Barthes, "I am not hidden in the text, I am merely unlocatable. My task is to move, to relay systems whose prospects stop neither at the text nor at myself."[6] Lacan's revolutionary view of the subject, then, may help us understand something that eludes thematic, rhetorical, and even psychological analysis. A text exists in and as the pulsation (*battement*) of different systems whose operations constitute, in effect, its real subject. In the article on aphanisis already referred to, I suggested very briefly how Thomas Pynchon's *Gravity's Rainbow* was constructed precisely on the idea of the "in-between," the gap between 0 and 1. Its method is, exactly like the work of reading described by Barthes, "topological."[7]

It might be interesting to turn now for another very brief verification, to a writer whose work does not seem to invite such an approach. With Pynchon, William Gaddis, and a good many other "postmodernist" writers, it is relatively easy to see how the subject has been shifted toward a mechanism, a mode of operation, a dominant metaphor (Metafiction is no more than the recognition of such a shift, perhaps the point at which it slides into formalism). With Donald Barthelme, things are less clear. No single mode of operation can account for the writing, which resists classification and epistemic reduction. For instance, Barthelme, as opposed to many other writers, deals with affects. Not sentiments attached to a particular fictional character, but affects in their pure, "floating" state.[8] Another example would be the use of conventional fictional figures or situations in a manner that is neither parodistic nor merely residual. One such figure, in particular, deserves our attention for the way it is handled by Barthelme: the father.

The figure of the father looms large in Barthelme's writing. Some of its major aspects have been studied in Robert Con Davis's excellent essay,[9] and my intention is merely to point to the manner in which disturbances or transformations in the system of codes can be signalled through the handling of a stock fictional figure. R. C. Davis studies the father principally as a "principle of order," a narrative function that "floats freely, to a considerable extent, without mooring in images of the father, either social or personal, because it is a structural aspect of narrative: it prohibits mere repetition and mere sequentiality, lapses into narcissism, in effect forbidding an untold story, either in the form of silence or in the mechanical repetition that imitates silence" (p. 171). This principle of order is continually promised (it is what all narratives in a sense promise), but its articulation is deferred, sometimes indefinitely, so that Barthelme too would seem to take his place in an inbetween, a tension between surrender to the principle of order (in which case his writing would merge into the vast nebula of conventional narratives) and the perpetual deferment of it (in which case the connections with narrative form would be progressively severed until the writing verged on pure lyric or nonsense).

But considering the father as a principle of order in this manner (even if it is as a "free-floating" principle) is seeing it as a figure of the imaginary, not of the symbolic. Rightly considered (i.e., as a symbolic figure), the father can only exist in the tension described above, between revelation and deferral. Neither complete avoidance of nor direct encounter with (much less complete mastery of!) the father are possible. The question, then, is how this tension can be taken into account in the writing itself; what formal strategies are summoned for its staging and what do they tell us about "the great contemporary neurosis."[10]

"Views of My Father Weeping" shows this tension admirably. The story is composed of two "lines," interwoven in the form of irregularly alternating paragraphs of varying length. One deals with the narrator's inquiry into his father's death, his search for an explanation; the other consists in a series of evocations or "views" of the father in diverse postures. The first strand constitutes the story proper (even though it remains inconclusive). It is in the line of traditional narrative (the "family romance"): in this case it takes the form of an investigation into the father's murder (an archetypal narrative if there is one). Because it is accompanied by very powerful feelings of guilt in the young man, it becomes when he hears the murderer's name, an encounter with the unbearable:

"When I heard this name, which in its sound and appearance is rude, vulgar, not unlike my own name, I was seized with repugnance, thought of dropping the whole business."[11]

And indeed, the matter is in a sense dropped, left unresolved. The desire to know, to see, encounters in true Oedipian fashion the blinding recognition of one's own secret desire. The story ends with the young man drinking with the murderer, listening to *his* narrative, perhaps believing him, *wanting* to believe that it was only an accident.

The second strand is made up of short, disconnected "views." As in dreams, these little scenes alternate and condense affirmation and disavowal: "Yet it is possible that it is not my father who sits there in the center of the bed weeping" (p. 3); "The man in the center of the bed looks very much like my father" (p. 5); "But perhaps it is not my father weeping there, but another father: Tom's father, Phil's father, Pat's father, Pete's father, Paul's father. Apply some sort of test, voiceprint reading" (p. 5); or "I don't know whether it is time to flee or will not be time to flee until later" (p. 5).

Like dreams, the text shows the disregard of the unconscious for contradictions, as well as the work of condensation. The latter is seen for instance in the word *peccadillo* defined by Barthelme as the "result of a meeting on the plains of the west, of the collared peccary and the nine-banded armadillo," (p. 4), but which of course condenses guilt and its simultaneous negation (a peccadillo being a minor fault or offense). Guilt, however, returns powerfully in the recurring scene of the father weeping on his bed. This scene triggers several reactions in the child, mostly a desire to flee the father's wrath, the threatening gush of his virility ("he is spewing like a fire hydrant with its lock knocked off," p. 5). But in opposition to this fear of the castrating "ambition" of the father, there is also the attitude of treating the father like a child. The father is seen writing on the wall with his crayons, playing with a doll's house, and wearing a hat with blue and yellow plastic jonquils; in other words being everything (daughter or son) but the father. For if he can be called up, fantasized as other than the father, then he will not be seen weeping, the guilt associated with his death will not obtain, and it will be possible to write other scenarios.[12] The story, then, follows the Oedipal pattern, up to the Freudian narration of the inquiry into the father's death and the son's guilt, which can be said to combine the original narrative (the myth of Oedipus) *and* its modernist retelling (in the form of Freud's version of it, his metanarrative). Barthelme writes in the space of this ambivalence, between the original and its many duplicates, in the consciousness of his "belatedness." But although the story shows an awareness of its position in the play of narratives (between the original scenario of the secret, and the metascenario of its elucidation) it remains caught in the powerful affects generated by the basic situation.

The Dead Father is an attempt precisely to escape this situation (that there should be a need to escape it is of course inherent in the situation itself, one of its symptoms). *The Dead Father* is no longer a quest (or inquest) narrative. Indeed, it seems as if the narrative code (already severely undermined in "Views of My Fathers Weeping" by the dissociation of the two story lines) had collapsed entirely. What remains is the journey, that of the dead father being dragged by a party of men to his grave. But the emphasis here is not on death (the dead father is *not* dead as well as dead); neither is it on the constitution of a bizarrely decentered narrative point of view that would exploit this peculiar situation (as is the case, for instance, in Faulkner's *As I Lay Dying*). *The Dead Father* proposes, in effect, a post-Freudian version of the question of paternity. It does so not by placing the father in the privileged position of a point of origin or of reference in a story of identities, but rather by constructing him as a kind of artifact, half giant, half mechanical device. By doing so, the text articulates the father in two widely different ways or "times":

the primitive time of the totem, on one hand, and on the other the indefinite present of the "great contemporary neurosis" in which the father appears as the improbable instrument of a collective reconciliation. The dead father is dead and *not* dead, alive and mechanical. He is a totem. Totemism, as we know, is the religion of the sons, a religion that conserves what it destroys.[13] *The Dead Father,* beyond the slow and farcical ritual of dragging the father to his grave across the American landscape, is a replay of the murder of Moses, itself a repetition of the murder of the *Urvater.* But it now concerns a caricature of the charismatic figure, a dummy assembled from the different attributes of paternity.

Already, in "Views of My Father Weeping," this process was beginning to be at work. The narrator's father was dissolving into "anybody's father," *a* father, a fatherliness. Here the father figure becomes radically objectified, especially in a section of the novel called "A Manual for Sons."[14] The instructions there read partly like a compendium from *Totem and Taboo* and partly like a handbook in how to defeat fathers; how, in effect, to exorcise the whole question: "Fatherhood can be, if not conquered, at least 'turned down' in this generation—by the combined efforts of all of us together" (p. 145).

In one respect, then, *The Dead Father* would seem to return to a very archaic image of the father, whose figure remains impacted in every individual (every "son"):

The death of fathers: When a father dies, his fatherhood is returned to the All-Father, who is the sum of all dead fathers taken together. (This is not a definition of the All-Father, only an aspect of his being.) The fatherhood is returned to the All-Father, first because that is where it belongs and second in order that it may be denied to you. Transfers of power of this kind are marked with appropriate ceremonies; top hats are burned. Fatherless now, you must deal with the memory of a father. Often that memory is more potent than the living presence of a father, is an inner voice commanding, haranguing, yes-ing and no-ing—a binary code, yes no yes no yes no yes no, governing your every, your slightest movement, mental or physical. At what point do you become yourself? Never, wholly, you are always partly him. That privileged position in your inner ear is his last "perk" and no father has ever passed it by (p. 144).

But in another respect, the "Manual for Sons" makes for an acceptance of, a compromise with, the unshakeable facts of fatherhood. Instead of the old Oedipal strategies of conflict or parricide, it suggests avoidance, playing down ("turning down") the whole question; something that amounts to a reconciliation with the unacceptable—in Freudian terms, a triumph of repression.[15] The old guilty conscience of tradition up to modernism has now made room for a postmodernist fantasy of reconciliation. The scene for it is that of a culture steeped in innumerable textbooks on how to maximize one's potential, avoid pain, and take care of oneself; thoroughly familiar with the catchwords of psychoanalysis and determined to beat it at its own game.[16] Such is the landscape Barthelme writes in in *The Dead Father*. That he does so ironically should not conceal the importance of the shift taking place, with the many questions it raises in its wake. The old guilt-ridden, paranoid system, in which sons were forever competing with the fathers while they lived and took the burden of their death upon their shoulders, is being replaced by a softer technology of father-sons relations, a situation in which the father is "impacted," safely tucked away in a corner of the memory, while the son remains a son ("A son can never, in the fullest sense, become a father," p. 33). What stories will there be to tell in this fantasy world of compliance and reconciliation, of narcissism and monotony and endless doublings? Barthelme's may be the first of a new generation whose stories owe little to the old subject, the old secrets.

11

Living On/Off the "Reserve"

Performance, Interrogation, and Negativity in the Works of Raymond Carver[1]

Marc Chénetier

> *"What we cannot speak we must pass over in silence."*
> Wittgenstein, Tractatus
>
> *First anonymous hand: "When one has nothing to say, one should stop talking." (Wittgenstein)*
>
> *Second anonymous hand, underneath: "WELL SAID!"*
> *(Seen on the walls of the Sorbonne in May 1968)*

S OMEWHERE BETWEEN Sherwood Anderson and Ring Lardner, if that axis had been prolonged through the refractive experimental wave of the 1960s and 1970s; somewhere between William Carlos Williams and Charles Bukowski, if literary categories had not prohibited the practice of genre solecism; somewhere between Grace Paley, Tillie Olsen, and the last works of Richard Brautigan, if gender politics had not befuddled the eye in search of the common revelations hidden under daily trivia; somewhere between George Bellows, Edward Hopper, and Jasper Johns, should *ut pictura poesis* apply: there writes Rymond Carver. Not that such rough localizations necessarily echo his own set of debts and reverences. A card above his writing desk highlights one of Ezra Pound's admonitions: "Fundamental accuracy of statement is the ONE sole morality of writing."[2] Hemingway, Tolstoy, and John Gardner, for different reasons (conciseness, a taste for the implicit, and personal contacts, respectively), loom large on Carver's mental and artistic horizon. But his existential and aesthetic concerns clearly have much in common with writers preoccupied with picturing the amazement of the quotidian. Whence the near-exclusive attention given to the thematic layout of his work by his few reviewers and critics. After each collection, reviews cautiously appear, sketching one or two of Carver's concerns and tentatively announcing the arrival of a "new realism." Repetition is the order of the reviewing day. Of serious investigation, there is precious little: there are courageous assessments by Thomas Le Clair and Alain Arias-Misson and one long interesting article on *Will You Please Be Quiet, Please?* where David Boxer and Cassandra Phillips foreground and analyze major thematic features.[3]

Overall, "what Carver talks about" has dominated presentations to such an extent that the last thing one is tempted to do is add yet another examination of a writer advertised as a mere witness to the lame joys and devastating limbic sorrows of lower-middle America. But Carver's is a voice that brings to contemporary fiction more than a low-key and unlyrical commentary on protagonists "butchered out of their souls a thousand years" (as Allen Ginsberg puts it in *Howl*), a voice that never endeavors merely to bring forth a picture of the American mind paralyzed by the contradictions of might and want or of soul-handicapped gropings for a minimal sense of self, a voice that owes its richness and worth to the revisiting of rhetorical possibilities rather than to the talented redaction of another installment of Gogol's *Dead Souls.*

Needless to say, Carver's "world," unique and idiosyncratic to the point of having preemptively ruined a whole generation of young epigons, is worth exploring. But its conscientious exploration leads to further and, in critical terms, more fertile interrogations. Should Carver's "world" be so explicitly and "realistically" accurate, other explorers of the way in which "the other half" lives were not missing. But his fiction is not tit-for-tat, sign-for-thing journalistic investigation into the existence of mainstream alienation and marginality of the self. Narratives that begin with a bang and move on to strange muteness, that document hollowness by omission, have a "message" that amply transcends the linear and sequential deciphering of the words appearing on the page.

Raymond the Menace: On Performance and Waking Up Blind

On the most immediate of levels, Carver's stories are studies in embarrassment. The violent economy of his short stories ("Get in. Get out. Don't linger. Go on."[4]) forces the reader *in medias res,* almost kicking him upon the stage. The curtain opens, the suspended heartbeats of cleaved lives abruptly resume as Carver, using imperative and unjustified deictics bludgeons presence upon the reader: "*This* old station wagon with Minnesota plates pulls into a parking space in front of *the* window"[5]; "*That* morning *she* pours Teacher's over *my* belly and licks it off."[6] But past the opening lines the text proceeds to unravel into misdirection, hesitatingly gropes its way into rough-dug channels over whose less than abrupt shoulders it constantly threatens to flow.

The "selves" depicted in his pages have so little sense of attachment, belonging, and identity that the very plurality of the main protagonist in "Fat" forces him to refer to himself in the first person plural (" 'We're ready to order now', he says"[7]). Loose, at large, and often utterly lost, their existence depends, for the duration of each story, on the concentrated exploration of the potential meanings attached to a single incident, whether minor or traumatically unsettling. Thus, for a minute, can a provisional sense of identity be chosen from among the variety of open-ended experiences which constitute their patchy lives. Identity is process and this process is what Carver's stories trigger, from crisis to crisis. There is hardly any sense ever given of the reasons why or ways in which one ever reached the opening of these superficially anecdotal moments; sudden entrances upon the page point to the characters' absence of control over lives consistently rendered through a language of vagueness and pointlessness.

Suspended between mysterious and unclear origins or causes and what I shall describe as preseismic endings, the stories are themselves explorations of mystery and vague sketches of revelation. Carver designates a sentence by Chekhov as the epitome of the effect he strives for: "And suddenly everything became clear to him."[8] But such blossoming knowledge is all but transitive for Carver: "I find these words filled with wonder and possibility. I love their simple clarity, and the hint of revelation that's implied. There is mystery, too: What has been unclear before? Why is it just now becoming clear? What's happened? Most of all—what now? There are consequences as a result of such sudden awakenings. I feel a sharp sense of relief—and anticipation."[9] To use another natural metaphor, Carver's stories follow the ripples made by a stone in water. The reader is too late to catch a glimpse of the stone before it sinks and must be content with the detailed analysis of the ripples it has produced on the surface of the pond. Nor is he ever allowed to witness the agonizing break of the ripples against the shore. Carver's stories, with rare exceptions, are totally comprised in the surface covered and organized by the

rings, excluding both the original point of impact ("Everything has changed since Harry's death," one story begins, but
one never knows either about Harry or his death[10]) and the
final slushy smack against the bank ("He said, 'I just want to
say one more thing'. But then he could not think what it could
possibly be."[11]). Carver's devotion to the circumscribed surface
on which the wider and wider circles of ever fainter and fainter
suggestion are the only evidence of clean brutal shocks may
account for the lack of solidity of all information and the
lability of diegetic arrangements, for the feeling of helpless
drift conveyed by bobbing protagonists. Going from A to B
without delimiting A or B leaves us with pure change, the
space in between, natural change, as in "furious *seasons*," moods
and meteorological alterations, the endless process of reor-
ganization and drive for coherence whereby nature attempts
to equate being and meaning, the suspended seconds between
blinding thunderbolt and crashing thunderclap. Such be-
tween-ness constitutes an important part of Carver's sense of
"reserve."

Let us shift from water to fire for a final set of metaphors;
the author himself suggests it whose most beautiful stories
("Dummy," "So Much Water So Close to Home," and "Distance") use the creeks and streams of *Near Klamath*[12] and mix
them with the *Fires* of creation, influences, and feverish anger
into the *bona fide* "ordeals" of his characters' lives. Tidal waves
and volcanic rumblings, sparks and ominous drops, flares and
drownings scan one important and inconspicuous thematic
dominant of a fictive world both irresistibly awash and timidly
agleam.

One might say that Carver fuses his stories so that they
detonate a few minutes after one has read them. The explosion never takes place between the covers of a collection, even
though two examples may act as the useful exceptions that
confirm the rule. The explicit violence that concludes "Tell
the Women We're Going"[13] is one; it considerably weakens

the story. Another, less explicit, concludes the tiny masterpiece called "Mine" in *Furious Seasons* and "Popular Mechanics" in *What We Talk About:* parents fighting over possession of a baby pull its limbs in different directions. The last lines hint at the possibility of some atrociously revisited judgment of Solomon:

> She would have it, this baby [FS:"whose chubby face gazed up at them from the picture on the table"]. She grabbed for the baby's other arm. She caught the baby around the wrist and leaned back. But he would not let go [FS: "He would not give."]. He felt the baby slipping [FS: going] out of his hands and pulled back very hard. [FS: "and he pulled back hard. He pulled back very hard."]
>
> In this manner, the issue was decided. [FS: "In this manner they decided the issue."][14]

The changes brought about by the revision of the tale point to Carver's masterful handling of ambiguity and suspension. The presence of the picture in the first version allowed metonymy to be a refuge against horror; but what active mode was still necessary in the original last sentence to make aggressivity manifest is replaced, in the more recent version, by a passive "the issue was decided" that takes out of the ending a modicum of the active violence born of the disappearance of the picture.

Such delicate balances are engineered to keep the reader tottering on the brink of certainty, which is much closer to it than the characters themselves ever get. Such is the ironic and distancing power of a voice of which Alain Arias-Misson could quite accurately say that "Carver has not given a voice to his characters; he has given his characters to a voice."[15]

And this is still as dangerously explicit as Carver ever gets. On the whole, his stories end in relative indeterminacy, but only after he has made sure that the reader will take the ultimate step they seem to require. By means of ellipsis and the implicit, they acquire an inescapably preseismic nature. Intimations of the nefarious lurk at all times as an important part of what Iuri Lotman would call the "arch-seme" of the texts. Carver has gone on record as repudiating the word "theme," an understandable stand on the part of a writer operating on the thin edge between meanings nascent and gone, pursuing cruelly indefinite states of "dis-ease," as he calls the evils to which William Kittredge's characters fall prey.[16] He would rather talk of "obsessions," he tells us in the afterword to *Fires*(p. 187), and he describes in similar terms his permanent elusive quest for the meaning of his own productions (p. 188). Stories written as explorations in "process" rather than in "fixed positions" (p. 188) need take us clearly away from established notions of theme. One is constantly reminded of stories by Flannery O'Connor ("A View From the Woods," for example), in which grace has no currency. Incipient change, hints, possible directions, and aborted realizations replace plainly affirmative statements. "Pastoral" ended, before it was reworked as "The Cabin" for *Fires,* with the following sentence: "He stared at the wordless distorted things about him."[17] The creation of stories devoid of a fixed telos invites repeated revision. Carver has identified with the process O'Connor described in her essay "Writing Short Stories." He does not know any more than she did how his stories will end as he begins writing them. Shortened, prolonged, altered, simplified, or made more analytical each revision, Carver's texts are not rewritten for improvement so much as because they programmatically demand to be. When prolonged, their original texture is of necessity altered to redistribute inklings towards a modified telos dictated by the rereading of a *primus lector inter lectores pares.* "The Bath," an extraordinarily threatening story in *What We Talk About* thus becomes the longer and mellower "A Small Good Thing" of *Cathedral,* signalling in this latest volume a movement away from threatening ambiguity, a working towards hope rather than horror, and the abandonment of features Carver may have come to consider akin to the narrative "gimmicks" he has always denounced.

The "reserve" in his texts thus seems to have shifted ground, and with that shift has come another in the arch-seme itself, if not in the referential contents of the tales. The accent used to fall on the apparently unaccentuated part of the canvas, over the spots where the ground was bare, devoid of color, the place where fears and desires could be projected as hinges. Now, however, a certain affirmative explicitness—however damning—has invaded *Cathedral;* from the title story to the new version of "A Small Good Thing," in the form of the rather dark pigments covering the ground. In places, then, where the arch-seme used to consist of the very set of mutely deductive unifying suggestions underlying the disconnected fragments of the text, a certain chromatism of the brush may now be attempting to connect them through harmonic—and more harmonious—echoes. A spark of hope in "Fever" and in "Cathedral" tends to give a potentially new agenda to stories whose ultimate promise seems to remain that blindness unavoidably undercuts all awakenings. Commenting on Carver's characters, a reviewer wrote that the "only way for them to validate themselves is through the performance of some act— any act—that gives them the illusion of free will."[18] One could also suggest that if such blind gropings are intransitive they aim at modifying the orientation of a field of forces felt to be adverse, forces materialized by objects, appearances, conversations, attitudes, and behaviors that seem to demand that one be constantly on one's guard, uncommitted, and more or less passively receptive to their message of anguish. What is, threatens, and what is not, threatens even more. Moving away from present visible menaces one is just as much at risk to fall into hidden pits and suggested abysses. Gesticulations on the surface may be gestures for survival, but they tend to be just as effective as mindless thrashing over ice floes or quicksands. A strictly phatic use of language may signal presence with insistence but it hardly gives it any dynamism or sense of direction. Thus performing may spell disaster too and the "quietistic" form of the short story, in which Osip Mandelstam saw the canonical form of lower class alienation and which he opposed to the "Napoleonic" mastery of the novel, is particularly adapted to the need for cover of Carver's characters.

A sense of menace is the arch-seme that not only goes into or comes out of Carver's stories but also activates them and invites their constant reexploration and rewriting. Whatever "thematic" dressing that foundation is given matters far less than the problematic that provides the energy for discursive exploration. "I think a little menace is fine to have in a story. For one thing, it's good for the circulation. There has to be tension, a sense that something is imminent, that certain things are in relentless motion, or else, more often, there simply won't be a story. What creates tension in a piece of fiction is partly the way the concrete words are linked together to make up the visible action of the story. But it's also the things that are left out, that are implied, the landscape just under the smooth (but sometimes broken and unsettled) surface of things."[19] Discussing Carver's stories one cannot *know* "what we talk about when we talk about them" without considering the rhetorical model governing the manner in which, time after time, Carver performs them. The way they are *about* anything is what must now concern us.

Indeterminacy and Questioning: The WH Factor

The promotional material on the jacket of *Cathedral* not unexpectedly emphasizes the pervasive atmosphere of stories that ominously mine the motherlode of threat. It uses for that effect terms with which no one could disagree, but contains, one objective that may lead astray the reader on the lookout for the underpinnings of Carver's art: "uninflected." I would like to argue here that the portion of the canvas left uncovered by the pigments of his prose contains nonetheless a complex weave of inflections, an underlying fabric whose warp and woof confer on the texts their direction and pattern while providing the power, and drawing the limits, of their meaning. These stories whose conclusions are inflected rather than inflicted upon us suggest that rhetorical considerations may be better suited to our analysis than thematic queries concerned with whatever is shown.

The interesting feature of Carver's writings is that they do not point to or at events, actions, and states of being to make plain their significance through a positivistic gesture of monstration so much as they define spheres from within and without, reveal limits and porous partitions between what is and what might be, explore the osmotic layer of contact between hypothetic realizations and tangential absences. Carver likes to define fiction as the bringing of the news from one world into another. But this process of communication is rather one that relies on suggestion, through ellipsis and indeterminacy, than one that endeavors to fill us in on what lies in the other world through a process of translation, be it metaphorical or grounded in referential illusion.

Indeterminacy

In "On Writing," Carver says: "The words can be so precise they may even sound flat, but they can still carry" (p. 18). Out of flatness, hollowness, and the systematized emptying of referentiality from lexicon and structure alike, he comes close indeed to a definition of literature by Umberto Eco in *L'Opera Aperta* that marks one step toward the question of negativity: "The determinate denotation of an indeterminate object."

Carver's strategic goal is to designate what is left out of a landscape of people and objects qualified by Thomas LeClair as "Hopper-plain."[20] The tactical operations lexically bear on the use of indefinites (the recurrence of "it," "what," "something," and "thing" is paramount here); a permanent recycling of words from one sentence to the next that generates semantic abrasion and anaphorically carries the reader away from the original and already moderately contextualized occurence; the use of objects as unexplained and disquieting symptoms (a word printed in hand on a banknote, the bridle in the story of that title, or the set of false teeth sitting on top of the T.V. set in "Feathers").

Syntactically, parataxis feeds the elliptic and so does the uniformization of tense in narratives that weave memories, present situations, and speculations on becoming. The possibilities for bifurcation abound, lodged under the elliptic hinges between passages that seem to eliminate the idea of progression by their use of circular and repetitious dialogue; most passages must rely on the drastic reorientation of attention generated by alineas and permanent "reprises" to wrench themselves away from the burrowing effect of voices apparently unable to get away from under their own weight by logical subordination or anything resembling reasoning. Events and gestures, however minor and unmotivated, dominate the articulative possibilities of the characters to such an extent that their frequent randomness, taking over all responsibility for the concatenation of paragraphs, points systematically to the collagelike quality of an apprehension of the real unable to rely on the analytic and organizing powers of consciousness. Indeterminacy thus complements the sense of a lack of control and direction; reified paragraphs assume the dramatic consecution of minds jerked or brutalized from one moment into the next, haphazardly pushed into realization by novel dispositions of the familiar.

The overall structure of the stories promotes the impression founded on this local analysis. In generalizing the use of what Roman Ingarden might call "spots of indeterminacy" and of what Wolfgang Iser might call "blanks" into the self-defeating "progressions" of narratives devised to get as close as possible to Cynthia Ozick's "foreknowledge of nakedness" (but no closer), Carver has extensive recourse to diegetic itineraries that fold back upon themselves, to analeptic recollection, circularity, and phatic redundancy. One might say that these are stories without an elsewhere, stories that extend no opportunity to transcend experience. Discourses biting their own tail parallel the self-enclosed circularity of lives that can merely recycle their problems into pretenses of temporary solution. Most of the characters' lives, unable to debouch outside of a past that has merely cornered them, are told by drilling out of the pregnant event motivating the story all that could pass for worthy relevance. In "Careful," a conversation that would account for the original situation does *not* take place and is metaphorically relayed by a plugged up ear. "Vitamins" is the story of an affair that does *not* take place, the energy-providing goods that the protagonist's wife peddles being ironically denied by flattened lives. "The Compartment" presents a crucial trip the ultimate justification for which vanishes along the way and makes room for a nonjourney strewn with nonincidents. Such slackening of the narrative spring, one that slowly unwinds without ever snapping into action, may be considered to render mimetically existential itineraries. But formal analysis reveals the paradoxical accomplishment of an author who has simultaneously "fused" his stories in the ways described above and has made his structures exercises in defusing the usual sources of narrative energy.

The dialogue, for example, demonstrates an increase of tension by hollowing out the conative with the absurdly extreme ingrowth of phatic conversation: "She said, 'I think I'll go upstairs and put on my robe. I think I'll change into something else. Robert, you make yourself comfortable,' she said. 'I'm comfortable,' the blind man said. 'I want you to feel comfortable in this house,' she said. 'I am comfortable,' the blind man said."[21] "Feathers," "Preservation," and "Where I'm Calling From," to cull three examples at random from *Cathedral*, dramatize the sort of time-stuffing achieved by oral language so desperate to have nothing to hitch on to that it is compelled to maintain an endless recycled babble, a recourse as hollow and as minimally life-preserving as inflatable jackets.

The analytic exploitation of an opening situation (that of "Sacks" or "Distance," for instance, the latter convincingly re-titled "Everything Stuck to Him" in the passage from *Fires* and *Furious Seasons* to *What We Talk About*) is such that all endings are only minimally ahead of the first lines of each story. The tiniest overlap extends into the semblance of a knot a narrative thread that mostly feeds on past occurences. "The Lie" covers all the space of its slim three pages with a sym-metrical and reversed movement of denial that redoubles the central theme and refuses progression. From "It's a lie"[22] to "Lying is just a sport for some people (p. 125)," through the admission, exactly halfway through, that the lie wasn't a lie and that the denial of that truth was a lie in itself, the female character demonstrates in a perfectly circular manner the emptiness of a text which is "about" nothing but its own struc-ture. We know nothing of the alleged original lie, the accu-sation is not part of the text, and the main effect consists in the general unsettling of an ill-defined situation, in the throw-ing off balance of a "normality" that is at no time detailed. "I want the truth" (p. 31), the male protagonist says, two para-graphs before the end, and this is exactly what the overall structure of the text makes sure the reader cannot attain, having merely been prodded into an assessment of exasper-atingly unconfirmable probabilities. In all typographical jus-tice, Carver's stories should open and close with question marks, suspended as they are between untold causes and problematic developments.

Carver provides the ironical impression that all answers lie ahead while making sure we understand, as his characters should, that their most important elements lie somewhere before the pretexts he uses as events. The innumerable un-answered questions of his stories do not so much embody an interrogation of the future as they reveal the mysteries of an implicit past. In instances where dialogue only promotes and deepens misunderstanding, one is reminded of "Prufrock": the paralytic investigation of inane possibilities masquerades as a search for causes, a search that culminates on the admission of broken communication: "That isn't it! That is not what I meant at all!"[23]

The systematic emptying of the narrative moment through a variety of tactical suggestions of indeterminacy makes us mistake wonderment about what got the characters there for a sense of impending threat. We are not afraid of what may lurk ahead so much as we are afraid of our growing consciousness that present disasters and stases cannot be mended through the efforts of the lame disabled consciousness that allowed them to happen in the first place. Carver's sense of menace is not necessarily born of the vast and vacant spaces lying beyond the final period of each story, even though that area may be where the reader initially projects his or her own misgivings. Much rather, Carver is most threatening when one can say of a character, whose minimal articulateness we know will not allow him to disentangle himself from that impenetrable brush, what a poet could say, twenty years ago of "speculative hipsters": "He had got, finally,/ to the forest/ of motives."[24]

Questioning

Such reaching for mute causes and moot consequences prepares us for an examination of negativity in Carver's work, that which Iser defines as the "non-formulation of the not-yet comprehended."[25] Negativity, then, is the unformulated double, the background or reverse side suggested by omission, concealment, and cancellation. But before we examine negativity, we must turn to another set of linguistic elements constituting what we might tentatively describe as the most visible and practical windows opened by the text onto its necessary obverse, or else as the combination of beckoning signs and black holes that forcefully draw us into or through the fabric in quest of what it simultaneously covers, denies, implies, rejects, and suggests. Which is where, of course, "reserve" takes on an altogether new meaning: what we might call the "WH factor" does not only consist of Carver's strategic indeterminacy but also of his insistent use of interrogations, interrogative structures, and indefinite centers one can only define and fill with queries. *What, why, when,* and *which* scan writings that are always, in one manner or another, interrogations and wonderments. There is, of course, the astonishing number of titles with questions: "Where Is Everyone?", "Why Don't You Dance?", "Will You Please Be Quiet, Please?", "Are You A Doctor?", "What's in Alaska?", "What Do You Do in San Francisco?", "Why Honey?", "How About This?", and "What Is It?". Such stories, mostly included in *Will You Please Be Quiet, Please?*, systematically pit the implicit and the subterraneous against explicit narratives aiming at some kind of resolution. Going unanswered, such questions linger in the mind during and after the reading of the texts, inciting one to look among the blanks and negations for answers feeding on transcended literal meaning, activating another multifarious set of questions where none is explicitly made to appear, and compelling to recycle mere suggestions and possibilities into new keys successively placed at the opening of the score. In which case, of course, less becomes more as willful expansion of what is merely hinted at becomes the necessary requisite for implementing the temptation of all transitive readings.

But such "questions" can also do without their final characteristic typographical mark. As a matter of fact, the passage from *Will You Please* to *What We Talk About* seems marked by a transition from recognizable questions to implicit ones. "What we talk about," being constantly defined by the very vagueness of such a lack of definition,[26] is a recurrent notion that operates "en creux," the vague geometrical locus determined by the various points where thrusts at definition come to expire.

A sense of internal puzzlement replaces the typographical marker where it does not appear; one could describe the internal shift in economy from *Will You Please* to *What We Talk About* as one regulated by an injection of ellipsis and irresolutions into texts stripped of their avowedly interrogative program. Sparer, more trimmed and elusive, more elliptic, sketchier (a sizeable number of them are reworked from the contents of *Furious Seasons,* and always in a reductive manner) the stories contained in *What We Talk About* have lost the questions of their titles and compensated them by a larger proportion of blanks within them or in their ending. For example, "Why Don't You Dance?", the only questionlike title in *What We Talk About,* ends in a significant way that leaves the question operational while shutting the story down: "She kept talking. She told everyone. There was more to it, and she was trying to get it talked out. After a time, she quit trying" (p. 10). Conversely, the story entitled "Mr. Coffee and Mr. Fixit" in *What We Talk About* has a question for its title in *Fires*; there, in its much longer version as "Where Is Everyone?", it makes plain a number of details that remain quite puzzling in the shortened text. Simultaneously, in *What We Talk About* parataxis is pushed to limits it never quite reached in *Fires*. The barest skeleton necessary for suggestion remains and a number of incidents that can be read as explanation in "Where Is Everyone?" are left as mere questions or unclear allusions in "Mr. Coffee and Mr. Fixit". The thermos jug filled with vodka, the death of the father, the side affair with Beverly, and all the details that made for "understanding" or "answering" a story in the interrogative mode have been toned down and have lodged the interrogations dismissed from the title at the heart of the text itself.

The ratio of question-titles to internal explicitness appears rather constant and seems to confirm Roland Barthes's definition: "A question is never anything but its own scattered answer, dispersed in fragments among which meaning erupts and escapes at the same time."[27] Judging by the ends of the stories, the tendency seems to be that the more clearly formulated the question is, the less diffuse and uncertain the answer becomes;[28] the most plainly "affirmative" title will be the one that retains the greatest level of explicit indeterminacy.[29] To borrow categories from Barthes's *S/Z*, even though both the proairetic and the hermeneutic codes can be traced in all stories, they are all too often superposed and alternately but nonexplicitly activated. The interrogative mode, foregrounded or clandestine, in turn activates one or the other at the expense of the one left dormant. Where the hermeneutic code is foregrounded by interrogative sentences, the proairetic assumes a more stabilized form. Let the proairetic dominate and the entire text—from lexicon to overall structure via syntactic choices—is activated as a tantalizing hermeneutic device. But in neither case is resolution clearly brought about. Diversely implanted in the mind of the reader, all manners of questions remain while Carver interrupts rather than ends his narratives. All hollow spots must be invested by the reading mind in sympathy or solidarity with the protagonists' inability to choose and decide. Very much like Samuel Beckett, in a text that derives its title from systematic use of the "WH Factor" (*What Where*), Carver always whispers: "Make sense who may. I switch off."[30]

Negativity

Eerily echoing Carver's definition of fiction,[31] Wolfgang Iser writes: "Fiction may be defined as a form of communication since it brings into the world something which is not already there." And he adds: "That which literature brings into the world can only reveal itself as negativity."[32] It is within this context of negativity that Carver's fictions may perhaps be assessed in the most satisfactory manner. In effect, Carver's voice does not feel justified to damn or judge the various fictitious situations it depicts. Irony, always a bearer of blasting torches and sardonic piques, is not suited to the purposes of a writer who merely wants to make plain a consciousness of the abyss without pushing his characters into it as sacrificial and vaguely redemptive victims. His art is therefore one that wants to make manifest whatever, precisely, cannot be pointed at; whatever ails his protagonists may have causes they are unable to discover and consequences that we cannot fathom more than they. By activating in the midst of a rather meagre diegetic landscape a suggestive structure pointing, so to speak, to having-beens or might-bes, Carver makes plain the essential negative thrust of his endeavors. This process, to particularize a more general view of Iser,

> does not consist in giving a determinate solution to the determinate problems posed, but in the transformation of events into the discovery of the virtual cause. Meaning thus emerges as the reverse side of what the text has depicted. The world of the text appears in a state of alienation, and this alienation effect indicates that meaning is potentially there, awaiting redemption from its potentiality. In consequence of this, the unwritten text is constituted by a dialectic mutation of the written . . . Meaning coincides with the emergence of the reverse side of the represented world . . . We see the twofold structure of negativity—as the cause of the deformation it is also the potential remedy, and is thus the structural basis for communication. (P. 228–29)

Carver exploits negativity rather than irony to invalidate the reality his texts manifest. By pointing consistently to that which "has not yet been comprehended"—and another suggestion of his stories is that the characters themselves, not being quite equipped for the task, are pushed all the deeper into the process of alienation—Carver favors contact between the struggling nature of the object of representation and the decoding attitudes of the reader at the reception end of the line. The mediating effects of the interrogative structure, of the elements of indeterminacy, and of the undecidable prolongation of the diegetic end transform his narratives into far less and far more than what most reviewers and critics have been tempted to pigeonhole as "realism" or "minimalism."

Even thematically, lessons have to be drawn from Carver's refusal to designate his characters' fate as failure or incompletion. His work goes squarely against the grain of a tradition that considers literature as a generally cathartic or resolutive gesture, a tradition that culminates with the modernist hypostatization of Art as redeeming construct. Adorno, militating against the expulsion of negativity from art, which he read as a form of quietism, argued in favor of an art, such as Raymond Carver's, that refused to defuse the contradictions and quandaries out of which it was born, against a pre-Lacanian, vulgar-Freudian vision of expression as outlet, overflow, respite, or evacuation: "The conformist acceptance by psychoanalysis of the popular view of art as beneficent to culture corresponds to aesthetic hedonism, which banishes all negativity from art, confining it to the conflicts that gave rise to the work and suppressing it from the end-product. If an acquired sublimation and integration are made into the be-all and end-all of the work of art, it loses that power through which it transcends the life which, by its very existence, it has renounced."[33] Irresolute endings, texts strewn with puzzling gaps, and opening situations progressively destabilized toward a sense of loss and disorientation thus add an aesthetic, moral, and ideological impact to a set of systematic formal disruptions. Nestled at the center of a paragraph that thrives on vagueness and the indefinite, a sentence in "Fever" may well be Carver's ultimate aesthetic statement of the question: "She also sent Carlyle long, rambling letters, in which she asked for his understanding in this matter—*this matter* [Carver's italics]—but told him that she was happy. Happy. *As if, Carlyle thought, happiness was all there was to life* [my italics]. She told him that if he really loved her, as he said he did, and as she really believed—she loved him too, don't forget—then he would understand and accept things as they were."[34]

Such refusal to let the text solve the issues that gave it birth can perhaps be best exemplified, both technically and hermeneutically, by two privileged tropic gestures in the works: halving and the status of metaphor.

Life on Division Street

Reading Carver, one cannot but be struck by abundant occurences of what I will call here "halving." Interestingly enough, Boxer and Phillips's article on "dissociation" exploits a number of images and dramatic situations pointing to "a sense of disengagement from one's own identity and life, a state of standing apart from whatever defines the self, or of being unselfed."[35] It also notices that most of the existential states of what I would personally refuse to call "selves" are states of "suspended animation," being *between* semesters, stories, marriages, jobs, alcoholic bouts, sleeping, and waking. But such disconnection from the familiar flow of a "normal" existence cannot only be traced to practical matters of life organization. Thematically exploiting the fact, underlined by Iser, that "if the basic reference of the text is to the penumbra of excluded possibilities, one might say that the borderlines of existing systems are the starting point for the literary text,"[36] Carver makes a point of having his characters choose, as refuge, places of the body and mind that stand halfway between possibilities, places through which the flow of information "from one world to another" will be channeled in a privileged manner, birds of omen flying through high passes. The impossibility of exhausting or even of getting at tantalizing meanings tends to place all characters in a position of extended reaching, makes them teeter on verges and cuts driven through their experience. They beckon to the other lying on the opposite slope with a vaguely hopeful gesture of completion, to "the other life," as the title of a poem puts it, where "my wife is in the other half of this mobile home."[37] The "Poem for Karl Wallenda, Aerialist Supreme" depicts him "midway between hotel and hotel,"[38] a reminder of the couple provisionally caught on the landing between two doors in "Neighbors."[39] Similarly, all moments are taken as dividing time into an unsolvable past and an improbable future. The abundance of connecting devices such as "next morning" or "afterwards" as paragraph openers makes plain the perpetual division operated in time and space by lives in quest of what escaped. Subrevelatory moments will occur over a double gate ("I Could See the Smallest Things") or during the meetings of parallel couples, meetings that formally evidence the precariousness of balances as much as they dramatically trigger debilitating comparisons and promote an extensive recourse to the vicarious ("Neighbors," of course, but also "They're Not Your Husband" or "What's in Alaska?" in *Will You Please* and "Feathers," "The Train," "Fever," or "Cathedral" in *Cathedral*). As the narrator of "What Do You Do in San Francisco?" puts it: "The situation was close enough to get me thinking." (p. 109) Things half-told go along with stories halved by revision, stories where halving is either the dramatic outcome ("Mine" in *Furious Fires,* and "Nobody Said Anything," where a trout has replaced the fated baby), the dramatic source of tension (the half-realized affair of "Are You a Doctor?"), or a part of the circumambient decor (the half-light of "Sixty Acres" drowning incomplete actions and realizations, the half-glances exchanged in all the stories); there are stories in which mirrors and the vicarious are tentatively used as doomed processes of completion. Desire and contradiction are the paralyzing forces that prevent these characters from getting away from vague pains and half-realized torments. The following passage features a rare density of binary structures that spells out the character's indecision before it is made plain in the conclusive sentence: "My wife *brought me up here the first time.* That's when we were still *together,* trying to make things work out. *She brought me here* and she stayed around for *an hour or two,* talking to Frank Martin in private. *Then* she left. *The next morning* Frank Martin got me aside and said 'We can help you. If you want help and want to listen to what we say.' But I didn't know *if they could help me or not.* Part of me wanted help. But there was another part."[40]

Divided within or severed from a counterpart ("Whatever they did from now on, each would do it without the other," (p. 184), uncertain of or cut off from their reasons and motives, questions without answers, most characters emphasize the other half of the bed, the next room, next-door life, previous days, tomorrows, and coming opportunities as well as favor half-truths while failing to articulate anything *in toto.* The vaguely ominous nature of objects is born out of their belonging and not belonging, of their potential for otherness, and their power of defamiliarization. Reversals, parallels, contradictions, and paradoxes (from "Dummy" fished out of his own fish pond to "The Lie" via "What We Talk About When We Talk About Love" and "The Fling") perpetually suggest that surfaces tend to have two sides and that the one we see is not the one that matters; they encourage us to turn all things over to look at their underbelly and install negativity at the heart of the written. All indefinites accrue to negative definition, and one is always closer to the stilled "endurance" of Faulknerian fame than to more traditional triumphant resolutions. Blind and silent, the fish of this poem is content with such provoked balance of forces as its minimal, repetitious, and non-affirmative stemming gesture can afford: "There's one that comes—/ heavy, scarred, silent like the rest, / that simply holds against the current, // closing its dark mouth against / the current, closing and opening / as it holds the current."[41] Equally blind and silenced by impoverished languages fed them by the media that fascinates them and shapes their reactions, Carver's characters are such fish, blind, scarred, half-way up or down river, face down in the water, contemplating a bottom obscured by the pale emission of their own paltry roe, reserving judgment, and moving laterally towards the edges.

Against Metaphor

It can be argued that the metaphorical process can be considered either as ally or enemy of negativity. Inasmuch as it makes manifest the unstoppable dissemination of meaning in the doomed movement of seizure of what must always remain radically other, the metaphorical can indeed be seen as a downstream representation of the unformulated that structures the text upstream and thereby appears as an inverted effect of negativity. Since it "would be impossible for language to formulate both the deformation of human situations and the remedy in one and the same instant", [therefore] "language can never explicitly state the meaning: it can only make itself felt by way of the apparent deformations and distortions which the formulated text reveals."[42] The metaphorical can be taken as such deformation and resorted to for effects that remain programmatically negative.

However, such distortion can also be apprehended from the point of view of its powers of translation, as the inscription into the text of what must remain more indefinite for negative purposes, the embodiment of that which must not be defined, the necessary hostage of the symbolic. Carver's refusal of metaphor strengthens a strategy that makes use of open-endedness not as a perpetual possibility for redefinition but as the programmatically limnal quality of the utterance, what A. R. Ammons calls "boundaried vacancies."[43] With Carver, the metaphorical perpetually rests on this side of its realization. His reliance on "thing," "it," "what," and "whatever it was" betrays a desire not to bridge the space that separates negativity from articulate meaning. Given the context of the stories and their thematic drive, metaphor would appear as translation against the logics of a text feeding on grounds where no obvious meaning is supposed to grow, as the defining instrument of the negative spring. Jumping, so to speak, over negativity into the known and the controlled would necessarily signify that meaning has been reestablished by short-circuiting the devices that kept it strategically at bay. Looking at a disturbing moon, the woman narrating "I Could See The Smallest Things" dismisses the necessity of such a jump: "A big moon was laid over the mountains that went around the city. It was a white moon and covered with scars. *Any damn fool could imagine a face there.*"[44] Not that overall situations cannot, in Carver's stories, be constructed metaphorically. Indeed, when the protagonist of "The Compartment" loses in turn his watch, the belongings in his suitcase, and his destination,[45] one gets a clear sense of allegorical treatment that flirts with the metaphorical. Similarly, the overall ominous signified of "ugliness" hovers over "Feathers," a story that pits horrid baby and false teeth against the archetypal peacock[46] to point out potential and realized existential bifurcations. But the texts themselves retain a flatness and an indeterminacy, an untranslated quality of experience that at the most allows for illustrative similes but will not resort to metaphorical mutation. The quest for meaning appears legal when undertaken laterally, "on the side," but appears unacceptable, because denaturing, when conducted "from above". Meaning can be plucked from neighboring things, in the margins, by comparison, in the same plane, as happens with lives vicariously lived or characters in search of missing halves. Complements are allowed in, but all obvious supplements are ruled out. Language retains throughout Carver's collections such deliberate flatness of tone that any word slightly out of the ordinary bounds or kelter sounds odd and vaguely metaphorical in itself (for example, "regarded" for "looked at," in several instances, and "assessment" in "Careful"). The heavy rhetorical inflections of the texts condemn the metaphorical index to remain at an hy-

pothetical zero degree above which it is seldom allowed to
rise. Even plain demonstrative signifiers are relegated by characters to the reserve wherefrom it is not always necessary to
retrieve them: "We both knew it was a peacock, sure, but we
didn't say the word out loud. We just watched it" (p. 7). By
the same token, the prodigious recreation of the shapes of
cathedrals in "Cathedral," when a seeing man lets a blind
man's hand ride his own over the contours of a drawing, seems
to indicate that the "always-already" metaphorical nature of
language can be dispensed with and make way for the greater
powers of performative communication. Passing on to his
characters' handling of their narratives a lesson taught students by one of the rare artists in his stories, a lesson he may
have taught himself, Carver could I suppose account for the
quality of their speech by making of its impoverishment the
reason of their inability to transcend their fate. But he could
also, making of paltry necessity an interesting set of virtues,
make it that of his own refusal to make things easy on us:
"You've got to work with your mistakes until they look
intended."[47]

To my mind, the features of Carver's writing examined in
this essay throw into question his present reputation as a "real-
ist." Even though he has clearly reintroduced a modicum of
social depiction in his stories, it seems clear that his strategic
choices favor the work as construct over an obsolete mimetic
conception of the use of literary language. A text that feeds
on reader's reaction and filling in, that operates by substrac-
tion of explicitness and clearly outlined conclusions, cannot
be said to rely on traditional categories of representation.
What mimetic dimensions the texts retain have to do with a
somewhat imitative exploration of the radical "béance" or gap
that yawns at the heart of experience, in the presentation,
rather than the representation, of a world of fractures, a world
whose chief activity is a linguistically deprived attempt at mak-

ing minimal sense. Thus, if Carver can be said to be a "minimalist"—a term he resents—the adequacy of the term must be attributed to a quality of experience more than to a representational mode. The dominant rhetorical inflections of his texts make sure that, as Adorno put it, "everything . . . as regards form and material, spirit and matter, has emigrated from reality into the works, and in them has been deprived of its reality."[48] Denouncing the easy and abusive association of many literary products with *bona fide* mimesis, Iser rightly refuses

the assumption that such texts are simply copies of a depraved world.
  If the deformations are signs of a hidden cause, [he adds,] and if this cause has to be rooted out by the reader's conscious mind, then, clearly, the *function* of the text (and hence the function of its negativity) far transcends that of simply copying reality. Negativity brings about the deformations which are the basic question posed by the text—a question that sets the text in the context of reality. Actualization of the virtual cause then opens up the possibility of finding the answer (which is potentially present in the formulated problems of the text). Negativity, then, embraces both the question and the answer, and is the condition that enables the reader to construct the meaning of the text on a question-and-answer basis.[49]

Furthermore, as if to demonstrate that no writer could come out of the 1960s and 1970s unaffected by two decades of innovative experimentalism, Carver—however keen his ear and eye and whatever his imitative talents—does not only write in defiance of traditional concepts of realism in literature. He also stands neatly within the boundaries of a literary world that gradually sets itself free from the honored premises of modernism. His practical recognition of the irresolutive nature of the text removes him from a tradition expectant of meaning equated with the resolution of the opening tensions. Seemingly removed from the most vanguard experiments of our time, important aspects of Carver's prose could nonethe-

less be described by this assessment of Samuel Beckett's revolt
against classical and psychological aesthetics:

> With Beckett . . . we become aware that meaning as a relief from
> tension embodies an expectation of art which is historical in nature
> and consequently loses its claim to be normative. The density of
> negations not only lays bare the historicity of our concept of meaning
> but also reveals the defensive nature of such a traditional expecta-
> tion—we obviously anticipate a meaning that will remove the illog-
> icalities, conflicts and indeed, the whole contingency of the world in
> the literary work. To experience meaning as a defence, or as having
> a defensive structure, is, of course, also a meaning, which, however,
> the reader can only become conscious of when the traditional concept
> of meaning is invoked as a background, in order for it to be
> discredited.[50]

Another contemporary helps us give a measure of Carver's
achievement. Speaking of the things that he left out, A. R.
Ammons invites us to hear "the hum of omissions," "the chant
of vacancies, din of/ silences," claims that he is "aware / of
them, as you must be," as the reader of Raymond Carver's
stories must be

or you will miss

the non-song

in my singing: it is not that words *cannot* say
what is missing: it is only that what is missing
     cannot
  be missed if
spoken: read the parables of my unmaking . . .[51]

12

David Mamet, a Virtuoso of Invective

Guido Almansi

THE RECENT PRODUCTIONS of the latest play by David Mamet, *Glengarry Glen Ross,* first at the National Theatre in London in 1983, then in March 1984 on Broadway, have forced the experts to reconsider the development of American theatre in the last ten years. Few critics had foreseen that Mamet would explode so soon on the stage with such a masterpiece.

Glengarry Glen Ross, which thrilled me both in London and in New York, has compelled me to reread all Mamet plays available in print, from *Lakeboat* (1970; but only published in 1981[1]) to *Edmund* (performed in 1982). A comprehensive reading of his work reveals a strong line of plays in which characters are exclusively men who display all the male prejudices about women, those "soft things with a hole in the middle," according to Stan's definition in *Lakeboat.* Mamet is the poet and critic, chronicler and parodist, of the stag party and of all social occasions and situations precluding women. His best plays are immune from any female contamination; the existence of women only filters on the stage through the preconceived ideas of the opposite sex. These comedies grow in a male-chauvinist conservatory in which only the worst prejudices blossom. *Lakeboat,* a juvenile work though under-rated by the critics, is a remarkable specimen of the all-male play. It is set on the *T. Harrison,* a cargo boat whose route takes it round the main harbors of Lake Michigan. The cast represents the members of the crew, mainly of the lower ranks in the hierarchy of freshwater sailors. *American Buffalo,*[2] which among Mamet's plays has had so far the greatest success with the press and the box office, takes place in a junk shop where the three male characters, somewhere between small trade and petty criminality, meet, argue, and fight. The latest play, *Glengarry Glen Ross,*[3] deals with a group of real estate salesmen in an agency on the outskirts of a large metropolis. These are Mamet's best plays "according to me"; but this expression means little, as Teach reminds us in *American Buffalo*: "According to me, yes. I am the person it is usually according *to* when I am speaking." But even in the other plays the best scenes are the exchanges between males, for instance the dia-logues of Bernie and Danny in *Sexual Perversity in Chicago*[4] (as with Witold Gombrowicz's *Pornography,* the text fortunately does not keep the title's promises), which are more lively than the scenes in which Deborah and Joan appear. I am thinking also of a few brief exchanges in *Duck Variations,*[5] snatches of mindless conversation between two old-age pensioners about the life and philosophy of ducks. The only exception—in my opinion, of course—is *A Life in the Theatre.*[6] Although it has only two male characters (a middle-aged actor and a young one), it does not seem to be very successful at reading level; it might have a certain impact on the stage, but I have never seen it performed.

Much less interesting, to my taste, are the plays with both male and female characters: for example *Edmund,* which de-scribes a young man fleeing the safety of his family and his job in search of sex and adventure in the low life of a great city; or the allegorical tale *The Water Engine,*[7] concerned with the inventor of a contraption that runs on distilled water in the years of the American Depression (the play is set at the time of the *Century of Progress Exposition* in Chicago in 1934), who is brutally crushed and eliminated by the forces of big business; or *Reunion,*[8] about the meeting of an ex-alcoholic and his daughter after twenty years of separation. Not that Mamet is unable to portray female characters: the girl in *Reunion* is not badly drawn, with her ambivalent feelings towards her father and her husband. But the playwright's ear is especially attuned to the sounds, rhythms, cadences, allusions, contradictions, vulgarities, dirty and stupid anecdotes, interjections, and exclamations that fill the conversation between two pals, working and drinking mates, colleagues, or rivals. The subject of their complaints is often a woman, or that more forward, buxom, and aggressive woman, America, who has bestowed upon them a dream, the Great American Dream, only to prove a prick-teaser, or that other woman, more mammary, plump, and vigorous yet, Mother Nature, a female God, rancorous and vindicative, who fucks up every single thing and every single man (Teach in *American Buffalo* about a bacon sandwich: "Aaaahh, they always fuck it up . . . This time they fucked it up too burnt"). Mamet does not necessarily belong to the ghetto of the male-chauvinist lingo; but this lingo, says the writer, you have to love it in order to use it (and if you love it the spectators end up by loving it too). Moreover, beside loving it, "you have to need it."[9] And through this love and need for a degraded language, this craving to use it, Mamet expresses the *cahier de doléances* of the fucked-up male against Mother Nature and her deputies in this world, the "soft things with a hole in the middle."

Mamet's best plays are necessarily comic: they denounce life's tragedy through the false liberation of the audience's laughter rather than the false participation of the audience's tears. Therefore, when a character speaks, his words have an ulterior meaning. Besides the meaning of the words, the act of speech itself *signifies*. A comic character can never be the writer's mouthpiece. He says "Au voleur, au voleur, à l'assassin, au meurtrier," as Harpagon in *L'Avare*, but an ulterior voice insinuates itself between the lines and silently comments on the absurdity of the miser's complaint. A character says "soft things with a hole in the middle," but someone somewhere thinks that it is a rather eccentric definition of women. Yet with the most alert modern playwrights, say from Harold Pinter onwards, this voice is kept as muted as possible. It was Shaw's generation who boosted the authorial voice; Pirandello, for instance, was such a clumsy manipulator of irony that he always had to give his power-of-attorney to one character—the horrid Laudisi, for instance, in *Cosi é, se vi pare*—who ponderously lashes the other characters and their blunders. The new playwrights, on the other hand, do not seem to care if the innocence (the purity) of their judgements is corrupted by the prejudices and emotional outbursts of their creatures. This gives a special ambiguity to the authorial voice, be it Pinter's, Stoppard's, or Mamet's. The verbal explosions of the characters come through with exceptional vigor, as if the "au voleur, au voleur" were not an "au voleur, au voleur" conditioned by the ulterior irony of the author, but an "au voleur, au voleur" absolute, unalterable, and unqualifiable. If in a musical a comic character says that women are "soft things with a hole in the middle," the whole context condemns this partial view of femininity and mocks the limitations of the speaker's sexual experiences. Yet in the ideal production of *Lakeboat* I have staged in my mind, Stan's phrase has an apodictic value. For the duration of the play women *are* "soft things with a hole in the middle." We must not only love and need this language: we must pretend that it conveys the truth, in a suspension of disbelief that defiles the audience to the level of the protagonists (and the process might not be very different when we watch *Ubu Roi* or *Macbeth,* for that matter).

Of course, society as represented and described by this sectorial language and its absurdist connotations is tragic; it is an empty world from which all traces of transcendence have been erased (whereas a craving for something beyond, albeit variously camouflaged, appears in the *other* plays by Mamet: *The Water Engine, Reunion,* and *Dark Pony*[10]). This is an entropic world, as postmodernist critics are wont to say, which crumbles down as the remnants of traditional values are washed away, existential possibilities are crushed, and social institutions overthrown. There is a waste of all possible values. Family, friendship, society, career, and love are words that have barely managed to survive, but in the process they have changed meaning. They are not yet empty words but are in the process of being emptied.

In order to have a plot, in life or on the stage, one must possess (and cherish) a sense of finality; the plot proceeds towards its completion, comic or tragic, positive or negative, of re-birth or re-death. But, as Christopher Bigsby notes in an upcoming essay,[11] Mamet's plays have no plot because their characters' existences are plotless. They live aimlessly, not so much because they are social failures (as in the plays of Tennessee Williams or Edward Albee) but because the very concept of aim has disappeared."

This is the great failure of the American dream, which was a dream of communication as much as of success. If communication between the various components of the nation is as efficient as the telephone company, everything is possible. Society becomes a huge network in which the shoeshine boy can communicate with the American president. In *The Water Engine* and in *Mr. Happiness,*[12] broadcasting is not "an electronic convenience, but an expression of our need to create and to communicate and to explain."[13] Hence the importance of the postal system in modern American literature, from *The Crying of Lot 49* by Thomas Pynchon to *The Water Engine* by

David Mamet, with its continuous references to a chain letter. To the clandestine circuits of this system of unofficial communication the future is entrusted, when the inventor sends the blueprints of his water engine to the name on top of the chain letter. This is the dream; but all methods of communication, official or alternative, fail. Mamet's characters pretend to speak, to communicate, and to relate with other people, in a world where everyone is isolated. The wires have been cut. As in *Tropic of Capricorn*, the delivery boys do not deliver telegrams any longer. The words family, friendship, love, and liberty, as we mentioned before, are being emptied and survive only as a parody of their former selves, for instance in the splendid speech about a citizen's rights in *American Buffalo*— a grotesque reversal of the American constitution. Don's cracker-barrel philosophy and Teach's barroom wisdom are topsy-turvy versions of native American virtues: independence, enterprise, tenacity, exacerbated individualism. Larceny = business, therefore it becomes a kind of commercial and economic institution based on the right of the individual to look after himself and mind his own business. As Teach says in *American Buffalo*: "The Freedom . . . of the *Individual* . . . To Embark on Any Fucking Course that he sees fit . . . In order to secure his honest chance to make a profit." But his "honest chance" includes burglary with a gun in his pocket, in case the owner of the burglarized house should turn out to be "some crazed lunatic who sees you as an invasion of his personal domain. Guys go nuts." Therefore, with such guys on the loose, it is better to be cautious and armed. And a revolver "makes me comfortable," says Teach. The American dream is still hovering in the wings, tantalizing the imagination of the characters, yet definitely out of reach. Perhaps it is just a quesion of a small chance: "All I want is a chance," says Levene in *Glengarry Glen Ross,* taking up a recurring plea of American fiction. The situation in Europe is different. Who has ever heard a European peasant, in life or in literature, in

Calabria or in Verga, in Auvergne or in Giono, in Yorkshire or in Thomas Hardy, who says "All I want is a chance"? The New York unemployed in *Tropic of Capricorn* knock at the door of the Cosmodemonic Telegraph Company of North America, asking the manager for a job, begging "for a chance, Christ almighty, just another chance."[14] But there is no chance left because there is no justice, neither in this world nor on yonder, nor in the alternative universe of our illusions. "There is NO LAW . . . there is no *history* . . . there is just *now,*" shouts the protagonist in *Edmund.* And Teach, thinking of his "whole cocksucking life," repeats the same litany: "The Whole Entire World. There Is No Law. There Is No Right Or Wrong. The World Is Lies. There Is No Friendship." "Every Fucking Thing," he concludes without comment, because "Every Fucking Thing" is terminal: it is the final, absolute argument. This is why Teach ends up trashing the junk shop with "a strange object," a dead-pig sticker, "a thing that they stick in dead pigs to keep their legs apart until all the blood runs out": a useful symbol for contemporary violence. When faced with such sentimental desolation, the paranoia of the individual is no longer a mental aberration but a sign of existential awareness. It is not Salvador Dali's *méthode paranoico-critique,* rather a *méthode paranoico-acritique,* leaving to others the responsibility of a critical attitude. "Someone's against me, that's their problem," says Teach in *American Buffalo.* Underneath the apparent nonsense, the joke goes far: consider it for a minute, and it will send shivers down your spine.

Of course Teach is paranoid: people he "works" or plays cards with are always cheating him; people he just knows are always mocking him; people he doesn't know, "guys like that, I like to fuck their wives" (I still remember the way in which Robert Duvall delivered this frightening line), or "The only way to teach these people is to kill them." Yet Mamet conveys the impression that Teach's paranoia is not the exception but the norm. Is it the only solution in this present life? The

Rolling Stones, champions of the frenzy and the despair of the last generation but one, used to sing: "Time / is on my side, / yes it is." But few realized the ironic potential of this statement. Mamet's characters also opt for the presentness of the present, as against the temptation of nostalgia: "What do you think it is, the Middle Ages?" Teach asks Don in *American Buffalo*. And Bernie to Danny in *Sexual Perversity in Chicago:* "These are modern times. What do you think it is, *the past?*" But Mamet's modern modern times are more disturbing than Charlie Chaplin's ancient modern times, so gently automatized after all. Nowadays we do not know any more what is happening in a world where people say: "There are numbers of such magnitude that multiplying them by two makes no difference at all" (Aaronow in *Glengarry Glen Ross*). Our degree of incomprehension and alienation is much higher.

I do not know whether it is possible to love Mamet's characters; but one ends up by cherishing their way of talking, gesticulating, swearing, and lying. Mamet is compelling in his description of a culturally deprived—even pauperized—milieu, be it the brutal crew of a lakeboat, an incompetent gang of petty thieves, or a ruthless team of con salesmen. He takes the vulgar, ruthless, discordant, and obscene sounds produced by this riff-raff and makes music out of them according to the canons of an aesthetics of ugliness. In this sort of dialogue the musicality of the phonetic rhythm counts at least as much as the plausibility and consequentiality of the narrative sense. "If it's not poetic on the stage, forget it," claims Mamet. "If it's solely serving the interest of the plot, I'm not interested." A critic insists on this point: "Plot is subordinated not so much to character as to the harmonics and dissonances of language."[15] These declarations of aestheticism ought however to be qualified. Mamet's complex orchestration of the brutal sounds of plebeian life reaches its apex in turpiloquy: and it is on that dangerous ground, dirty words, that narrative rhythm, psychological consistency and musicality ought to be checked and controlled. Theatrically, Mamet's plays may not convince everyone, but it would be difficult to deny his prominence as poet of swearwords, artist of invectives, and virtuoso of obscene expressions. He is the prince of contemporary blasphemers, and his predecessor, a few years back, was Louis Ferdinand Céline; the mastership of literary outrageousness runs through a noble lineage. "Fuckin' Ruthie, fuckin' Ruthie, fuckin' Ruthie, fuckin' Ruthie, fuckin' Ruthie," states Teach when entering the stage in the first act of *American Buffalo*. And when Don asks, "What?" Teach stresses his point: "Fuckin' *Ruthie.*" Later, Ruthie becomes that "Southern bulldyke asshole ingrate of a vicious nowhere cunt." The sequence of obscenities, which has its own internal music, is also in tune with Teach's character, as it is spat out with magniloquent fury, though emerging from the inarticulate sounds of bubbling rage.

Glengarry Glen Ross, written to my opinion in the best American idiom to be found on the contemporary scene, has one of the highest percentage of obscenities and swearwords on the market. But it is difficult to successfully use expressions like "fucking," "asshole," "shit," and "cocksucker," and give the impression that these words are *necessary,* perhaps even more difficult than speaking of "the honor of the family," "the pride of one's class," "the intensity of passion." Mamet manages to convey the inevitability of such language, both stylistically and strategically. The salesmen in *Glengarry Glen Ross* who tear each other to pieces cannot do without these swearwords and obscenities. The sublimation (or should we say *humilization,* since we are dealing with a *sermo humilis* and not with a *sermo sublimis?*) of their anxiety occurs through a catharsis of the obscene. The characters in this play need swearwords as badly as they need the food they eat, the air they breathe. Turpiloquy is not used to titillate the taste of a low-brow audience (it might do that as well, but we are not concerned with this), but to save the character from despair. I swear therefore I am

("turpiloquor ergo sum"). The musicality of the swearing se-
quences, the orchestration of insults, and the vast gamut of
perverse expressions are no mere virtuosism. There is as much
drama in a "fuck you" in *Glengarry Glen Ross* as in the emotional speculations of *Death of a Salesman*. Roma, one of the
con men, to his boss, Williamson: "You know your business I
know mine. Your business is being an asshole." Levene, back
at the office with a signed contract forced upon a gullible
man: "I closed 'em! I *closed* the cocksucker." Moss, jealous of
Levene's selling exploit: "You did that?" Levene: "Yeah." Moss:
"Fuck you." Fuck and shit are holy words in this language,
and with them the characters escape, through the gateway of
the obscene, from the pettiness of their social and psychological contract. Because this is the point: fuck and shit are better
words than the unuttered ones that would describe the pure,
uncontaminated reality of their life and trade. Anything, even
the lowest obscenity, is preferable to an objective representation. Mamet's text is musical because the subject lends itself
to symphonic treatment, and his subject is linguistic redemption through swearwords and obscenities.

In this degraded world, as everywhere else, sex is a problem
(even the ducks, in *Duck Variations,* have sexual difficulties).
Sex appears mostly parcelled up, subdivided in its various
bodily components, hence the reduction of women to "soft
things with a hole in the middle." Bernie, talking about his
sexual preferences in *Sexual Perversity in Chicago:* "Not that
I'm a tit man . . . I mean, I *dig* tits . . . but I wouldn't go out
of my way for a pair of tits . . . The way I see it, *tits* . . . are
what you make out of 'em . . . But an *ass* . . . is an *ass*." The
final tautology transforms the mental stuttering of this randy
idiot in a verbal triumph. In Mamet's plays sex is a metaphor
for violence and vice versa. Able-bodied Seaman Fred recalls
his first sexual experience: after the movies they are dryhumping in the living room when "all of a sudden the whole
thing becomes clear to me. I mean in a flash all this horseshit

about the Universe becomes clear to me, and I perceive meaning in life: I WANT TO FUCK. I want to stick it inside her. Screw dryhumping. I want to get it wet." And the way to get laid is "TO TREAT THEM LIKE SHIT." So next time, when they are alone, "I hit her in the mouth. I don't mean slap . . . I mean hit, I fucking pasted her . . . Not a word did I speak, but off with her dress, panties . . . Smacko, spread the old chops and I humped the shit out of her." After a fanciful reconstruction of her ecstatic bliss, he goes to the door and says: "Not another word, you cunt." If the reader does not like this scene, does he think that sailors speak and think less brutishly?

But filth is not the apanage of a concentrational, all-male, society, like a lakeboat. The situation does not substantially alter when Mamet moves to the freer sexual circulation of a large metropolis. Sex is at most a technicality: who is good, who is not so good at it, like football or billiards. In *Sexual Perversity in Chicago* Danny and Deborah separate after having lived together for a while, and they both recriminate about each other's competence. Danny: "Your friend, *Joan,* is a better fuck than you are . . . and she's a lousy fuck. Aren't you going to tell me I'm a lousy fuck?" Deborah: "You *are* a lousy fuck." Danny: "You're fulla shit." On the whole, there is not much to be gotten out of sex. It is much better at the race track, where everything is "clean." "The track is clean. It's like life without all the complicating people. At the track there are no two ways. There is win, place, show, and out-of-the-money. You decide, you're set. I mean, how clean can you get? Your bet is down and it's DOWN . . . It's poetry. It's a computer" (from *Lakeboat*). Even drinking is clean; to drink becomes a way of life, like zen. "I could tick off my life in beercaps," says Stan, while Mamet winks over his shoulder to the audience with the reference to T. S. Eliot. Stan's father could drink: "Drink it by the fifth. He never lacked for booze, that man. That's one thing I can say for him." As to himself, Stan, well,

he is a man, whereas the cunts, "what do they know of booze
... They don't understand it. It's a man thing, drinking. A
curse and an elevation. Makes you an angel. A booze-ridden
angel. Drinking? I know my alcohol, boyo. I know it and you
know I know it. And I know it." Almost a handbook of the
perfect alcoholist, perfect, because uncontaminated by other
interests.

Even culture—in this case the culture of violent films—
assumes an unexpected purity in this macho world. The best
scene in *Lakeboat* is the discussion between two sailors of the
respective strength of two Kung-fu heroes. "He's no fucking
good," says Fred, defending his champion with sarcasm. "That's
why he didn't take five fucking guys in that barroom using
only one pool cue." And he insists: "All I know is like you say
any guy who fucks all night and drinks a shitload of cham-
pagne and can go out at five the next morning and rob a bank
without a hitch has to be no fucking good." These epic deeds
only happened on the screen, but the demarcation between
fiction and reality has been obliterated. Mamet usually manages to avoid a condescending tone in his quick raids upon a
degraded culture; he seems to admire and invites us to share
his admiration for the purity and simplicity of these mental
schemes.

In *American Buffalo* the petty thieves were above all incompetent, even as petty thieves. Brendan Gill, in a review published in the *New Yorker,* complained about it: these characters,
"of low intelligence and alley-cat morals . . . appear to know
no more about their squalid means of survival . . . than we in
the audience have long since learned from reading the papers
and watching T.V." But this is perhaps precisely the point.
Mamet does not exalt a degraded life in the manner, say, of
Genet or William Burroughs. He is neither the moralist scourge
nor the mystic advocate of low life. He just tries to understand
its internal logic, so alien to our criteria of value and judgment.
At times, he manages to catch some instances of beauty in

squalor. Teach, in *American Buffalo,* is not only a louse: he is a louse who does not even know his job as a louse. His greatness lies in his magnificent incompetence. If I were to find a literary antecedent, I would recur once again to that mine of inspiration for contemporary literature, Henry Miller's fiction. Bob Ramsay in *Black Spring* might be taken as a parallel to Teach, though the latter displays a sort of useless activism, the former of useful inactivity:

I remember that everybody liked Bob Ramsay—he was the black sheep of the family. They liked him because he was a good for nothing and he made no bones about it. Sundays or Wednesdays made no difference to him: you could see him coming down the street under the drooping awnings with his coat over his arm and the sweat rolling down his face; his legs wobbly, with that long, steady roll of a sailor coming ashore after a long cruise; the tobacco juice dribbling from his lips, together with warm, silent curses and some loud and foul ones too. The utter indolence, the insouciance of the man, the obscenities, the sacrilege. Not a man of God, like his father. No, a man who inspired love! His frailties were human frailties and he wore them jauntily, tauntingly, flauntingly, like banderillas. He would come down the warm open street with the gas mains bursting and the air full of sun and shit and oaths and maybe his fly would be open and his suspenders undone, or maybe his vest bright with vomit.[16]

Bob Ramsey is not like Teach, but they are both studies in squalor. And how difficult it is to study humanity at that level.

Glengarry Glen Ross is a different case altogether: the sharks of the estate agency are skillful operators. We see one of them, Ricky Roma, as he is robbing a customer. This latest play still describes the empty, sordid world of Mamet's former works, but it explores a new dimension in it—the poetics, as well as the rhetoric, of salesmanship. This area of contemporary life has been hitherto almost unexplored by literature.[17] Fiction, the theatre, and the cinema have had little to say about the millions of people who devote their lives to this activity. Not long ago I saw the Broadway production of *Death of a Salesman* with Dustin Hoffman in the main role. Although Miller's play has aged remarkably well, it seems rather irrelevant and inadequate to the problem of salesmanship, as if it were mainly a question of locomotion—aching feet after carting heavy suitcases of samples and tired eyes from driving too long. These are mere side-effects. As to the qualities of a salesman, Miller mentions only sympathy, i.e., the passive capacity to ingratiate oneself to a customer. There is nothing about the active requirements to the profession: persuasion, aggressiveness, tenacity, imagination, eloquence, and shamelessness.

In our society a salesman does not usually perform a public service, for all the assertions of Madison Avenue. His job is much closer to plunder; there is money lying waste in the pockets of potential customers, and he insures that this flow of cash will be channeled in the proper direction. The salesman is a new version of the highway robber, who uses a biro instead of a gun. For millions and millions of salesmen, the act of selling, of forcing a customer to sign a contract, is the culminating moment of their life. The world exists in order that the salesman can sell a Hoover, and this sale is the dominating thought. From dawn to dusk, from St. Stephen's to Christmas, from the beginning of their career to retirement age, this is their main preoccupation: how to sell a Hoover. I am not speaking of monomaniac freaks, but of our next door neighbor, whose secret obsession with Hoovers normally escapes us.

In the nineteenth century, on the crest of enthusiasm for industrial revolution and commercial expansion, writers were not so coy. But nowadays we seem somewhat ashamed of the enormous diffusion of induced, or even forced, selling. We would rather forget how important the purchase or the sale of a Hoover has become. So we choose to obliterate the Hoover salesman from our minds, though we give his activity ample space in newspapers, on the box, in mail advertisements, on posters, in the shops, everywhere. *Glengarry Glen Ross* therefore stands out as an exception, because it forces us to examine the macroscopic phenomenon of salesmanship: the total involvement of the salesman, his intense emotional interest, the aggressivity and pugnaciousness—sometimes even the virtuosity—he displays in a sale.

Reviewers have been struck by the evil and the despair emanating from the characters: hungry birds of prey fighting over their scarce victims. The salesmen are trying to sell some plots of worthless land in Florida to gullible citizens; they are waiting for *leads,* addresses of potential customers who have been stupid enough to write to the agency for information.

The top salesman will get a Cadillac, the runner-up a set of carving knives; the others are out. It is the law of the jungle, but this is a time of famine: there are not enough *leads,* and the birds of prey are getting hungry. This is the basic story, and the most authoritative critics have seen the play as an exploration of the lowest level of national business, on the border of illegality, and even petty crime. But before being criminals—or, even worse, diabolical *Confidence-Men*—the characters are just plain salesmen. They are a bunch of paranoids—ruthless, immoral, aggressive and rapacious—whose language is totally false except when they swear or insult each other. This seems to me a model of normalcy. They are not very different from our neighbor who dreams all night of selling or not selling Hoovers to pliant or rebellious customers and starts on his round in the morning determined to sell Hoovers to anyone, whether it is needed or not. *Glengarry Glen Ross* is the norm, not the exception; and the emphasis put on the low life aspect is just there to establish dramatic tension. This is different from *American Buffalo:* it is America *tout court.*

As all other salesmen in the world, the con men of *Glengarry Glen Ross* have vested their whole emotional capital in their work. At times, the displays of love, hate, envy, emotion, hostility, and rage may seem disproportionate compared to their limited aim. But it is not the case: trying to sell bits of Florida to Chicagoans who are unlikely ever to set foot there does actually require all the resources of the salesman's imagination, emotion, and intelligence. You cannot be a *good* salesman unless you are obsessed by selling; you cannot be a *great* salesman (they exist. Wasn't Humbert Humbert's uncle "a great traveller in perfumes"?) unless you are untouched by any moral scruple. The customer must appear as an enemy to be annihilated: a "cocksucker," in fact, who must be forced to kneel and humiliated into signing the contract.

In the magnificent scene in which Levene tells Ricky Roma about his exploit, the sale of eight units for eighty-two thousand dollars, the tension arises from the opposition of the roles of the predator and the predated. On the one side is Levene, the armed robber, fountain pen in hand, ruthless, obsessive, and persistent, waiting for the moment of truth. On the other side the two victims, twitching in the last spasms of their defeat. Levene is silent, because everything has already been said. He is awaiting the last move that will seal his triumph as a salesman:

"Now I want you to sign."
I sat there. Five minutes. Then, I sat there, Ricky, *twenty-two minutes* by the kitchen *clock*. Not a *word*, not a *motion*. What am I thinking? My arm is getting tired? No. I *did* it. I *did* it. Like in the *old* days. Like I was taught . . . Like, like I *used* to do . . . I did it. [And the culminating moment finally arrives:] I looked on them. All on them, nothing on me. All my thoughts are on them. I'm holding, the last thought that I spoke: "Now is the time." . . . They signed, Ricky. It was *great*. It was fucking great. It was like they wilted all at once. No *gesture* . . . nothing. Like together. They, swear to God, they both kind of *imperceptibly slumped*. And he reaches out and signs, he passes it to her, she signs. It was so fucking solemn.

What a great erotic scene. Nothing is lost of the intensity of life experience as it goes through the filters of writing or staging. This is the intensity of coition: Levene has buggered his customers. If the audience refuses to get carried away by *Glengarry Glen Ross,* it is not because of the brutality of the text, but because it is too faithful a mirror to our consumer's society.

To sell is important and difficult, and *Glengarry Glen Ross* proves that it is not only an all-absorbing, harassing activity, but also an occasion for virtuosity, which we can admire apart from moral considerations. Doctor Dulcamara is a common figure in our society: the streets of the nation are full of people who could sell windsurfs to Eskimos and snowploughs to Bedouins. How do they do it? In *Glengarry Glen Ross* we are given a glimpse of this high virtuosity in the scene with Roma and Lingk in a Chinese restaurant. The salesman guides the conversation—but so gently, so smoothly, so nonchalantly—from philosophical considerations on the nature of life to the qualities of a piece of land in Florida. One might condemn the cynicism of the operation, but one is compelled to admire its sheer virtuosity. Only one artist could move with such ease from one theme to the next: Arthur Rubinstein.

13

Sam Shepard
Word and Image
Christopher Bigsby

S AM SHEPARD EXEMPLIFIES two major developments
in the American theatre of the 1960s and 1970s. He is a
product both of Off-Off Broadway theater and of the growth
of regional theater. His career began in October 1964 at Theatre Genesis, a new theatre created by Ralph Cook in St.
Mark's Church in-the-Bowerie in New York City; it developed
in later years through his association with the Magic Theatre
in San Francisco. He showed little interest in Broadway, and
Broadway responded by showing little interest in him.

Sam Shepard was born in November 1943 in Fort Sheridan,
Illinois, the son of an army officer. For the first twelve years
of his life he moved from one army base to another, ending
up in Guam. On his father's retirement, the family moved to
California, eventually settling on an avocado ranch in Duarte,
and it is his California experience that is such a marked feature
of his work. It was also in California that he first became
involved in acting, joining the Bishop's Repertory Company,
a religious group that performed in churches and church

halls. He left home at the age of nineteen and moved to New York, where he became a busboy at the Village Gate. The head waiter was Ralph Cook and Shepard's plays formed the first double bill at Cook's new theatre. Thanks largely to a favorable review in the *Village Voice,* Shepard was encouraged to continue; his plays appeared at the Cherry Lane Theatre and at La Mama as well as Caffe Cino.

Despite his success, however, he received little or no money and had to continue working as a waiter. But his work seemed to dominate Off-Off Broadway, being performed at the Judson Poet's Theatre and the American Place Theatre, as well as at Off-Broadway's Martinique Theatre. An Obie Award in 1966 provided him with increased visibility, and his plays began to be produced outside of New York, at the Firehouse Theatre in Minneapolis and at the Mark Taper Forum in Los Angeles. He also began writing for the cinema and was associated with Antonioni's *Zabriskie Point.* Fellowships and grants now released him from his financial problems and in the early 1970s he spent some time in England, interested in particular in the music scene. But his works remained rooted in American concerns, with the myths, the images, and the values that led him to say of the 1970s that, "you could hear the sound of America cracking open and crashing into the sea."[1]

His is a drama that seems to respond to a sense of paranoia, an anxiety that expresses itself in fragmentary images or in a language dense with ambiguity. In a culture for which style becomes simultaneously both a necessary act of concealment and a revealing truth, he creates plays in which style becomes a primary language and a key to private and public meaning. In some of his early works the logic was disturbed by drugs and, in the case of *La Turista,* illness; the result of an allusiveness that remained a distinguishing characteristic in later works that, as far as I know, benefitted from neither. Shepard's plays share something with the "fractured world" that he observes and that he sees as constituting reality for those who assemble their sense of the real from the detritus of the media or the disassembled fragments of experience. His plays tend to deal with people who understand little of the forces that operate on them. His characters find one another mysterious and alarming; they appear to need the very relationships that torment them. Nothing is quite what it appears, not merely because deceit and concealment seem a necessary part of experience but because the reality of relationships escapes them. They seem trapped in plots that they do not themselves generate. In *True West,* where the two principal characters do seem to produce their own texts, insofar as they write or simply invent movie scenarios, they end up in effect dissolving into those texts, characters in a drama no more plausible than the one they take themselves to be inventing. Their mother, meanwhile, seems to be little more than a stereotype lifted from some other text or from the world of popular myth. Indeed, Shepard's work relies on intertextuality, on a complex series of fictional and mythic cross references that pull his work in the direction of a fictive universe of signs rather than a world dense with social observation.

In *Fool for Love* the very constituent parts of the past are problematic. Alternative texts compete. Versions of the real coexist with no privilege granted to any one of them. What does appear to be granted is some authority to feeling, though this is inconstant, characterized by fluctuating pressure, pulses of attraction and repulsion that suggest an uncertain sense of the real or at the very least a real that shifts disturbingly at the level of language, image, and relationship. Forces do seem to exist—usually perverted, distorted, and distended—but they seem to originate less in a self projecting its own environment or a range of possibilities than in biologic or metaphysical coercion. Like Pinter's early plays, Shepard's works are frequently comedies of menace, with the paranoia located less in the individual than in the culture. If we see through a glass it is not so much darkly as distortedly. The threat comes from the shape of emotions or social possibilities that are seldom engaged directly. We recognize the presence of determining pressures not by confronting them directly but by observing their effects.

There is a kind of romantic fatalism in his work that is akin to that to be found in the plays of Tennessee Williams. A form of doom is implied by mismatched sensibilities, by hints of apocalypse (embodied in images of destruction—the crashing plane in *Icarus's Mother,* the domestic mayhem of *True West,* or the flickering flames that close *Fool for Love*), and by the sense of a closed system suggested by plots that turn back on themselves or exhaust themselves, as though energy were being leached away from the very structure of the play as from the characters themselves. But where Williams' characters can often reach down into themselves, tap into some reservoir of lyricism that can sustain them if never quite overcome the power and the prosaic literalness of the world, Shepard's figures have no such resources. They are stranded. Outside is a desert—sometimes literal and sometimes symbolic—but it mirrors their own aridity. What they observe is a fragmentation of thought, emotion, and social context but they lack any means to gain a purchase on it. All they are offered is myths generated by the media, myths that, unlike those rooted more securely in the sensibility, are, finally, evidence of that fragmentation rather than gestures of resistance. And the sense if not the knowledge of that fact leaves a residue of anxiety and alarm. Something seems to be buried behind the blankly menacing face of social alienation—a child of that anxiety and alarm, a nameless horror which may indeed have been conceived by those who feared their own capacity to project a human future as devoid of manifest feeling as the human past, the aborted evidence for an apocalypse engendered by, rather than visited upon, them. On the other hand, the evidence of disintegration may itself imply some more radical disjunction, some final threat of dissolution beyond the powers and capacities of Shepard's characters to resist. As he says in an introductory note to *The Unseen Hand,* for those who are caught up in the "fractured world . . . What's happening to them is unfathomable but they have a suspicion. Something unseen is working on them. Using them. They have no power and all the time they believe they're controlling the situation."[2] The irony implied by this is unavailable to the characters. They are, thus, victims, unable even to identify the nature of the threat that, nonetheless, they feel.

Shepard's first play was, in his own words, an ersatz Tennessee Williams drama in which a young girl is raped in a barn (a later play, such as *Buried Child,* is not entirely free of William's influence, both in its gothic touches and in that concern with the nature of the real that came to concern Williams in a play such as *Outcry*). It was followed by a number of works in which the spontaneity of vision was taken to have an authority and authenticity of its own. It was an assumption that was not without its naiveté. On the other hand, they are disturbing precisely by virtue of their arbitrariness. And yet for all his insistence on this arbitrariness there is a consistency in these images. The consistency lies in a sense of loss, of threat, of anxiety, and of tension. The source of that disturbance is not immediately apparent but it exists as a pressure in his work, a force that threatens to deform language, character, and imagery. There is no substantiality to characters who seem little more than gestures, even, at times, caricatures, invested with a force and vividness that is borrowed from their mythic status or from their performative energy or from the sheer fascination of style. So, the cowboy, the pop singer, and the clichéd figure assume a role that lifts them above their origins. Their very emptiness implies the reification that his work explores. Something is missing that could sustain the density of experience and personality. The threat is both from within and without. There is an air of the temporary about his characters.

Like him, they tend to derive from a world without roots, a world without a history and, more menacingly, without a future. And that sense of a timeless moment predominates. As Shepard has explained, his images "come from all kinds of things, they come from the country, they come from that particular sort of temporary society that you find in Southern California, where nothing is permanent, where everything could be knocked down and it wouldn't be missed, and the feel of impermanence which comes from that—that you don't belong to any particular culture."[3] And that is the special horror of Shepard's plays. If there is a shared past it is problematic, while ahead there seems to lie the possibility of apocalypse. The only coherence seems to lie in images that work on and emerge from the subconscious. And those are dominated by the possibility of annihilation. Thus, in *Icarus's Mother*, whose very title implies the possibility of catastrophe, a fragmentary plot is held together only at the level of image as a jet plane apparently crashes to earth while a group of people in a park prepare a barbecue and fireworks apparently soar into the sky. Consonance is a product only of the imagistic rhyme constituted by fire. Thus, the plane may or may not have written $E = MC^2$ across the sky; it may or may not have crashed. But whatever the various individuals see is linked by associational logic. In all their minds the sound of the aircraft is related to fire, and fire in turn implies the possibility of extinction. In a sense it is a play that shares something with Edward Albee's plays, *Box* and *Quotations from Chairman Mao Tse-Tung*, in which apocalypse is simultaneously both a present possibility and an established fact. In *Icarus's Mother* we are told, "the whole sky is lit. The sirens come and the screaming starts . . . and the tide breaks open and the waves go up . . . The water goes up to fifteen hundred feet and smashes the trees, and the firemen come. The beach sinks below the surface. The seagulls drown in flocks of ten thousand. . . And the pilot bobbing in the very centre of a ring of fire that's closing in . . . His hand reaching for his other hand and the fire moves in and covers him up and the line of two hundred bow their heads and moon together with the light in their faces."[4] The pattern is not elaborated by the individual characters; it coheres in the minds of an audience responsive to images all too securely rooted in the contemporary psyche.

Nor is the anxiety necessarily a response to nuclear catastrophe, though plainly that is a dominant motif; it owes something, too, to Shepard's sense of a society, fragmenting and fragmented, destroying itself as effectively from within as without. Like many of his other plays, it is a work in which mood and tone are a primary concern. His plays are simply not susceptible of analysis in conventional terms. The response they demand is not primarily a rational one. The harmonics owe nothing to psychology nor even primarily to social satire; they assume a level of shared apprehension as ironically the only source of communality. In his plays, lovers, brothers, parents, or friends are at odds, not least because they have no sense of sharing anything more than their fears or the storehouse of values and ideals paraded for public consumption by the media. Past and present are problematic; the only certainty lies in feelings, which are denied even as they are articulated. And, indeed, that is a primary problem for his characters; they are denied access to their own inner lives, enacting experiences whose meaning is denied to them. Events seem unrelated, and experiences carry no weight of knowledge, being compounded of no coherence that can offer more than temporary consonance. Instead, their lives are compacted of disparate events forced together only by the fact of sequentiality.

John Hawkes, in 1964, spoke of plot and character as the enemies of the novel. In other words, he reacted against a model of the novel that implicitly accepted a particular version of experience and a particular paradigm of identity, not to mention the manner in which experience is organized and identity expressed. Reacting against an emphasis on setting and theme, he chose to stress instead structure, verbal and psychological coherence. Much the same would seem to be true of Sam Shepard, with the exception that Shepard seems to reject even the notion of psychological coherence. Indeed, that kind of stability becomes in a sense a danger, a threat. For his characters are potentially the victims of a particular kind of plot, a plot which ultimately threatens their existence. In *Fool for Love* they do battle over the authority of the very fictions that they parade with such assurance (as elsewhere his characters deploy style as weapons, engage one another with images or with a language attenuated and deformed by social pressure). Each tries to incorporate the others into his or her own fiction. They each offer a plot into which the other characters are invited to accommodate their lives. The only constancy comes from the moments of passion, moments seldom sustained but none-the-less authentic for that. There plainly is no singular truth to be appreciated or defined. The moments of resistance, the denials and the evasions, are no less true than the emotions that they thereby seem to negate. Incompletions and fragmentariness seem to have an authority of their own. The completions exist in the minds and imaginations of those who watch and who have their own necessities. And in several of his plays his characters do address that audience directly, thereby appealing to experiences that take them beyond the page and the stage. Meaning is not to be wholly circumscribed by the play that needs to preserve its mysteries. The fear, indeed, is of a world in which all meaning surrenders itself too completely, a world in which the surface becomes the only reality.

Myth becomes the only grounds on which Shepard's characters can meet. *Mad Dog Blues* (1971) brings together Marlene Dietrich, Mae West, Captain Kidd, Paul Bunyan, and Jesse James. And if in a sense they represent closed systems, completed myths, once brought into conjunction they become elements in a shifting kaleidoscope of meanings. As he has explained, myth "speaks to everything at once, especially the emotions"; but, for him, myth implies "a sense of mystery and not necessarily a traditional formula."[5] But this does not imply that his work should be seen as part of that revolt against language that, inspired in part by Antonin Artaud, became a feature of some Off-Broadway groups. Indeed, he sees in the rhythms of language a necessary means to provoke what amounts almost to a mystical sense of being. He has spoken of the desire to "evoke visions in the eye of the audience,"[6] finding in American Indian poetry a religious and spiritual sense of the world that exists behind the word and that the word may liberate; and in a sense that amounts to a description equally of his style and his objective.

The play that comes closest to engaging the immediate realities of the American political system and to objectifying the sense of threat implicit in his early work is *Operation Sidewinder* (1970), first performed at Lincoln Center. This play concerns a class of mythologies—those of a contemporary scientistic, militaristic culture in which the machine becomes a god, worshipped for its destructive power, against those of an older world in which personal and public values are fully integrated. The former is embodied in an Air Force computer, fashioned into the form of a giant metallic snake; the latter in the snake once it is dismembered and claimed as a symbol of eternity, a god not of science but of a restored unity between man and nature. If it is also an image of the fall it is an image that can be deflected from its logic only by a transformation, a resurrection of hope and a rediscovery of human values. And redemption is a possibility that the play celebrates, drawing on familiar images from a decade in which the body's resistance to the machine was celebrated as a political and metaphysical fact. The patent arbitrariness of Shepard's gestures, the degree to which he relies on public stereotypes as "ready mades" for his drama, makes him vulnerable to attack, students at Yale seeing the black revolutionaries in the play as offensively racist. But he is consciously dealing in public images. *Operation Sidewinder* is an ironic play whose own *deus ex machina* (a UFO descends to rescue the pure in heart and spirit from a corrupt world) is a deliberate provocation but the redemptive mood seems real enough, a product of a decade that saw such symbolic acts of resistance as credible and liberating articles of faith.

By the time he wrote *Angel City* (1976) the optimism, if that is what it was, has largely collapsed. The city of the angels resolves itself into a bleak Los Angeles, the bright visions into a third-rate horror movie, while liberation becomes little more than the pursuit of the self down the narrow by-way of solipsism. Once again the plot seems to absorb its own characters, as the jaded script writers slowly turn into the monsters they write about.

But if social criticism is an element of Shepard's work it is not a dominant one. The ironies in his work are the product of more than the injustices of a particular system. The loneliness that seems to characterize his figures is not a pure product of social alienation. The irony is more profound than that generated by a space between image and reality. There is something of the absurdist in Shepard as he deploys characters with no substance whose persistent optimism becomes the root of irony. As a character remarks in *Buried Child,* which won Shepard a Pulitzer Prize in 1978: "You're all alike you hopers. If it's not God, then it's a man. If it's not a man, then it's a woman. If it's not a woman then it's the land or the future of some kind. Some kind of future."[7] Certainly, here, no character can bear the weight of the desperate appeal in the same play: "We can't not believe in something. We can't stop believing. We just end up dying if we stop. Just end up dead."[8] But if the basis for this faith can scarcely be found in the plays themselves, the need is perhaps implied by plays that so rigorously exclude it. And in a work that he developed with Joseph Chaikin in 1981, *Savage/Love*, he did finally create a celebration of love that seemed a resource that could go some way towards neutralizing the alienations that otherwise seem a birthright in his plays. But there is another resource, another image for the consonance for which his characters long but which they can see no way of attaining; that resource is music. Shepard is himself a musician and he sees in the structural and rhythmic fixities and the coexisting freedoms some kind of image of his characters' plight. Indeed, the process of constructing and performing a play is not itself radically dissimilar so that the metatheatrical gestures that recur in his work are themselves, perhaps, suggestions of the extent to which the theatre reenacts the experience it chooses to engage. They imply, simultaneously, the ironies of the absurd and the possibility of transcendence.

Shepard's is a theatre of images. Language remains a subtle instrument and a means of implying a world behind the word (shades, perhaps, of Whitman); but what is most striking in his work is the visual imagery. The stage becomes a tableau; his settings have metaphorical force; his characters seem to live allegorically. It may be true that as he says, "language is a veil hiding demons and angels"[9] and he is undoubtedly one of the most linguistically impressive of America's dramatists, particularly in terms of his sense of the rhythms of rural and urban America, but it is the "images which shine in the junk"[10] that are finally the most compelling feature of his work.

Those images, however, are not the isolated symbols of Tennessee Williams's work, forced to carry the burden of his meaning. They are the essence of his plays, as characters, style, and the rhythms of speech cohere to create powerful and disturbing metaphors for an alienation that connects the social, the psychological, and the metaphysical.

His characters are always about the business of penetrating mysteries; they are all in some sense on a quest—for meaning, for completion, and for some kind of restored consonance.

That that meaning never resolves itself, that the quest never reaches its objective, and that meaning somehow never coheres (when the buried child is discovered it deepens rather than dissolves the mystery) is in part a testament to Shepard's sense of the absurd and in part a testament to his desire to protect mystery as potentially the source of redemption. For though the movie scripts that his characters write are banal and though the man with a gift for second sight deploys it only to select winners in a dog race, there are other visions that may be worthwhile and there are myths that are not the cynical product of a society that revolves around the concept of consumption. And that, too, gives his work a special fascination. Highly sensitive to style and to the images deployed by the media—which we somehow manage to share without their creating a real sense of community—he still seems to see these aspects of contemporary life as evidence of a longing that is not satisfied by such substitutes. We may not come together in the real—a concept holding little meaning in his work—but we do perhaps in our mutual struggle to shape experience into form, to understand the painful contradictions of love and to be moved by what we do not fully understand. Perhaps, he seems to imply, meaning lies less in the tune that we try to detect than in the occasional harmonies and in the rhythms to which we respond instinctively with the senses rather than the analytic mind. Perhaps much the same meaning applies to his work.

Notes
Biographical Notes
Index

Notes

Introduction

1. A previous and partial attempt was made in a book limiting itself to French views: Ira D. Johnson and Christiane Johnson, eds., *Les Américanistes* (Port Washington, NY: Kennikat Press, 1978). A number of others are in progress under the general editorship of the European Association for American Studies.
2. See for example Harold Bloom, "The Central Man," *New York Review of Books* 31, no. 12 (19 July 1984): 5–6.
3. Guy Davenport, *Tatlin!* (New York: Scribner's, 1974), 211.
4. *Funk and Wagnalls' Standard College Dictionary,* s.v. "critical angle."
5. See my article on the subject in *New Literary History* (Spring 1985).

Chapter 1. The Real Thing

1. Gilbert Sorrentino, *Mulligan Stew* (New York: Grove Press, 1979), 420.
2. Clarence Major, *Reflex and Bone Structure* (New York: Fiction Collective, 1975), 56.
3. Clarence Major, *Emergency Exit* (New York: Fiction Collective, 1979), 25.
4. In Jerome Klinkowitz, *The Life of Fiction* (Urbana: Univ. of Illinois Press, 1977), 15. See also in the same volume Ronald Sukenick's "Twenty Digressions toward a Non-definition of Art."
5. See Jerome Klinkowitz, *The Practice of Fiction in America* (Ames: Iowa State Univ. Press, 1980).
6. Ronald Sukenick, *98.6* (New York: Fiction Collective, 1975), 11.

7. Clarence Major, "Reality, Fiction, and Criticism," *par rapport* 2, no. 1 (1979): 68.
8. Wolfgang Iser, *The Act of Reading* (London: Routledge and Kegan Paul, 1978), 68.
9. Iser, *Act of Reading*, 65.
10. See Gérard Genette, *Nouveau discours du récit* (Paris: Seuil, 1983), 54.
11. Major, *Reflex and Bone Structure*, 1.
12. Lionel Trilling, "Manners, Morals, and the Novel," *The Liberal Imagination* (New York: Viking Press, 1950), 203.
13. Tzvetan Todorov, "Du vraisemblable que l'on ne saurait éviter," *Communication* 11 (1968): 146.
14. Sorrentino, *Mulligan Stew*, 2.
15. Gérard Genette, "Vraisemblance et motivations," *Communications* 11 (1968): 20; reprinted in *Figures II* (Paris: Seuil, 1969).
16. Robert I. Edenbaum, "The Poetics of the Private Eye: The Novels of D. Hammett," in *The Mystery Writer's Art*, ed. F. M. Nevins, Jr. (Bowling Green: Bowling Green Univ. Popular Press, 1970), 99.
17. Sorrentino, *Mulligan Stew*, 30.
18. Major, *Reflex and Bone Structure*, 3.
19. Tzvetan Todorov, *Introduction à la Littérature fantastique* (Paris: Seuil, 1970).
20. See also the distinction between "fact" and "fiction" in Mas'ud Zavarzadeh, *The Mythopoeic Reality* (Urbana: Univ. of Illinois Press, 1976), 20.
21. In discussing what David Lodge calls the "short circuit" between reality and fantasy in postmodern fiction, Christine Brooke-Rose suggests that it is "simply a fusion of semantic categories"; see *A Rhetoric of the Unreal* (Cambridge: Cambridge Univ. Press, 1981), 360.
22. Jonathan Baumbach, *Reruns* (New York: Fiction Collective, 1974), 78.
23. Sorrentino, *Mulligan Stew*, 1.
24. See Philippe Hamon, *Le personnel du roman* (Geneva: Droz, 1983), 107.
25. Sorrentino, *Mulligan Stew*, 2.
26. For "double referentiality" see Guido Carboni, "La finzione necessaria: considerazioni sulla *postmodern fiction* negli Usa, " *Calibano* 7 (1982): 67–73.

Chapter 2. Modernism/Postmodernism

1. This central problem of "rezeptionsäesthetik" is discussed in the introduction to Rainer Warning, ed. *Rezeptionsäesthetik* (Munich: Fink, 1975), 19.
2. Stephen Spender, *The Struggle of the Modern* (1963; reprint, London: Macmillan, 1965), 83.
3. Frank Kermode, "Revolution: The Role of the Elders," in *Liberations: New Essays on the Humanities in Revolution,* ed. Ihab Hassan (Middletown, CT: Wesleyan Univ. Press, 1971), 87–99.
4. I am at this point leaving the most general level of the discussion and beginning to argue predominantly, and then exclusively, in terms of conventions of narrative. My reasons for this procedure are twofold. One is that the relationship between modernism and postmodernism as period styles has been conducted almost exclusively with reference to prose fiction. The second one is that both terms in a very general and very vital way concern themselves with the relation between the text and the world out there—that is, with questions of *mimesis,* which are (in our time) primarily dealt with by the criticism of narrative.

   But in the background of the argument there is a constant awareness that, in a sense, it just duplicates the approach of, for instance, Conrad Aiken's review of the *Waste Land,* "An Anatomy of Melancholy," *New Republic,* 7 Feb. 1923; reprinted in *T. S. Eliot, The Waste Land,* eds. C. B. Cox and A. Hinchliffe (London: Macmillan Casebook Series, 1968; reprint 1975), 91–99.
5. Spender, *Struggle of the Modern,* x.
6. I am adapting—without, at this point, being able to go into extended justification of the approach—Charles William Morris's notion of semiotic *dimensions: Foundations of the Theory of Signs* (Chicago, 1938; reprinted in *Writings on the General Theory of Signs, Approaches to Semiotics,* vol. 16, ed. Thomas A. Sebeok [The Hague: Mouton, 1971], 13–71). The three dimensions of signs—designated semantic, pragmatic, and syntactic—constitute three directions in which the sign reaches out: towards objects, towards subjects or users, and towards other signs. Texts, in my view, can base their contextualization, or the way in which they are perceived as wholes of sorts, more or less restrictively on one or the other of these dimensions. They can rely on the objects to which they refer to come together as a world; they can rely on

the reader to whom they appeal to (re)construct a wholeness of meaning in them that is not semantically based; or they can rely on their parts coming together as signs, in purely formal configurations.

Chapter 3. Yours Faithfully, the Author

1. Donald Barthelme, *Snow White* (New York: Atheneum, 1967), 44. Subsequent references to this edition are given in parentheses in the text.
2. Paul Watzlawick, "Patterns of Psychotic Communication," in *Problems of Psychosis,* eds. Pierre Doucet and Camille Laurin (Amsterdam: Excerpta Medica, 1971), 44–53.
3. Henry James, *Turn of the Screw* (New York: Macmillan, 1898).
4. William Gass, "Tropes of the Text," in *Representation and Performance in Postmodern Fiction,* ed. Maurice Couturier (Montpellier, France: Delta, 1983), 39.
5. Thomas Pynchon, *The Crying of Lot 49* (1967; reprint, Harmondsworth: Penguin Books, 1974).
6. John Barth, *Letters* (New York: G. P. Putnam's Sons, 1979), 44.
7. Pynchon, *Crying of Lot 49,* 31. Subsequent references to this edition are given in parentheses in the text.
8. Tony Tanner, *Thomas Pynchon* (London and New York: Methuen, 1982), 71.
9. Jean Guenot, *Ecrire* (Saint-Cloud, France: Chez Jean Guenot, 1982), 17; my translation.
10. Maurice Couturier, "Interview with Michel Butor," in *Representation and Performance in Postmodern Fiction,* ed. Maurice Couturier (Montpellier, France: Delta, 1983), 204; my translation.
11. Nabokov, *Look at the Harlequins!* (New York: McGraw-Hill, 1974), 62. Subsequent references to this edition are given in parentheses in the text.
12. Nabakov, *Ada* (New York: McGraw-Hill, 1969).
13. Jurgen Ruesch, *Disturbed Communication* (New York: Norton, 1957).
14. Barthelme, *Snow White,* 4.
15. Eureca Uri Comturi, *La Polka piquée* (Lausanne: L'Age d'Homme, 1982), 120–22.

Chapter 4. A Room of One's Own

1. See Jacques Derrida, "Living On: Border Lines," in *Deconstruction and Criticism*, Harold Bloom, Paul de Man, Geoffrey Hartman, James Hillis Miller, and Jacques Derrida (New York: Seabury Press, 1979), 75–176.
2. See Julia Kristeva, "Bakhtine, le mot, le dialogue et le roman," *Critique* 23 (1967): 438–65.
3. Thomas Mann, "Meerfahrt mit 'Don Quijote'" [Sea-Voyage with 'Don Quixote'], *Gesammelte Werke*, vol. 9 (Oldenburg: S. Fischer, 1960), 432. "This is a literary death out of jealousy—but this jealousy, to be sure, bears witness at the same time to the heartfelt and proudly defensive bond between the poet and the ever peculiar child of his intellect, a deep feeling, no less earnest for finding expression in whimsical literary precautions against outside resuscitation attempts"; my translation.
4. See Philip Stevick, *The Chapter in Fiction: Theories of Narrative Division* (Syracuse, NY: Syracuse Univ. Press, 1970), 57–73.
5. Robert Coover, *Spanking the Maid: A Novel* (New York: Grove Press, 1982), 86.
6. Maurice Blanchot, *La folie du jour* (Paris: Editions fata morgana, 1973), 20. "Finally I became convinced that I was face to face with the madness of the day. That was the truth: the light was going mad, the brightness had lost all reason; it assailed me irrationally, without control, without purpose," ("The Madness of the Day," trans. Lydia Davis, *Tri-Quarterly* 40 [1977]: 172).
7. Blanchot, *La folie du jour*, 30. "Oh, I see the daylight, oh God," ("The Madness of the Day," trans. Davis, 176).
8. Blanchot, *La folie du jour*, 9. "I feel boundless pleasure in living, and I will take boundless satisfaction in dying," ("The Madness of the Day," trans. Davis, 168).
9. John Barth, *Chimera* (1972; reprint, Greenwich, CT: Fawcett Crest Book 1973), 212. Subsequent references to this edition are given in parentheses in the text.
10. Italo Calvino, *Se una notte d'inverno un viaggiatore* (Torino: Guilio Einaudi editore s.p.a., 1979), 101. "The true authors remain those who for him were only a name on a jacket, a word that was part of the title, authors who had the same reality as their characters, as the places mentioned in the books, who existed and didn't exist at the same time, like those characters and those

countries," (*If on a winter's night a traveler,* trans. William Weaver [New York: Harcourt, 1981], 101).

11. Calvino, *Se una notte,* 263. "Just a moment, I've almost finished *If on a winter's night a traveler* by Italo Calvino," (*If on a winter's night a traveler,* trans. Weaver, 260).

12. Barth, *Chimera,* 320.

13. Derrida, "Living on: Border Lines," 83.

Chapter 5. Figure and Ground

1. *Selected Letters of Robert Frost,* ed. Lawrence Thompson (London: Jonathan Cape, 1965), 419./

2. I have followed the account by Julian Hochberg in "The Representation of Things and People," in *Art, Perception, and Reality,* eds. E. H. Gombrich, J. Hochberg, and M. Black (Baltimore and London: John Hopkins Univ. Press, 1972), 50–52.

3. Jean Piaget, *The Psychology of Intelligence* (London: Routledge and Kegan Paul, 1950), 59–60.

4. Ibid., 65.

5. Jacques Derrida, "Structure, Sign, and Play in the Discourse of the Human Sciences," in *Writing and Difference* (Chicago: Univ. of Chicago Press, 1978), 278–93.

6. Jean Piaget, *Structuralism* (London: Routledge and Kegan Paul, 1971), 53, 55.

7. Erich Auerbach, "Figura," in *Scenes from the Drama of European Literature* (Gloucester, MA: Peter Smith, 1973), 11–76. This collection of essays is to be reprinted as volume nine in the Theory and History of Literature series from the University of Minnesota and Manchester University presses.

8. Henry David Thoreau, *Walden and Civil Disobedience,* ed. Owen Thomas (New York: Norton, 1966), 66.

9. Martin Heidegger, "The Origin of the Work of Art," *Poetry, Language, Thought,* trans. Albert Hofstadter (New York: Harper Colophon, 1975), 15–87.

10. Jacques Derrida, *La Vérité en peinture* (Paris: Flammarion, 1978), 328, 330.

11. *The Poetry of Robert Frost,* ed. E. C. Latham (London: Jonathan Cape, 1977), 296.

12. See Dennis Welland, "The Dark Voice of the Sea: A Theme in American Poetry," in *American Poetry,* ed. I. Ehrenpreis, Strat-

ford-upon-Avon Studies 7 (London: Edward Arnold, 1965), 196–219.

13. A. R. Ammons, *Selected Poems 1951–1977* (New York: Norton, 1977), 43.

14. *The Collected Poems of Wallace Stevens* (London: Faber and Faber, 1955), 72.

15. J. Hillis Miller, "Stevens' Rock and Criticism as Cure," *Georgia Review* 30 (1976): 345. This two-part article valuably discusses "line" and "ground" in the context of *mise en abyme.*

16. Ammons, *Selected Poems,* 101–2.

17. *Poetry of Robert Frost,* 34.

18. See J. R. Smitten and A. Daghistany, eds., *Spatial Form in Narrative* (Ithaca and London: Cornell Univ. Press, 1981).

19. Ralph Waldo Emerson, *Nature, Addresses, and Lectures* (Boston and New York: Houghton Mifflin; Cambridge, MA: Riverside Press, 1891), 30.

20. John Ashbery, *Rivers and Mountains* (New York: Ecco Press, 1977), 44.

21. *Selected Journals of Henry David Thoreau,* ed. Carl Bode (New York and Toronto: New American Library, 1967), 40.

22. John Ashbery, *Self-Portrait in a Convex Mirror* (New York: Penguin, 1976), 72.

23. John Ashbery, "Callibiography," in *Narrative Art,* eds. T. B. Hess and J. Ashbery (New York: Macmillan, 1970), 58.

24. E. C. Traugott and M. L. Pratt, *Linguistics for Students of Literature* (New York: Harcourt, 1980), 275.

25. Roman Jakobson, "Shifters, Verbal Categories, and the Russian Verb," in *Selected Writings,* vol. 2 (The Hague: Mouton, 1976), 130–47.

26. Ashbery, *Rivers and Mountains,* 31.

27. John Ashbery, *Shadow Train* (New York: Penguin, 1981), 25.

28. John Dixon Hunt, *The Figure in the Landscape: Poetry, Painting and Gardening during the Eighteenth Century* (Baltimore and London: Johns Hopkins Univ. Press, 1976), 201, 206.

29. See C. Norberg-Schulz, "Existential Space," *Existence, Space, and Architecture* (London: Studio Vista, 1971), 17–36.

30. Kenneth Clark, *Landscape into Art* (Harmondsworth: Penguin, 1966), 17.

31. Rainer Maria Rilke, *Selected Works, vol. 1: Prose,* trans. G. Craig Houston (London: Hogarth Press, 1967), 7.

32. *Collected Poems of Wallace Stevens,* 372.

33. Jeffry Spencer, *Heroic Nature: Ideal Landscapes in English Poetry from Marvell to Thomson* (Evanston, IL: Northwestern Univ. Press, 1973), xi.
34. John Ashbery, *The Double Dream of Spring* (New York: Ecco Press, 1978), 50.
35. John Ashbery, *Houseboat Days* (New York: Viking, 1977), 32.
36. Ashbery, *Double Dream of Spring*, 36.
37. This paper was previously presented, in a different form, to the annual conference of the British Association of American Studies at Nottingham in 1982.

Chapter 6. The Exile of Binx Bolling

1. Percy had first chosen to entitle his novel *The Confessions of a Moviegoer* (Simone Vauthier, "Title as Microtext: The Example of *The Moviegoer*," *Journal of Narrative Technique*, Sept. 1975, 220– 21).
2. How does he read *The Charterhouse of Parma?* Immediately . . . or mediately?" (Walker Percy, *The Moviegoer* [New York: Knopf, 1961]: 214). Subsequent references to this edition are given in parentheses in the text.
3. Jean Baudrillard, *Simulacres et simulation* (Paris: Galilée, 1981), 208.
4. "The impossibility of determining what is the remainder of the other characterizes the phase of simulation and the agony of distinct systems, a phase where everything becomes remainder and residual" (Baudrillard, *Simulacres et simulation*, 209).
5. "Copies are the secondhand possessor, well-grounded claimants, guaranteed by resemblance; simulacra are like false claimants, constructed on a dissimilitude, a perversion, and a misappropriation that are all essential. It is in this way that Plato divides the domain of image-idols: on one side the icon-copies, on the other simulacra-phantasms" (Gilles Deleuze, "Simulacre et philosophie antique, " in *Logique du sens* [Paris: Minuit, 1969], 296– 97).
6. Kate: "Only in time of illness and disaster are people real. I remember at the time of the wreck—people were so kind and helpful and *solid*" (p. 81).

   Binx: "I too once met a girl in Central Park, but it is not much to remember. What I remember is the time John Wayne killed three men with a carbine as he was falling to the dusty street in *Stagecoach*" (p. 7).

7. Wrongly, because the real can be thought of and represented (evoked by the volatility of words) as a subtle or fluid principle. Michel Serres emphasizes the historical connivance of the imagination of the real and of the imagination of the solid (the triumphant mechanics of solids), the secret alliance of the truth and of consistency in the Western imagination, to the detriment of the hydrostatic and the mechanics of fluids—volutes and turbulences (Michel Serres, *Naissance de la physique* [Paris: Minuit, 1977], 32, 182–84).

8. "Be it life or death, we crave only reality." And the only sacred instrument will be Thoreau's "Realometer" (Henry David Thoreau, *Walden* [New York: Norton, 1966], 66).

9. In this case, space and time are, strictly speaking, tropes (trophies). So that they may be recognized in their multiplicity, according to Binx, one should distribute to travelers exiting train stations "a little trophy of local space-time stuff" (p. 201).

10. "That is to say . . . an operation dissuading any real process by means of its operational double, a metastable descriptive machine, programmatic, impeccable, which provides all the signs of the real and short-circuits all its vicissitudes" (Baudrillard, *Simulacres et simulation*, 11).

11. "Les Champs Elysées," a pure simulacrum: in the supposed reality of the fiction (the avenue in New Orleans so baptized), nothing corresponds to the normal connotations of the name. What defines this avenue, on the contrary, is the absence of any Elysian element: "We live . . . on Elysian Fields . . . Though it was planned to be like its namesake, the grandest boulevard of the city, something went amiss" (p. 9).

12. Discourse could trigger this eternally threatening contagion of an ideology of the serious because of its heuristic, ethical, and mimetic value; it is from the depths of his exile that Binx gives meaning to the message: "It can only mean one thing" (p. 4). There is no sickness worse than that of "meaning" and only a long exile can cure us of this cancer.

13. Jean Ricardou, *Le nouveau roman* (Paris: Seuil, 1978), 30–31.

14. If signs themselves make no difference and no longer make the difference, we have the entropic empire of the "same." Without difference, no energy remains available in closed systems; such is the terminal stability of heat death.

15. Objectivity never bodes anything good. For Binx, Aunt Emily's tone of objectivity is frankly "ominous" (p. 220).
16. In their nighttime conversations on their porch, the Bollings like to dissipate mysteries and, for example, to decide on the size of the universe.
17. In the way in which Deleuze uses the word *myth:* "Active Gods are the myth of religion, as fate is the myth of a false physics, and Being, the One, the All, the myth of a false philosophy saturated with theology" (Deleuze, *Logique du sens,* 323).
18. "I no longer write or receive letters" (p. 87). It is interesting to note that the first disengagement of Binx, his first deconstruction, has as its object the postal message and the formidable apparatus of values conveyed by the postal system: letter, literature, sending, journey, receiving, destination, fate, code, and communication (Jacques Derrida, *La Carte postale* [Paris: Aubier-Flammarion, 1980]). Could the letter, whether it be alphabetical or postal, whether purloined or delivered, be the last prison-house of the imagination? (Claude Richard, *Le Timbre-Poste* [Paris: Orange-Export, 1981]).
19. See Clément Rosset, *Anti-Nature* (Paris: PUF, 1973), where this is the central theme, in particular chapter 2, "Nature and Religion," pp. 41–43); Martin Heidegger, for whom the word "nature" is the fundamental word of metaphysics" ("Comment détermine-t-on la physis?" in *Questions,* vol. 2 [Paris: Gallimard, 1968], 182); and Francois Wolff, *Logique de l'élément* (Paris: PUF, 1981), especially in his brilliant conclusion, "La 'nature des choses' contre la nature" (pp. 257–66).
20. Wolff, *Logique de l'élément,* 165–71.
21. The titles of "fundamental works" all refer to the unique: history (*A Study of History*); life (*What is Life?*); and the universe (*The Universe as I See It* [p. 69]).
22. The fact that Binx lives in the world of simulacra after his initiation and that he learns to enjoy it is shown by the lucidity with which he recognizes the "simulacrum of a dream" (p. 54).
23. "A universe where the image ceases to be secondary in relation to the model, where the imposture claims truth, where finally there is no more original but an eternal scintillation where the absence of origin is dispersed in the bursting of the detour and return" (Maurice Blanchot, "Le Rire des Dieux," *NFR* [July 1965]: 103, quoted in Deleuze, *Logique du sens,* 303).

24. The dividends paid by this firm, whose names associates life with the accidental, are prodigious: "If you had invested a hundred dollars in 1942, you'd now be worth twenty-five thousand" (p. 196). Should we read the profits on this investment in a figurative sense?
25. "Wonder"—Kate's domain—is above all a liberating feeling. Women's liberation will go through the same process as men's liberation—to be liberated from the yoke of the cause and effect chain, of determinism, of the concept of destiny, in other words the order of reason. "He . . . suggested we look into the reasons. . . . What if there is nothing? That is what I have been afraid of until now—being found out to be concealing nothing at all. But now I know why I was afraid because I felt that I must *be* such and such a person. . . . Now I am saying good-bye, Merle. And I walked out, as free as a bird. . . . But I know I am right or I would not feel so wonderful" (p. 115).
26. "This one fact the world hates, that the soul becomes" (Ralph Waldo Emerson, "Self-Reliance," in *Essays* [London: Dent, 1955], 44).
27. Herman Melville, *Moby Dick* (New York: Norton, 1967), 16.
28. "You never know what happened to Binx Bolling: it's sort of *up in the air*," Percy answers J. Gerald Kennedy and Ben Forkner ("An Interview with W. Percy," *Delta* 13: 10). *The Moviegoer* is a novel that does not close.

Chapter 7. The Energy of an Absence

1. William Gaddis, *The Recognitions* (New York: Harcourt, 1955). Subsequent references to this edition are given in parentheses in the text.
2. Harold Bloom, *The Anxiety of Influence* (London, Oxford, New York: Oxford Univ. Press, 1973), 26.
3. Gerald L. Bruns, *Inventions: Writing, Textuality, and Understanding in Literary History* (New Haven, London: Yale Univ. Press, 1982), 7.
4. Steven Moore, *A Reader's Guide to William Gaddis's "Recognitions"* (Lincoln, NB, and London: Univ. of Nebraska Press), 118. Suicide is once hinted at in a very oblique way when Mr. Feddle quotes Tolstoy's play *Redemption* and "inadvertently puts the idea

of suicide into Benny" (Moore, *Reader's Guide*, 41). This will happen in a later chapter.

5. Moore, *Reader's Guide*, 40.

6. When Stanley adds apologetically, "I don't read Voltaire of course" (p. 617), he points to the fact of his being a Roman Catholic and, as Moore observes (*Reader's Guide*, 243), Voltaire's works are on the *Index*.

7. See my "Gaddis and the novel of entropy," *TREMA* 2 (1977): 97–107 for a further discussion of this point.

8. See for instance George Steiner's chapter "In a Post-culture," in *In Bluebeard's Castle* (London: Faber, 1971), 51–74.

9. George Steiner, "Crossed Lines," *New Yorker* 26 Jan. 1976, 108.

10. John O'Brien, "An Interview with Gilbert Sorrentino," in the Gilbert Sorrentino number of *Review of Contemporary Fiction* 1, no. 1 (1981): 6.

11. J. D. O'Hara, "Coteries and Poetries," *Nation* 2–9 Jan. 1982: 20.

12. Gilbert Sorrentino, *Imaginative Qualities of Actual Things* (New York: Pantheon, 1971).

13. Gilbert Sorrentino, *Mulligan Stew* (New York: Grove Press, 1979). Subsequent references to this edition are given in parentheses in the text.

14. Malcolm Bradbury wrote, "There are some books that deserve unstinting acclaim not because they are perfect (few are) but because they set out to qualify or displace the whole idea of perfect literature" ("Writing Mocking Writing," *New York Times Book Review* 26 Aug. 1979:9). See also Harold I. Brown, "L'Autoréférence en Logique: L'Exèmple de 'Mulligan Stew'," *Diogene* 118 (1982): 144: "Il reste à dire une chose à propos de ce livre étrange, c'est qu'en dépit de son lourd handicap, *Mulligan Stew* est un chef-d'oeuvre . . . *Mulligan Stew* contient une proportion affligeante de morceaux de bravoure exécrables—et pourtant le roman 'marche', et la méchante qualité de cette prose contribue à son efficacité." Brown describes this as a confusion of hierarchies.

15. John O'Brien, "Gilbert Sorrentino Tilts at Language," *Washington Post Book World* 22 May 1983.

16. "But foost away, O masted Imperato, and I'll scrample up my cerebellata for the responders oll korreck," for example (Gilbert Sorrentino, *Blue Pastoral* [San Francisco: North Point Press, 1983], 61). There are obvious echoes from James Joyce, an author deeply revered by Sorrentino. Subsequent reference to this edition are given in parentheses in the text.

17. "Lines are missing (but missing from *what?*)" (O'Brien, "Gilbert Sorrentino Tilts at Language").
18. Gilbert Sorrentino, "The Various Isolated: W. C. Williams' Prose," *New American Review* 15 (1972): 196–97.
19. "A poem does not mean anything," Sorrentino stated in "An Interview Conducted by Barry Albert Westbeth," *Vort Magazine* 6 (7 April 1974): 7.

Chapter 8. Between Latency and Knowledge

1. Nabokov, *Ada* (New York: Penguin, 1980– 1981), 9. Subsequent references to this edition are given in parentheses in the text.
2. Nabokov, *A Russian Beauty* (New York: Penguin, 1973). Subsequent references to this edition are given in parentheses in the text.
3. This is a literal translation of the notion of "lecture-écriture" introduced by Roland Barthes.
4. In the following, and somewhat technical, study of the set-phrase I am indebted to Gérard Deléchelle, whom I want to thank here.
5. See Maurice Couturier, "Sex vs. Text: From Miller to Nabokov," *Revue Francaise d'Etudes Américaines* 20 (1984): 243–60.
6. This definition of the degree zero of the metaphor is different from what Elizabeth Cardonne-Arlyck calls "degré zéro de la métaphore" in her excellent study of the metaphor (in *La Métaphore Raconte*, ed. Julien Gracq [Paris: Klincksieck, 1984]). It rather corresponds to what she calls "métaphore-cliché" in the definition she gives of the figures of "deviation" (in French, "l'écart"). She differentiates the cliché-metaphor that is absorbed in the sentence from the trope that breaks the isotopy, the diegetic comparison from a comparison that is heterogeneous to the narrative milieu.
7. John Fowles, *The Collector* (London: Jonathan Cape, 1963), 5.
8. See Gérard Genette, "Métonymie chez Proust," *Figures* 3 (Seuil), 48.
9. This is my translation. Many of the following remarks have been inspired by the excellent commented catalog of the exhibition that includes articles by Antonin Artaud, Klossowski, and Starobinski. The quotation is from "La Jeune Peinture Française," originally written in Spanish by Artaud (in *Balthus* [Paris: Centre Georges Pompidou, 1983], 43).

10. Nabokov, *Bend Sinister* (New York: Penguin, 1947), 117.

11. Michel Foucault, *Ceci n'est pas une Pipe,* ed. Bruno Roy (Scholies: Fata Morgana, 1973), 47–48. This is my translation. I want to thank Leslie Coward for her numerous suggestions and her friendly help.

Chapter 9. "An exact precession . . ."

1. André du Bouchet, *Défets* (Paris: Clivages, 1981), unpaginated.

2. Guy Davenport, "Au Tombeau de Charles Fourier, " *Da Vinci's Bicycle* (Baltimore and London: Johns Hopkins Univ. Press, 1979), 91.

3. Leonardo da Vinci, *Codex F* (Paris: Bibliothéque de l'Institut de France), 49v; my translation. See for example the drawing folio 88 in the *Codex Huygens* (New York: Pierpont Morgan Library, ms. 1139), which shows the sun in five different positions with the corresponding shadows on the earth. The Epicurean theory of simulacra is also a recurring theme in Leonardo's work; see Paul Valéry, *Introduction à la méthode de Leonardo de Vinci* (1894; reprint, Paris: Gallimard, 1957, 1153–99). I am especially indebted to Franc Ducros' work on Leonardo; see "Entre l'oeil et la main," *Prévue* (22 Jan. 1983, 47–67) and *Ombre lointaine* (Aix-en-Provence: Alinea, 1983).

4. Davenport, "C. Musonius Rufus," *Da Vinci's Bicycle,* 18.

5. Gertrude Stein, *Geographic History of America* (New York: Random House, 1936), 58n.8.

6. Davenport, "Au Tombeau de Charles Fourier," 98.

7. Martin Heidegger, *Sein und Zeit* (Tubingen: Max Niemayer, 1927).

8. Leonardo da Vinci, *Codex Trivulziano* (Castello Sforzesco, Milano: Biblioteca Trivulziana), 34r; my translation.

9. Clément Rosset, *Le Réel, traité de l'idiotie* (Paris: Minuit, 1977). See also by Rosset, *L'Objet singulier* (Paris: Minuit, 1979).

10. Davenport, "Au Tombeau de Charles Fourier," 95.

11. Ibid., 65.

12. Leonardo da Vinci, *Codex H* (Paris: Bibliothéque de l'Institut de France), 141r; my translation.

13. Davenport, "The Invention of Photography in Toledo," *Da Vinci's Bicycle,* 121.

14. Davenport, "A Field of Snow on a Slope of the Rosenberg," *Da Vinci's Bicycle*, 180.
15. Stein, *Geographical History*.
16. Davenport, "A Field of Snow," 183.
17. Ibid., 180.
18. See Henri Maldiney, *Regard, Parole, Espace* (Lausanne: L'Age d'Homme, 1973), 19.

Chapter 10. The Case of Donald Barthelme

1. André Green, "The Unbinding Process," *New Literary History* 12, no. 1 (1980 [1971]): 12.
2. Régis Durand, "On *Aphanisis:* A Note on the Dramaturgy of the Subject in Narrative Analysis," *MLN* 98, no. 5 (1983): 860–70.
3. Jean Baudrillard, *Les stratégies fatales* (Paris: Grasset, 1983), 165; my translation.
4. See Brian McHale, "Modernist Reading, Post-Modern Text: The Case of *Gravity's Rainbow*," *Poetics Today* 1, nos. 1–2 (1979): 85–110, who points out that whereas modernist fiction called for a kind of critical paranoia ("the mind-set of *tout se tient*"), post-modern reading requires "negative capability," which is nothing here but the ability to be "rationally irrational" (pp. 107–8).
5. Lacan, *The Four Fundamental Concepts of Psychoanalysis*, ed. J. A. Miller, trans. Alan Sheridan (New York: Norton, 1978), 218.
6. Roland Barthes, *S/Z* (Paris: Seuil, 1970), 17; my translation.
7. For a further disscussion of the point of view of scientific epistemology, see Claude Richard, "Le Graal du Référent," *Fabula* 2 (1983): 9–28.
8. For a first approach of this question, see Maurice Couturier and Régis Durand, *Donald Barthelme* (London: Methuen, 1983).
9. Robert Con Davis, "Post-modern Paternity: Donald Barthelme's *The Dead Father*," *The Fictional Father: Lacanian Readings of the Text*, ed. R. C. Davis (Amherst: Univ. of Massachusetts Press, 1981): 169–82.
10. Lacan sees in the decline of the paternal image the nucleus of what he calls "the great contemporary neurosis." And he adds: "Our experience leads us to point to its main determination in the personality of the father, always deficient in some manner,

absent, humiliated, divided, or false" (*Les Complexes Familiaux dans la Formation de l'Individu* [Paris: Navarin, 1984 (1938)], 73).

11. Donald Barthelme, *City Life* (New York: Farrar, Strauss, and Giroux, 1971), 9. Subsequent references to this edition are given in parentheses.

12. This second element, of course, finds its theoretical narrative in Freud's discussion of the dream in which a man saw that "his father was alive once more and was talking to him in his usual way, but (the remarkable thing was that) he had really died, only he did not know it" (*Standard Edition of the Complete Psychological Works of Sigmund Freud,* vol. 5 [London: Hogarth Press, 1953], 430).

13. See, for example, a discussion relevant to this question in Jean-Francois Lyotard, "Figure foreclose," *L'Ecrit du temps* 5 (1984): 86: "If in repression the object is not excluded but included as figure (thing-representation) in the psychic system, it becomes understandable that totemism should be the religion of the sons: the son is the father suppressed and conserved" (my translation).

14. Donald Barthelme, *The Dead Father* (New York: Farrar, Strauss, and Giroux, 1975). Subsequent references to this edition are given in parentheses in the text.

15. The proper object of repression is reconciliation and compromise (in technical terms "compromise-formation").

16. See, for example, the scene in which Thomas, in a replay of the Oedipian situation, not only solves the riddle and escapes the monster but also goes away with a knowledge of his key signifier ("murdering"). The dead father considers the story "a tall tale," to which the Lacan-wise son replies: " 'No tale ever happened in the way we tell it . . . but the moral is always correct.'

" 'What is the moral?'

" 'Murdering,' Thomas said" (Barthelme, *The Dead Father,* 46).

Chapter 11. Living On/Off the "Reserve"

1. The notions explored in this article at times have been subsumed under the polysemy of the English words *reserve* and *reservation:* thus, the idea of mining or exploiting a reserve, of drawing on reserves, of reserving judgement, and of being on one's guard (the obsolete "on the reserve") cohabit with expressions such as "to have reservations" or to "live on a reservation." In all cases

the idea is of some physical or mental space set aside for or withheld from use.

However, one meaning of the French word *réserve* no longer carries over its harmonics into English and is fundamental to my endeavors. The *OED* (compact edition, p. 2056) still lists one old use in the way it is meant here: "Reserve: noun, II, 5, (1876) Hamerton, *Etching and Etchers:* Reserves of pure white amidst dark shading may be made at any time." *Réserve, riserva, ausgesparresfeld:* other European languages seem to have maintained that use. The paraphrases and circumlocutions now used by English-speaking art historians contain different harmonics: "spare part" smacks of the mechanical and "bare part" is too lame to serve erotic purposes.

By reserve, then, will also and above all be meant here the part of a painting that is left uncovered with pigment because the artist desires to use the ground color of the canvas, paper, or other material serving as ground, instead of the color of the paint.

This being the central, but "reserved," metaphor, further explicitness is hardly of the essence, but the notion will be seen to watermark the essay.

2. Raymond Carver, "On Writing," *Fires* (Santa Barbara, CA: Capra Press, 1983), 14.

3. Thomas Le Clair, *Contemporary Literature* 23, no. 1: 86–88; Alain Arias-Misson, "Absent Talkers," *Partisan Review* 49 (1982): 625–28; David Boxer and Cassandra Phillips, "Voyeurism, Dissociation, and the Art of Raymond Carver," *Iowa Review* (Summer 1979): 75–90.

4. Carver, "On Writing," 14.

5. Raymond Carver, *Cathedral* (New York: Knopf, 1983), 187.

6. Raymond Carver, *What We Talk About When We Talk About Love* (New York: Knopf, 1980), 21.

7. Raymond Carver, *Will You Please Be Quiet, Please?* (New York: McGraw-Hill, 1975), 1.

8. Carver, "On Writing," 15.

9. Ibid.

10. Raymond Carver, "Harry's Death," *Fires,* 139.

11. Carver, *What We Talk About,* 159.

12. Raymond Carver, *Near Klamath,* Poems (Sacramento, CA: Sacramento State College, 1968).

13. Carver, *What We Talk About,* 57–66.

14. Ibid, 125. References in brackets are to the version contained in *Furious Seasons* (Santa Barbara, CA: Capra Press, 1977), 93.

15. Arias-Misson, "Absent Talkers," 628.

16. Raymond Carver, Preface to *We Are Not in This Together,* William Kittredge (Port Townsend: Graywood Press, 1984).

17. Carver, *Furious Seasons,* 91.

18. James Atlas, *Atlantic Monthly* 247, no. 6 (June 1981):96–98.

19. Carver, *Fires,* 17.

20. Le Clair, *Contemporary Literature,* 86.

21. Carver, "Cathedral," *Cathedral,* 219.

22. Carver, "The Lie," *Fires,* 123.

23. T. S. Eliot, *Selected Poems* (London: Faber and Faber, 1961), 14.

24. Imamu Amiri Baraka, "A Poem for Speculative Hipsters," (1964).

25. Wolfgand Iser, *The Act of Reading* (Baltimore: Johns Hopkins Univ. Press, 1980), 229.

26. In the case of the collection bearing that title, the influence of Charles Bukowski seems strong, witness the poem "You Don't Know What Love Is," in Carver, *Fires,* 57–71.

27. Roland Barthes, "Literature and Signification," *Critical Essays* (Evanston, IL: Northwestern Univ. Press, 1972), 2–4.

28. Witness for example the end of "What Do You Do In San Francisco?": "I don't mind. It's all work one way or another, and I'm always glad to have it" (Carver, *Will You Please,* 119) or that of "How About This?": "'Harry we have to love each other,' she said" (Ibid., 192).

29. See for example the end of "Signals": "'I don't think he ever knew her,' Wayne said" (Ibid., 224) or that of "Gazebo": "'Duane,' Holly goes. "In this too, she was right" (Carver, *What We Talk About,* 29). See also my later discussion on Carver's use of "halving."

30. Samuel Beckett, *Collected Shorter Plays* (London: Faber and Faber, 1984), 316.

31. "Good fiction is partly a bringing of the news from one world to another" (Interview with Raymond Carver, *Paris Review* 88 [1983]: 221).

32. Iser, *Act of Reading,* 229.

33. Adorno, *Aesthetische Theorie,* Gesammelte Schriften 7 (Frankfurt: Fischer, 1970), 25.

34. Carver, "Fever," *Cathedral,* 164.

35. Boxer and Phillips, "Voyeurism," 75.

36. Iser, *Act of Reading,* 72.

37. Carver, *Fires,* 106.
38. Ibid.
39. Carver, *Will You Please,* 14.
40. Carver, *Cathedral,* 138.
41. Carver, *Fires,* 102.
42. Iser, *Act of Reading,* 229.
43. A. R. Ammons, "Unsaid," *Collected Poems 1951–1971* (New York: Norton, 1965).
44. Carver, *What We Talk About,* 31.
45. Carver, "The Compartment," *Cathedral,* 47–58.
46. Carver, "Feathers," *Cathedral,* 3–26.
47. Carver, "Cathedral," *Cathedral,* 172.
48. Adorno, *Aesthetische Theorie,* 158.
49. Iser, *Act of Reading,* 228.
50. Ibid., 223.
51. Ammons, "Unsaid."

Chapter 12. David Mamet, A Virtuoso of Invective

1. David Mamet, *Lakeboat* (New York: Grove Press, 1981).
2. David Mamet, *American Buffalo* (London: Eyre Metheun, 1978); first produced in 1975.
3. I read *Glengarry Glen Ross* in a typescript that circulated at the National Theatre in London.
4. David Mamet, *Sexual Perversity in Chicago* (London: Eyre Metheun, 1978); first produced in 1974.
5. David Mamet, *Duck Variations* (London: Eyre Methuen, 1978); first produced in 1972.
6. David Mamet, *A Life in the Theatre* (New York: Grove Press, 1977); first produced 1977.
7. David Mamet, *The Water Engine* (New York: Grove Press); first produced in 1977.
8. David Mamet, *Reunion* (New York: Grove Press); first produced in 1977.
9. I found this quotation in a leaflet issued by the National Theatre in London on the occasion of the world premier of *Glengarry Glen Ross.*
10. David Mamet, *Dark Pony* (New York: Grove Press); first produced in 1977.

11. I am referring to an unpublished chapter on Mamet in the second volume of Christopher Bigsby's *American Drama* (vol. 1, Cambridge: Cambridge Univ. Press, n.p.). I am grateful to Dr. Bigsby who has kindly allowed me to consult the manuscript.

12. David Mamet, *Mr. Happiness* (New York: Grove Press); first produced in 1978.

13. This is a quotation from Mamet that I found in Christopher Bigsby's manuscript, see note 11.

14. Henry Miller, *Tropic of Capricorn* (London: Granada, 1971), 30.

15. These quotations are from Christopher Bigsby's text, see note 11.

16. Henry Miller, *Black Spring* (London: Granada, 1974), 11–12.

17. The obvious exception is Stanley Elkin's *Franchiser* (Boston: Godine, 1976).

Chapter 13. Sam Shepard: Word and Image

1. Sam Shepard, *Hawk Moon* (New York, 1978), 12.

2. *Five Strange Plays by Sam Shepard* (London, 1967), 79.

3. Bonnie Marranca, ed., *American Dreams: The Imagination of Sam Shepard* (New York, 1981), 198.

4. *Five Strange Plays*, 46.

5. Marranca, *American Dream*, 216.

6. Ibid.

7. Sam Shepard, *Buried Child and Seduced and Suicide in B^b* (London, 1980), 52.

8. Ibid., 60.

9. Marranca, *American Dreams*, 216.

10. Kenneth Chubb, "Fruitful Difficulties of Directing Shepard," *Theatre Quarterly* 4, no. 15 (Aug.–Oct. 1974): 24.

Biographical Notes

GUIDO ALMANSI is Professor of English and Comparative Literature at the University of East Anglia, Norwich and writes regularly for Italian newspapers. He has coauthored a book on Harold Pinter (Methuen). His latest book, entitled *Amica Ironia*, was published by Garzanti (Milan).

CHRISTOPHER BIGSBY is Professor of American Studies at the University of East Anglia in Norwich. He is the author of the three-volume *Critical Introduction to 20th Century American Drama*, of *The Second Black Renaissance*, and of books on English and American theatre, popular culture, contemporary novelists, Dada, and Surrealism.

NANCY BLAKE teaches literature at the University of Montpellier and is a practising psychotherapist. Her critical works include *Henry James: Ecriture et Absence* and *Ezra Pound et l'Imagisme*.

ALIDE CAGIDEMETRIO has taught American Literature at the University of Venice since 1974. Her special interest is the historical transformation of fiction considered from a contemporary vantage point. She has written studies of Gertrude Stein, Virginia Woolf, James Purdy, and Robert Coover, and books on Djuna Barnes (*Una strada nel bosco,* 1980) and Western autobiography (*Verso il West,* 1938). She is now working on "a science-fiction of history" in the nineteenth century novel.

MARC CHÉNETIER is Professor of American Literature at the University of Orléans, chairs the René Tadlov Group for Research in Contemporary American Literature (Maison des Sciences de l'Homme, Paris), and edits the *Revue Française d'Etudes Américaines.* He is the author of a long study of Vachel Lindsay's aesthetics (*L'Obsession des Signes,* 1979) and of *Richard Brautigan* (Methuen, 1983), has edited Vachel Lindsay's *Selected Letters,* "Stanley Elkin" (*Delta,* 20),

244
Biographical Notes

and "Intellectuals in the United States" (*Revue Francaise d'Etudes Américaines,* 16), coedited *Impressions of a Gilded Age,* and published numerous articles on contemporary American fiction and twentieth century poetry.

MAURICE COUTURIER, Professor of English at the University of Nice, is a specialist of contemporary fiction. He is the author of *Nabokov,* he coauthored *Donald Barthelme* with Régis Durand, and is the editor of "Nabokov" (*Delta* 17) and author of "Sexualité et érotisme dans la littérature américaine" (*Revue Française d'Etudes Américaines,* 19). He also has written a novel, *La Polka Piquée.*

ELLMAN CRASNOW studied at Cape Town, Cambridge, and Yale. He lectures in the school of English and American Studies at the University of East Anglia, Norwich. He has written on Henry James, Edgar Allen Poe, and Wallace Stevens, and on Puritanism, Transcendentalism, and Modernism. He is presently working on the poetry of John Ashbery.

RÉGIS DURAND is Professor of American Literature at the University of Lille. He is the author of *Melville, signes et métaphores* (Lausanne: L'Age d'Homme, 1981) and coauthor, with Maurice Couturier, of *Donald Barthelme* (Methuen, 1983); he has also coauthored numerous articles on contemporary theory and literature. He is also an art critic and a poet.

PIERRE GAULT, Professor of American Literature at the University of Tours, has long been working on the fiction of John Hawkes. His book *La Parole Coupée* was published in 1984 (Paris: Klincksieck) and his edition of the issue of *Delta* dedicated to Hawkes was published in 1985. His main interest lies with "intimate" semiotic readings of fiction, as witness his analyses of Nabokov, Gass, and Kosinski. The convergence of his and Laurent Souchu's readings of the erotics of contemporary fiction has been noted in European circles.

HARTWIG ISERNHAGEN has earned a Dr. phil. (Freiburg, 1969), and a Dr. phil. habil. (Wurzburg, 1979). He is currently chair for American and Commonwealth Literature, Department of English, Basel University. His publications are on twentieth century fiction and theory.

CLAUDE RICHARD is a professor of American Literature at the University of Montpellier, editor of *Delta,* translator and essayist, and the author of *Poe, Jounaliste et Critique* (1979), *Le Timbre-Poste* (1981), *Le Sextant* (poems, 1984) and essays on Poe, Melville, Hawthorne, Flannery O'Connor, Walker Percy, John Barth and Thomas Pynchon.

JOHAN THIELEMANS teaches English at the Higher Institute for Translators and Interpreters in Ghent. He has contributed to J. Kuehl and St. Moore's *In Recognition of William Gaddis* and has interviewed such authors as Donald Barthelme, John Hawkes, Gilbert Sorrentino, Coleman Dowell, Kurt Vonnegut, and Walter Abish for the Third Programme of the Flemish Belgian Radio. In 1984, he taped an inverview with William Gaddis for Belgian television.

HEIDE ZIEGLER is Professor of American and English Literature at the University of Stuttgart. Her publications include a study of the short stories of William Faulkner and, together with Christopher Bigsby, a collection of interviews with American and English novelists. Her forthcoming publication is a study of irony in contemporary American fiction.

Index

247